reaching  llustrations

 rom

 hurch  istory

Ron Prosise

KRESS
BIBLICAL
RESOURCES

PREACHING ILLUSTRATIONS FROM CHURCH HISTORY
Published by Kress Biblical Resources
PO Box 132228
The Woodlands, TX 77393

Alphabet characters from the book, *The Picture Alphabet, for the Instruction and Amusement of Boys and Girls* by H. S. Otley, 1830

ISBN 978-1-934952-23-8

Cover design: Cherith Festa
Text design: Greg Wright (DiamondPointMedia.com)

Printed in the United States of America

2016—First Edition

10 9 8 7 6 5 4 3 2 1

To my beloved Donna, God's marvelous blessing and the joy of my life.

"Like a lily among the thorns, so is my darling among the maidens."

(Song 2:2)

CONTENTS

Contents

INTRODUCTION

Years ago John MacArthur preached a sermon entitled, *A Passion for the Lost.* As he will often do, MacArthur used an account from church history to illustrate his point, which was the importance of believers having a fervent concern for unbelievers. Referencing a book by Cortland Myers[1], he began his message with this account of Robert Murray M'Cheyne, one of Scotland's greatest preachers from the nineteenth century:

> Everywhere he stepped, Scotland shook. Moreover, he opened his mouth, and a Spiritual force swept in every direction. Thousands followed him to the feet of Christ.
>
> A traveler was eager to see where M'Cheyne had preached, and he went to the Scottish town and found the Church. And an old gray-haired sexton agreed to take him through the Church. And as he led the way in the M'Cheyne study, he said, "Sit in that chair." And the traveler hesitated a moment and then sat in the chair. On the table before him was an open Bible, and the sexton said, "Drop your head in that book and weep. That's what our minister always did before he preached," said the old man. He then led the visitor into the pulpit before the open Bible. "Stand there," he said, "and drop your head on your hands, and

---

[1]   Cortland Myers, *How Do We Know?* (Philadelphia: The Judson Press, 1927), 46

let the tears flow. That's the way our minister always did before
he began to preach.[2]

I have heard many sermons on evangelism, but this illustration of
M'Cheyne's passion for the lost immediately seized my attention and ignited
my imagination. It helped me to not only better understand but also motivate
me in seeking to have this kind of evangelistic fervor.

There are some who might question the use of illustrations in sermons,
wondering whether it shouldn't be sufficient just to teach the truths of God's
Word. In *Rediscovering Expository Preaching*, Richard Mayhue addresses this
issue, comparing the use of sermon illustrations to seasonings and sauces
in gourmet cooking. He writes, "The main meal, or the message, should
never be eclipsed by secondary features; nonetheless, these garnishings
can dramatically enhance the flavor/interest level of a meal/message well
prepared in other respects." Mayhue affirms that illustrations cannot "replace
the Holy Spirit's work of impacting people with the power of God's Word.
However, to ignore or minimize these proven features of good communication
makes a preacher negligent in exercising his human responsibility to be as
effective as possible."[3]

Bryan Chapell agrees with this when he writes,

> Illustrations are not supplemental to good exposition; they
> are a necessary form of exposition in which biblical truths
> are explained to the emotions and the will as well as to the
> intellect... They are integral to effective preaching, not because
> they entertain, but because they expand and deepen the
> applications the mind and heart can make."[4]

I have experienced the truth of this in my own preaching. I began
collecting sermon illustrations as a student in seminary, always on the

---

[2] John MacArthur, *The Passion of Jesus for the Lost*, Sermon 80-63, Grace To You, http://www.
    gty.org/Resources/Sermons/80-63

[3] Richard Mayhue, "Rediscovering Expository Preaching," *Rediscovering Expository
    Preaching*, ed. John MacArthur, Jr. (Dallas, Tex.: Word, 1992) 242

[4] Bryan Chapell, *Using Illustrations to Preach with Power* (Grand Rapids, Mich.: Zondervan,
    1992) 13

lookout for ones that appeared to be particularly potent. I soon learned that certain kinds of illustrations seemed more effective than others. In particular, I noticed my own reaction to illustrations from the men and women of faith from the pages of history. I discerned that when preachers effectively used these illustrations, several things happened. First, the point of the sermon was vividly clarified and reinforced. Second, I grew in my understanding and appreciation of these heroes of the faith. Third, I found that I was stimulated to godliness through the lives of these men and women.

John Piper affirms this when he writes, "Experience and Scripture teach that the heart is most powerfully touched, not when the mind is entertaining abstract ideas, but when it is filled with vivid images of amazing reality."[5] One of the best ways that this is accomplished is through God's truth lived out in the lives of His people, which can be used as powerful illustrations in preaching.

Similarly, over a century ago, John Broadus, in his classic work, *On the Preparation and Delivery of Sermons*, noted,

> Great as is the value for our purposes of Science, and the attention now bestowed upon it, we must not forget that History, from its narrative and descriptive character and its human interest, has a peculiar and almost unrivalled charm. And in some respects, this is especially true of Biography, both general and religious. Here there is the interest which always attaches to a person, to an individual human life... Spurgeon often used illustrations from the lives of devout men; and Richard Fuller employed all manner of historical and biographical incident, both secular and religious, with rare felicity and power.[6]

The great benefit of using illustrations from church history is that they do more than effectively illustrate sermons—they exhort us to holy living. Puritan Thomas Brooks said, "Example is the most powerful rhetoric."[7]

---

5 John Piper, *the Supremacy of God in Preaching*, (Grand Rapids, Mich: Baker Books, 1990), 88

6 John A. Broadus, *A Treatise on the Preparation and Delivery of Sermons, ed. Edwin Dargan* (New York: A. C. Armstrong and Son, 1903) 236-7

7 C. Bradley, ed., *The Select Works of The Rev. Thomas Brooks, vol. 1* (London: L. B. Seeley and Son, 1824), 34

Commenting on this, John MacArthur writes,

> What makes examples so powerful? Why is it "the most powerful rhetoric"? An example shows us what principles can't. Principles and precepts instruct us about our duty. But an example assures us the duty is possible because someone else is also performing it.[8]

John Piper agrees, writing,

> The aim of God's providence in the history of the world is worship flowing from the people of God. Ten thousand stories of grace and truth are meant to be remembered for their refinement of faith and the sustaining of hope and the guidance of love... The lives of our flawed Christian heroes are inspiring for two reasons: because they were flawed (like us) and because they were great (unlike us). Their flaws give us hope that maybe God could use us too. Their greatness inspires us to venture beyond the ordinary."[9]

This happened to me when I read an account in the life of Civil War General Stonewall Jackson. A friend of Jackson was talking with him about the difficulty of obeying the Scripture injunction, "Pray without ceasing." Jackson answered his concern, insisting that one could so accustom himself so that it could be easily obeyed. Explaining his own practice, he commented,

> When we take our meals there is the grace. When I take a draught of water I always pause, as my palate receives the refreshment, to lift up my heart to God in thanks and prayer

---

[8] John MacArthur, *In the Footsteps of Faith* (Wheaton: Crossway, 1998), 7

[9] John Piper, *Life as a Vapor* (Sisters, Oregon: Multnomah, Ore., 2004), 73-74. Also Cotton Matther, who wrote, "Examples do strangely charm us into imitation. When holiness is pressed upon us, we are prone to think, that it is a doctrine calculated for angels and spirits, whose dwelling is not with flesh. But when we read the lives of them that excelled in holiness, though they were persons of like passions with our selves, the conviction is wonderful and powerful." Cotton Mather, *Magnalia Christi Americana: Or the Ecclesiastical History of New England vol. III* (London: Thomas Parkhurst, 1702), 70

for the water of life. Whenever I drop a letter into the box at the post office, I send a petition along with it for God's blessing upon its mission, and upon the person to whom it is sent. When I break the seal of a letter just received, I stop to pray to God that he might prepare me for its contents, and make it a messenger of good. When I go to my classroom, and await the arrangement of the cadets in their places, that is my time to intercede with God for them. And so of every other familiar act of the day.[10]

Jackson's practical example spurs me on to fulfill this command of Scripture to "Pray without ceasing."

God's Word encourages reflection upon past history to learn the lessons it can teach. In Deuteronomy 32:7, Moses gives this exhortation: "Remember the days of old; consider the years of all generations. Ask your father, and he will show you, your elders, and they will tell you."

Another objection regarding the usage of church history that could be given is that it can seem academic and removed from real life. D. Martyn Lloyd-Jones argues just the opposite when he writes,

> It is always essential for us to supplement our reading of theology with the reading of church history. . . . If we do not, we shall be in danger of becoming abstract, theoretical, and academic in our view of truth; and, failing to relate it to the practicalities of life and daily living, we shall soon be in trouble.[11]

Lloyd-Jones is right—a good illustration from church history can help the listener see the teaching of God's Word lived out in personal example, a mighty fusion of "spirit and truth."

I have experienced the impact of historical illustrations in my own preaching. I once preached a sermon on Matthew 5:43-48, where Jesus teaches that believers are not to hate, but rather love their enemies. I wanted to show the inconsistancy of a believer nurturing and expressing

---

[10] J. Wm. Jones, "Appendix, Containing Personal Reminiscences," *Stonewall Jackson: A Military Biography*, John Esten Cooke (New York: D. Appleton and Company, 1876), 504

[11] David Martyn Lloyd-Jones, *The Puritans: Their Origins and Successors* (Edinburgh: Banner of Truth, 1987) 215-216

both hatred and love, and found the following illustration to drive this point quite forcefully:

> The English pastor Newman Hall wrote a booklet in the nineteenth century entitled "Come to Jesus" which led many thousand souls to the Savior. Later in life, he became engaged in a theological controversy which grew more bitter with each new stage of the discussion. At length, he prepared a paper which he intended to be a crushing and final reply. He closed the argument by an attack that would be irresistible and overwhelming. He showed his opponent no mercy and felt that he had beaten him to the ground. When the paper was finished, he read it to a friend, and asked triumphantly, "How do you think I have handled him?"
>
> "Well," said his friend, "you have effectually disposed of him. Have you thought of a title for your paper?"
>
> "No," Hall replied. "Have you anything to suggest?"
>
> His friend answered, "I propose that you call it, "Go to the Devil," by the author of "Come to Jesus."
>
> The paper was never published.[12]

Preachers have a wonderful opportunity to introduce history's men and women of faith to their congregations through sermon illustrations. There is a treasure trove of saints in church history awaiting your discovery and your listeners' edification—preachers and presidents, kings and commoners, faithful men and women, who loved Christ and lived for Him and though dead, still speak.

---

[12] J. Ritchie Smith, *The Wall: And The Gates, and Other Sermons* (Philadelphia: The Westminster Press, 1919), 120-1

Guidelines For Using
Historical Illustrations

There are five important guidelines concerning illustrations in preaching. These guidelines will safeguard from common dangers.[13] The preacher must be concerned with purpose, truthfulness, orthodoxy, appropriateness, and brevity.

Purpose

The purpose of sermon illustrations is not to amuse or entertain, and certainly not to liven up an otherwise dull sermon. Bryan Chapell rightly notes,

> Preachers who illustrate primarily to entertain ultimately destroy the foundation of their messages. An entertainment ethic creates shallow congregations and hollow pulpits. People who attend such a church are implicitly taught that their own desires and sensations are to be the object of their worship. Such persons learn to evaluate the success of a

---

[13] For further guidelines in the use of illustrations, see Richard Mayhue, "Introductions, Illustrations, and Conclusions," *Rediscovering Expository Preaching,* ed. John MacArthur, Jr. (Dallas: Word, 1992) 250; Bryan Chapell, *Using Illustrations to Preach with Power* (Grand Rapids, Mich.: Zondervan, 1992) 148-177; and Jack Hughes, *Expository Preaching with Word Pictures* (Ross-shire, Scotland: Christian Focus, 2001) 167-177

sermon not by the conviction of spirit it brings but by the lightness of heart it offers.[14]

Thomas Chalmers, who lived from 1780 to 1847, was "probably the most gifted and powerful preacher since John Knox in Scotland."[15] He was a preacher who had "neither appearance, nor manner, nor voice to recommend him."[16] Dr. John Mason, who was also a preacher, was asked the reason for Chalmer's great power in preaching. He replied, "It is his blood-earnestness."[17] There must be a holy, wholehearted seriousness to the preparation and preaching of God's word. This blood-earnest sense of purpose is seen in the Puritan preacher Thomas Shepard. When on his deathbed, he was visited by several young ministers. Shepard addressed them, giving them his wise and heartfelt counsel on preaching:

> Your work is great, and requires great seriousness. For my own part, I never preached a sermon which, in the composing, did not cost me prayers, with strong cries and tears. I never preached a sermon from which I had not first, got some good to my own soul. I never went up into the pulpit but as if I were going to give an account of myself to God.[18]

This keen sense of purpose includes the judicious use of sermon illustrations. Jack Hughes crystallizes the purpose of preaching and the use of sermon illustrations toward this when he writes,

> Your goal in preaching is to permanently fix the truth of God's word in the minds and hearts of your listeners. Your effectiveness as a herald is not determined by your ability to know what you are saying, but your ability to *get the people to whom you are preaching to know and understand what you are saying*. If you are going to do this, you must overcome the

---

[14] Bryan Chapell, *Christ-Centered Preaching* (Grand Rapids, Mich: Baker Books, 1994), 167

[15] David Larsen, *The Company of the Preachers* (Grand Rapids, Mich: Kregel, 1998), 423

[16] Ashbel Green, *The Christian Advocate, vol. 4* (Philadelphia: A. Finley, 1826), 162

[17] James Alexander, *Thoughts on Preaching* (Edinburgh: Ogle and Murray, 1864), 264

[18] Benjamin Brook, *The Lives of the Puritans, vol. III* (London: James Black, 1813), 106

obstacles standing between you and your people. You must achieve three things: (1) you must hold people's attention; (2) you must give them understanding; and (3) you must help them remember. Preaching with word pictures [*a term Hughes uses that includes illustrations and historical events*] helps to accomplish all three goals.[19]

And so, if he were preaching upon the subject of anxiety, the preacher could use the following illustration to accomplish these three objectives:

> Martin Luther writes about a time he was sorely vexed and tried by his own sinfulness, by the wickedness of the world, and by the dangers that beset the Church. One morning he saw his wife Katharina dressed in mourning. Surprised, he asked her who had died.
>
> "Do you not know?" she replied, "God in heaven is dead."
>
> Luther retorted, "How can you talk such nonsense, Katie? How can God die? Why, He is immortal, and will live through all eternity."
>
> Katie asked him, "Is that really true?"
>
> Luther replied, "Of course!"
>
> "And yet," she said, "though you do not doubt that, yet you are so hopeless and discouraged."
>
> Luther then realized the contradiction of his belief and his behavior, and overcame his anxiety[20]

This illustration will not only hold people's attention, but it will help hearers understand that anxiety is incompatible with a Biblical understanding and trust in God's character. And those who hear will certainly remember this vivid illustration of truth.

Truthfulness

Another essential guideline for the preacher to follow is to try to make sure that the illustration is true. If the illustration is false or questionable,

---

[19]   Hughes, 65-6

[20]   Emily Christlieb, *A Day in the Life of Luther* (London: James Nisbet and Co., 1883), 65

it can raise doubt about the truth it was meant to explain as well as the preacher who is communicating it. One popular book of sermon illustrations gives this account:

> Augustine, while puzzling over the doctrine of the Trinity, was walking along the beach one day when he observed a young boy with a bucket, running back and forth to pour water into a little hole. Augustine asked, "What are you doing?" The boy replied, "I'm trying to put the ocean into this hole." Then Augustine realized that he had been trying to put an infinite God into his finite mind.[21]

On the surface, this seems to be a wonderful illustration, and it is one that I included in my file when I first read it years ago. But upon further investigation, I discovered that this is an apocryphal account in the life of Augustine. According to legend, Augustine had a vision of a child on the beach, and after hearing the boy say what he was attempting, responded, "Child, it is impossible." The child then replied, "Not more impossible than to comprehend what you are now meditating upon," and immediately vanished.[22] The author of this illustration book presented this apocryphal account in a way that makes it appear this was an actual historical incident.[23]

When a preacher uses an inaccurate or erroneous illustration, it calls into question the truthfulness of the rest of his message. Several years ago,

---

[21] Michael Green, *Illustrations for Biblical Preaching*, (Grand Rapids, Mich.: Baker Book House, 1982), 389

[22] William John Thomas, et. al, *Notes and Queries* (Oxford: Oxford University Press, 1850), 440

[23] A true historical illustration on the Trinity, one used by James Montgomery Boice in *Foundations of the Christian Faith* (116) is the following:

> A Unitarian once asked the American statesman Daniel Webster regarding the Trinity, if he believed that one and three are the same thing. Webster replied, "Sir, I believe you and I do not understand the arithmetic of heaven."

Joseph Banvard, *The American Statesman* (Boston, Gould and Lincoln, 1856), 20

Boice comments, "The doctrine of the Trinity does not mean that three equals one, of course, and Webster knew that. It means rather that God is three in one sense and one in another. But Webster's reply nevertheless showed a proper degree of creature humility. We believe the doctrine of the Trinity, not because we understand it, but because the Bible teaches it and because the Spirit himself witnessed within our heart that it is so."

James Montgomery Boice, *Foundations of the Christian Faith* (Downers Grove, Ill., 1986), 116

I heard a radio Bible teacher use an illustration about an atheist university professor. As the account went, every year this professor would challenge his class with the existence of God by dropping chalk onto the floor of the classroom, defying God to preserve it intact. The chalk would always break into pieces. One year, when a student had the courage to confess his faith in Christ, the professor said, "If God existed, he could stop this piece of chalk from hitting the ground and breaking. Such a simple task to prove that He is God, and yet He can't do it." As the professor dropped the chalk, it slipped out of his fingers, off his shirt cuff, onto the pleat of his pants, down his leg, and off his shoe, rolling away unbroken on the floor. The shocked professor left the class, and the student then had the opportunity to share Christ with 300 fellow students.

This story was quite captivating, so I called the ministry to obtain the illustration, which I excitedly used in an upcoming sermon on faith. There was only one problem—it was not true, as one of my listeners later pointed out.[24] The use of a fictitious illustration can weaken the credibility of your sermon and you as a preacher. Beware of mixing the iron of Scripture's truthfulness with the clay of fictitious accounts. Take the time and effort to check on the accuracy of illustrations.[25]

It is also important to document the source of your illustration in your file. Many times, I have returned to an illustration I filed years ago, to find that I did

---

[24] Rich Buhler, "The Atheist Professor At USC Who Encountered God Through a Piece of Chalk-Fiction!" *TruthOrFiction.com,* http://www.truthorfiction.com/ rumors/c/chalk.htm

[25] A documented illustration on faith is the following, regarding Bernard Gilpin, a puritan preacher in the sixteenth century:

> When Bonner, the Bishop of London had secured a royal warrant for the arrest of Bernard Gilpin in 1558, he promised that he would be at the stake in a fortnight. Gilpin laid his hand on his house-steward, he said, "At length they have prevailed against me. I am accused to the Bishop of London, from whom there will be no escaping. God forgive their malice, and give me strength to undergo the trial."
>
> As soon as he was apprehended he set out for London, in expectation of death by fire. But on the journey he broke his leg, which unavoidably detained him some time on the road. Those conducting him maliciously threw at Gilpin one of his frequent sayings, "That nothing happens to us but what is intended for our good."
>
> When they asked him whether he thought his broken leg was so intended, he meekly replied that he had not doubt of it. He was proved right; before he was able to travel, Queen Mary died, and he was set free.

Benjamin Brook, *The Lives of the Puritans, vol. I* (London: James Black, 1813), 253

not record the source. Being unable to verify its validity, I have been reluctant to use it. As a preacher, you need to make the effort to verify and record the source when you file an illustration, which can then not only be preached with confidence, but shared with those who afterwards ask you for it.

Orthodoxy

Faithfulness to God's Word compels the preacher to always be "accurately handling the word of truth" (2 Tim. 2:15). But in historical illustrations, care must also be taken regarding the doctrine of the person featured. For example, this incident from the life of Sir Isaac Newton that appears in a sermon illustration book points to creation's testimony to its Creator:

> Sir Isaac Newton had a replica of our solar system made in miniature. In the center was the sun with its retinue of planets revolving around it. A scientist entered Newton's study one day, and exclaimed, "My! What an exquisite thing this is! Who made it?"
>
> "Nobody!" replied Newton to the questioner who was an unbeliever.
>
> "You must think I am a fool. Of course somebody made it, and he is a genius."
>
> Laying his book aside, Newton arose and laid a hand on his friend's shoulder and said: "This thing is but a puny imitation of a much grander system whose laws you and I know, and I am not able to convince you that this mere toy is without a designer and maker; yet you profess to believe that the great original from which the design is taken has come into being without either designer or maker. Now tell me, by what sort of reasoning do you reach such incongruous conclusions?"[26]

As good as this illustration is, it is mitigated in that Sir Isaac Newton was not an orthodox Christian, as he denied the doctrine of the trinity. And so, it is advisable that this illustration must be qualified, if used at all.

---

[26] Paul Lee Tan, *Encyclopedia of 15,000 Illustrations* (Dallas, Tex.: Bible Communications, Inc., 1998), 472

Interestingly enough, I discovered a similar account that appears in the biography of a famous agnostic. This illustration can be readily used, as it is not weakened by having an unorthodox individual as its subject:

> Pastor Henry Ward Beecher was friends with the renowned agnostic orator of the late nineteenth century, Colonel Robert G. Ingersoll. Beecher had a celestial globe in his study, a present from a manufacturer. On it was an excellent representation of the constellations and the stars which compose them. Ingersol was delighted with the globe. He examined it closely and turned it round and round. He exclaimed, "It's just what I wanted—who made it?"
>
> Beecher repeated, "Who made it? Oh, nobody, Colonel—it just happened!"[27]

Along with doctrine, character is another issue for consideration. Some time ago, I came across a striking illustration for conscience in a historical account of Sir Walter Raleigh:

> When Sir Walter Raleigh was led to his death by beheading in 1618, he was asked in what manner he would extend himself on the block. He answered, "So the heart be right, it is no matter how the head lies."[28]

Although Raleigh's beliefs were orthodox, his was not a life of godliness. So if a preacher wanted to use this illustration, he could preface it by saying, "Although Sir Walter Raleigh's life was not a model of holiness, his comment before his execution about the conscience is certainly true..." and then proceed to give the illustration. Another option is to use a different illustration on the conscience, such as this one of Elizabeth Welsh, who was the youngest daughter of John Knox:

---

[27]   Edward Garstin Smith, *The Life and Reminiscences of Robert G. Ingersoll* (New York: The National Weekly Publishing Company, 1904), 11

[28]   John Watkins, *Characteristic Anecdotes of Men of Learning and Genius, Natives of Great Britain and Ireland, During the Last Three Centuries* (London: Albion Press, 1808), 56

When the Scottish minister John Welsh, was banished to France in 1606, his wife Elizabeth, the daughter of John Knox, was told by King James that he might return to Scotland if he would acknowledge the authority of bishops. Elizabeth knew that this would be a violation of conviction and conscience, and so in reply, she raised her apron and said, "Please your Majesty, I'd rather kep [catch] his head there."[29]

Appropriateness

Another important guideline concerning the use of sermon illustrations is that they be appropriate. Far too often, sermon illustrations are used by preachers merely to add interest to a sermon, not to clarify or reinforce the truth of Scripture. I recall listening to radio preacher who spent a considerable amount of time in his sermon citing various entries from *The Guinness Book of World Records*. This was indeed interesting to listen to but did not help to explain the Scripture he was teaching, and I was left with no idea of what Biblical truth he was seeking to illustrate. It must always be in the forefront of the preacher's mind that the explanation of the truth of Scripture is the priority, and illustrations are a tool to this end. As Richard Mayhue points out, "Don't use an illustration just because it is a great illustration; make sure it illustrates your point from the biblical text."[30] A commitment to the acquiring of illustrations will help to ensure that you have a good collection from which to draw an appropriate illustration for your sermon.

Illustrations must be both appropriate to the teaching of the sermon, as well as to the goal of the sermon—never to impress men, but to serve God in revealing His Son and explaining His truth, as this account of Thomas Manton aptly illustrates:

> Puritan Thomas Manton was asked to preach upon some public occasion, and his sermon was noted as being "learned, ingenious, and eloquent." As he was returning home, an old gentleman pulled him by the coat, desiring to speak with him.

---

[29] James Anthony Froude, *Thomas Carlyle: A History of the First Forty Years of His Life, 1795-1835, vol. I* (London: Longmans, Green, and Co., 1882) 108-9

[30] Mayhue, "Rediscovering," 250

The doctor stopped, and the stranger said, "I was one of your auditory today: I went to be fed with the gospel, as usual, but have returned empty. Dr. Manton was not Dr. Manton this morning. There was, indeed, much of the doctor, of the florid and learned man, in the discourse, but little or nothing of Jesus Christ: it was, in short, no sermon to me."

Manton answered, "If I have not preached to you, you have now preached a good sermon to me, such as, I trust, I shall never forget, but be the better for as long as I live."[31]

Brevity

Yet another danger to guard against is allowing illustrations to hijack the sermon. Here, the hazard is not that the illustrations are uninteresting but that they overpower the teaching of the sermon. Some preachers employ multiple illustrations that become the focus of the sermon rather than the servant of the sermon. More attention and time is given to the illustrations than to the biblical text, and instead of clarifying, they distract. Charles Spurgeon gives the warning:

> While we thus commend illustrations for necessary uses, it must be remembered that they are not the strength of a sermon any more than a window is the strength of a house; and for this reason, among others, *they should not be too numerous...* Illustrate, by all means, but do not let the sermon be all illustrations, or it will be only suitable for an assembly of simpletons. A volume is all the better for engravings, but a scrap-book which is all woodcuts is usually intended for the use of little children. Our house should be built up with the substantial masonry of doctrine, upon the deep foundation of inspiration; its pillars should be of solid Scriptural argument, and every stone of truth should be carefully laid in its place; and then the windows should be ranged in due order" (italics in original).[32]

---

[31] Augustus Toplady, *The Works of Augustus M. Toplady, vol. IV* (London: Printed for the Proprietors and sold by W. Row, 1794), 179

[32] Charles Spurgeon, *Lectures to My Students* (Grand Rapids, Mich.: Zondervan, 1954) 352-535

An illustration does not need to be lengthy to be potent, as demonstrated by this pithy illustration of the priority and joy of holiness:

> The English Puritan preacher Philip Henry had a way of blessing his newly married friends that was very different and distinct. He would say to them, "Others wish you all happiness; I wish you all holiness, and then there is no doubt but you will have all happiness."[33]

Another danger of excessive illustrations is that they can become a substitute for the labor in the Word required to faithfully teach the truths of Scripture. God's preachers are commissioned to "work hard at preaching and teaching" (1 Tim 5:17) and to be diligent workmen in the word of truth (2 Tim 2:15). Good illustrations can aid that work but can never replace it. Only God's Word has the power to save the unbeliever and sanctify the believer. R. Albert Mohler emphasizes this when he asks, "What does it mean to be a servant of the Word? It means that our ministry is so prioritized that the preaching of the Word becomes so central that everything else must fall into place behind this priority—everything else."[34] This means everything outside the pulpit and everything in the pulpit, including illustrations, must be subservient to the God-ordained preaching of Scripture.

In the early nineteenth century, someone once had the opportunity to hear the preaching of the aforementioned Thomas Chalmers for the first time. One of his ardent admirers asked the man afterwards, "What do you think of Dr. Chalmers?"

"Think of *him*?" replied the man. "Why he has made me think so much of *Jesus* that I had no time to think of him!"[35]

May this be true in our preaching—may it never magnify the earthen vessels, but only serve to exalt the supreme treasure of Christ Jesus.

---

[33] Matthew Henry, *The Life of the Rev. Philip Henry* (London: William Ball, 1839), 111

[34] R. Albert Mohler, "The Primacy of Preaching," *Feed My Sheep: A Passionate Plea for Preaching,* ed. Don Kistler (Morgan, Penn: Soli Deo Gloria, 2002), 29

[35] Ashbel Green, ed., *The Christian Advocate, vol. IV,* (Philadelphia: A. Finley, 1826) 163

ILLUSTRATIONS

Accountability—to God

American statesman Daniel Webster was once asked, "What was the greatest thought that ever entered your mind?" Webster reflected for a moment and replied, "The thought of my personal accountability to God."[36]

Accountability—to God

When Adalbert was appointed bishop of Prague in 982, it seemed to give him little satisfaction, and he was never seen to smile afterwards. Being asked the reason, he said, "It is an easy thing to wear a mitre and a cross, but an awful thing to give an account of a bishopric, before the Judge of quick and dead."[37]

Accountability—to one another

In 1738, John Wesley formed an organization of small groups for the purpose of spiritual accountability. Those who wanted to join the groups were asked a series of questions before being admitted:

---

[36] *Christian Faith and Life, vol. III, no. 2, ed. by William M. McPheeters, et. al.* (Colombia, SC: The Bryan Printing Company, 1901), 61

[37] Joseph Milner, *History of the Church of Christ, vol. III* (Boston: Farrand, Mallory and Co., 1809), 246

1. Have you the forgiveness of your sins?

2. Have you peace with God through our Lord Jesus Christ?

3. Have you the witness of God's Spirit with your spirit that you are a child of God?

4. Is the love of God shed abroad in your heart?

5. Has no sin, inward or outward, dominion over you?

6. Do you desire to be told of your faults?

7. Do you desire to be told of all your faults—and that plain and home?

8. Do you desire that every one of us should tell you, from time to time, whatsoever is in his heart concerning you?

9. Consider! Do you desire we should tell you whatsoever we think, whatsoever we fear, whatsoever we hear concerning you?

10. Do you desire that in doing this we should come as close as possible, that we should cut to the quick, and search your heart to the bottom?

11. Is it your desire and design to be, on this and all other occasions, entirely open, so as to speak everything that is in your heart, without exception, without disguise, and without reserve?

For those in the group, the following questions "may be asked as often as occasion offers; the five following at every meeting":

1. What known sins have you committed since our last meeting?

2. What temptations have you met with?

3. How were you delivered?

4. What have you thought, said, or done, of which you doubt whether it be sin or not?

5. Have you nothing you desire to keep secret?[38]

---

[38] William Hurd, *A New Universal History of the Religious Rites, Ceremonies and Customs of the Whole World* (London: Richard Evans, 1814), 717

Admonishment

Adoniram Judson once sent for a native Christian woman who was about to engage in something which Judson considered would not be for her spiritual good. He pleaded with her, but she would not give it up. Finally, he said, "Look here," and snatched a ruler from the table, tracing a not very straight line upon the floor. "Here is where you have been walking. You have made a crooked track, to be sure—out of the path half the time; but then you have kept near it, and not taken to new roads; and you have—not so much as you might have done, mind, but still to a certain extent—grown in grace. And now, with all this growth upon your heart and head, in the maturity of your years, with ripened understanding of the goodness of God, here," bringing down the ruler with emphasis to indicate a certain position, *"here you stand.* You know where this path leads. You know what is before you—some struggles, some sorrows, and finally, eternal life and a crown of glory. But to the left branches off another very pleasant road, and along the air floats, rather temptingly, a pretty bubble. You do not mean to leave the path you have walked in fifteen years; you only want to step aside, and catch the bubble, and think you will come back again; *but you never will.* Woman, think! Dare you deliberately leave this strait and narrow path, drawn by the Savior's finger, and go away for one moment into that of your enemy? Will you? *Will you?* WILL YOU?"

The woman burst into tears, unable to speak for her sobbing. Judson then prayed that God would preserve her in her determination. Later in life she said that whenever she was unusually tempted, she would see Judson's finger pointing along the path of eternal life, the words "Will you?" coming from his lips as though it was the voice of God, and it would turn her back again in prayer to the Lord.[39]

Admonishment

Puritan pastor Joseph Alleine was very faithful in administering reproof. Once, when he set about to do this, he said to a friend, "I am now going about that which is likely to make a very dear and obliging friend become

---

[39] Francis Wayland, *A Memoir of the Life and Labors of the Rev. Adoniram Judson, D.D., vol. II* (Boston: Phillips, Sampson, and Company, 1854), 362-3

an enemy. But, however, it cannot be omitted; it is better to lose man's favor than God's." But the rebuke had the opposite effect—the man, grateful for Alleine's conscientious faithfulness to him, loved him the better ever after, as long as he lived.[40]

Admonishment

Thomas De Witt Talmage was a chaplain during the Civil War and pastor of the Central Brooklyn Tabernacle from 1869-1895. During a visit to the dentist, he was asked, "Does that hurt?"

Talmage immediately answered, "Of course it hurts. It is in your business as in my profession. We have to hurt before we can help."[41]

Admonishment

Alcohol was a problem for General Ulysses Grant that resulted in his resignation from the Army instead of a court-martial in 1854. It continued to be an issue for him during the Civil War, and he made a pledge to his chief of staff, General John Rawlins, that he would not drink again. When Grant broke that pledge, General Rawlins, a man of faith, put his friendship and his career on the line when he wrote a letter of rebuke to his commanding general, saying,

> You have the full control over your appetite, and can let drinking alone. Had you not pledged me the sincerity of your honor early last March that you would drink no more during the war, and kept that pledge during your recent campaign, you would not to-day have stood first in the world's history as a successful military leader. You cannot succeed in any other way...
>
> If my suspicions are unfounded, let my friendship for you and my zeal for my country be my excuse for this letter; and if they are correctly founded, and you determine not to heed the admonitions and the prayers of this hasty note by immediately

---

[40]   Richard Baxter, *Life and death of the Rev. Joseph Alleine* (New York: Robert Carter, 1840), 61-62

[41]   T. De Witt Talmage, *The Masque Torn Off* (London: Richard B. Dickenson, 1879), 246

ceasing to touch a single drop of any kind of liquor, no matter by whom asked or under what circumstances, let my immediate relief from duty in this department be the result. I am, General, yours respectfully, John A. Rawlins.[42]

Affliction

John Dod was a Puritan well acquainted with affliction. His wife died, he was suspended from his ministry by the bishop of Oxford, and he himself experienced extreme bodily suffering and almost died. But his view of affliction was refreshingly Biblical. He remarked, "Nothing shall hurt us but sin; and that shall not hurt us, if we can repent of it. And nothing can do us good but the love and favor of God in Christ; and that we shall have if we seek it in good earnest. Afflictions are God's potions, which we may sweeten by faith and prayer; but we often make them bitter, by putting into God's cup the ill ingredients of impatience and unbelief."[43]

Affliction

During a time of severe affliction with sickness, Edward Payson, an American preacher in the early 1800s, was asked by some of his friends if he could see any particular reason for it. He replied, "No, but I am as well satisfied if I could see ten thousand. God's will is the very perfection of all reason."[44]

Sometime later, a friend with whom he had been conversing on his extreme bodily sufferings, and his high spiritual joys, remarked, "I presume it is no longer incredible to you, if ever it was, that martyrs should rejoice and praise God in the flames and on the rack." He answered, "No, I can easily believe it. I have suffered twenty times as much as I could in being burnt at the stake, while my joy in God so abounded, as to render my suffering not only tolerable, but welcome."[45]

---

[42]   Donn Piatt, Henry Van Boynton, *General George H. Thomas: A Critical Biography* (Cincinnati: Robert B. Clarke & Co., 1893), 319

[43]   Benjamin Brook, *The Lives of the Puritans, vol. III* (London: James Black, 1813), 1-3

[44]   Edward Payson, *Memoir, Select Thoughts and Sermons of the Late Rev. Edward Payson* (Philadelphia: J. L. Gihon, 1858), 405

[45]   Ibid., 419

Affliction

Henry Martyn, missionary to India, died in 1812. In his last sickness he exclaimed, "Why should I murmer? Weakness, peril, and pain are but the ministering angels whose office it is to conduct me to glory."[46]

Affliction

In 1889, the pressure upon Hudson Taylor and his ministry in China was so great that he asked for renewed earnestness in prayer at home, saying, "It seems as if every native Christian and helper as well as missionary were being assailed." Yet he and his co-workers were learning deeper lessons of the sustaining power of God. In a letter, Taylor wrote, "The cross does not get comfortable, but it bears sweet fruit."[47]

Affliction—blessings in

At a worship service in the 1800s, several persons spoke of their trials, but said that their blessings more than counterbalanced them. At length Billy Bray rose; clapping his hands and smiling, he said, "Well, friends, I have been taking vinegar and honey, but, praise the Lord, I've had the vinegar with a spoon, and the honey with a ladle."[48]

Affliction—brings compassion

Thomas DeWitt Talmage, American pastor of the 1800s, once posed a question to someone about his pastor, who was a very brilliant man. He asked him, "Why is it that your pastor, so very brilliant, seems to have so little heart and tenderness in his sermons?"

The older saint replied, "Well, the reason is our pastor has never had any trouble. When misfortune comes upon him, his style will be different."[49]

---

[46]   W. E. Shipton, ed., *Lectures Delivered Before the Young Men's Christian Association*, vol. 16 (London: James Nisbet and Co., 1861), 339

[47]   Dr. and Mrs. Howard Taylor, *Hudson Taylor and the China Inland Mission* (London: China Inland Mission , 1918), 461-2

[48]   Frederick William Bourne, *The King's Son or A Memoir of Billy Bray Compiled Chiefly From His Own Memoranda* (London: Hamilton, Adams & Co., 1883), 40

[49]   T. De Witt Talmage, *The Pathway of Life* (New York: The Christian Herald, 1894), 60

Affliction—for the sake of Christ

When John Huss was condemned to die by being burned at the stake in 1415, a paper crown with three devils, with the title "Leader of a heretical movement" was placed on his head. Huss replied, "My Lord Jesus Christ, for my sake, did wear of crown of thorns; why should not I then, for his sake, wear this light crown, be it ever so ignominious?"[50]

Affliction—God's will in

In the 1800s, Pastor George Pentecost visited a lady who was in deep trouble because of great afflictions. When he went in her home, she was working on a bit of embroidery. As he talked with her, she dropped it wrong side up, and there it lay a mass of crude work, tangled, everything seeming out of order.

"Well," he said, "what is this you are engaged at?"

"Oh, she replied, "it's for a Christmas gift."

He remarked, "I should not think you would waste your time on that. It looks tangled, without design or meaning."

Surprised at the abrupt change of the subject and his opposition to her word she exclaimed, "Why, Mr. Pentecost, you are looking at the wrong side. Turn it over."

Then he said, "That's just what you are doing, you are looking at the wrong side of God's workings with you. Down here they seem tangled, but up there He is working from the right side."[51]

Affliction—God's purpose in

When the Puritan minister John Dod was experiencing trials, he consulted his father-in-law, who told him, "Son, son, when affliction lieth heavy, sin lieth light." This reply conveyed great encouragement to Dod, who would afterwards say, "Sanctified afflictions are spiritual promotions."[52]

---

[50] John Foxe, *The Church Historians of England: Reformation Period, vol. III, part II* (London: Seeleys, 1855), 493

[51] J. L. Nye, *Anecdotes on Bible texts, The Epistles of Paul the Apostle to the Corinthians and Galatians* (London: Sunday School Union, 1882), 77-78

[52] Benjamin Brook, *The Lives of the Puritans, vol. III* (London: James Black, 1813), 2-3

Affliction—God's will in

Marie Booth was the third daughter of William Booth, the founder of the Salvation Army. She had an accident at an early age that caused her to have convulsions which made her an invalid. A friend visiting one day said to her it was a pity that a woman so capable should be hindered by sickness from doing the Lord's work.

Marie replied, "It is great to do the Lord's work, but it is greater to do the Lord's will."[53]

Affliction—praise in

In 1931 missionary Amy Carmichael was badly injured in a fall, which left her bedridden, and for the last twenty years of her life until her death, she was confined to her room, in constant pain. Yet instead of bitterness, she chose blessing. During this time, she wrote, "'Glorify ye the Lord in the fires' (Isaiah 24:15), not when they have passed or you are out of them and they are only memories, but in them.[54]

Anger

Puritan Matthew Henry was once asked, "How can I be angry and sin not, as the apostle tells us?"

"Only in one way," he replied, "and that is, not to be angry with anything but sin."[55]

Anger

The English pastor Newman Hall wrote a booklet in the 1800s entitled "Come to Jesus" which led many thousand souls to the Savior. Later in life, he became engaged in a theological controversy which grew more bitter with each new stage of the discussion. Finally, he prepared a paper which he

---

[53] Ivan Henry Hagedorn, *Biblical Messengers of Encouragement* (New York: Pulpit Press, 1945), 78

[54] Amy Carmichael, *Candles in the Dark* (Fort Washington, Penn.: Christian Literature Crusade, 1982), 63

[55] H. A. Downing, *Anecdotes for the Family, Or, Lessons of Truth and Duty for Every-day Life* (Hartford, Conn.: Case, Lockwood & Company, 1862), 17

intended to be a crushing and final reply. He closed the argument by an attack that would be irresistible and overwhelming. He showed his opponent no mercy and felt that he had beaten him to the ground. When the paper was finished, he read it to a friend, and asked triumphantly, "How do you think I have handled him?"

"Well," said his friend, "you have effectually disposed of him. Have you thought of a title for your paper?"

"No," Hall replied. "Have you anything to suggest?"

His friend answered, "I propose that you call it, "Go to the Devil," by the author of "Come to Jesus."

The paper was never published.[56]

Anxiety

Martin Luther writes about a time he was sorely vexed and tried by his own sinfulness, by the wickedness of the world, and by the dangers that beset the Church. One morning he saw his wife Katie dressed in mourning. Surprised, he asked her who had died. "Do you not know?" she replied, "God in heaven is dead."

Luther retorted, "How can you talk such nonsense, Katie? How can God die? Why, He is immortal, and will live through all eternity."

Katie asked him, "Is that really true?"

Luther replied, "Of course!"

"And yet," she said, "though you do not doubt that, yet you are so hopeless and discouraged."

Luther then realized the contradiction of his belief and his behavior, and mastered his anxiety.[57]

Anxiety

The German reformer Philipp Melancthon so prized prayer that he actually feared to lose anxieties, lest he should lose the blessed relief of prayer. He said, "If I had no anxieties I should lose a powerful incentive to prayer;

---

[56]   J. Ritchie Smith, *The Wall: And The Gates, and Other Sermons* (Philadelphia: The Westminster Press, 1919), 120-1

[57]   Emily Christlieb, *A Day in the Life of Luther* (London: James Nisbet and Co., 1883), 65

but when the cares of life impel to devotion, which is the best means of consolation, a religious mind cannot do without them. Thus trouble compels me to pray, and prayer drives away trouble."[58]

Assurance

In the 1800s, English chemist and physicist Michael Faraday discovered benzene, electromagnetic induction, and the laws of electrochemistry, among other accomplishments. He was the first to convert mechanical energy into electric energy, inventing the electric dynamo, the ancestor of modern power generators. Faraday has been called by science historians the best experimentalist in the history of science. As Faraday neared his death, he was asked about his theories. He replied, "They are now over, and I am resting on certainties. I know whom I have believed, and am persuaded that He is able to keep that which I have committed to Him" [2 Tim 1:12].[59]

Assurance

When J. Wilbur Chapman was studying for the ministry, he heard D. L. Moody was to preach in Chicago. He speaks of meeting with him afterward:

> To my great joy Mr. Moody came and sat beside me. I confessed that I was not quite sure that I was saved. He handed me his opened Bible and asked me to read John 5:24; and trembling with emotion I read: "Verily, verily, I say unto you, He that heareth My word, and believeth on Him that sent Me, hath everlasting life, and shall not come into condemnation; but is passed from death unto life."
>
> He said to me, "Do you believe this?"
> I answered, "Certainly."
> He said, "Are you a Christian?"
> I replied, "Sometimes I think I am, and again I am fearful."
> "Read it again," he said. Then he repeated his two questions,

---

58   William W. Patton, *Prayer and its Remarkable Answers* (Chicago: J. S. Goodman, 1876), 24

59   W. W. Peyton, "The Resurrection: A Study in the Evolution of Religion, " *The Contemporary Review, vol. LXXV, January-June 1899* (New York: Leonard Scott Publication Company, 1899), 139

and I had to answer as before.

Then Mr. Moody seemed to lose patience and he spoke sharply, "Whom are you doubting?" and then it all came to me with startling suddenness.

"Read it again," said Moody, and for the third time he asked. "Do you believe it?"

I said, 'Yes, indeed I do."

"Well, are you a Christian?' and I answered, "Yes, Mr. Moody, I am." From that day to this I have never questioned my acceptance with God.[60]

Assurance

At one of his meetings Dwight L. Moody met a man who said to him, "I can't feel that I'm saved."

Moody replied, "I want to ask you a question: Was it Noah's feelings that saved him or was it the ark?"

The man answered, "Oh, I see it now!"[61]

Bible—disregard of

During his college studies, Thomas Goodwin once took a journey to hear Puritan John Rogers preach one of his weekday lectures. Rogers was at that time discussing the subject of the Scriptures and on this occasion admonished his hearers on their neglect of the Bible. He represented God as addressing them: "I have trusted you so long with my Bible; you have slighted it, it lies in your houses covered with dust and cobwebs; you care not to look into it. Do you use my Bible so? Well, you shall have my Bible no longer." He then took up the Bible from the cushion, and seemed as if he were going away with it, and carrying it from them; but immediately turned again, and personated the people answering God, fell down on his knees, wept, and pleaded most earnestly: "O Lord, whatever thou dost to us, take not thy Bible from us! Kill our children, burn our

60 Ford Cyrinde Ottman, *J. Wilbur Chapman: A Biography* (New York: Double Day, Page & Company, 1920), 29-30

61 Charles F. Goss, *Echoes from the Pulpit and Platform* (Hartford, Conn., A.D. Worthington & Co., 1900) 114

houses, destroy our goods, only spare us thy Bible." Then he addressed the people as from God: "Say you so? Well, I will try you a little longer; here is my Bible for you. I will yet see how you will use it; whether you will love it more, whether you will observe it more, whether you will practice it more, and live more according to it." By these actions the people who heard him were deluged in their own tears. Goodwin himself, when he left, wept on the neck of his horse for a quarter of an hour before he had power to mount, so great was the conviction by this admonishment for the neglect of the Bible.[62]

Bible—God's word

John Wycliffe has been called "The Morning Star of the Reformation." In the 1300s, the Scriptures were practically unknown.[63] Christianity had become grossly corrupt and superstitious.[64] Standing against the religious teachings and traditions of his day, Wycliffe taught that the Bible was the only authority of truth and faith. He wrote that "Holy Scripture is the faultless, most true, most perfect, and most holy law of God, which is the duty of all men to learn, to know, to defend, and to observe, inasmuch as they are bound to serve the Lord in accordance with it, under the promise of an eternal reward."[65]

Wycliffe translated Scripture into English and brought its light and life to England.

Bible—God's word

The Bohemian reformer John Huss treasured the Scriptures, which were his daily companion. In it he found "the gold of wisdom, the silver of eloquence, the gems of virtue, lavishly poured forth in heavenly grace."[66] It was this that Huss was called to preach, and he could not be silent, declaring,

---

[62] John Howe, "The Principles of the Oracles of God," in *The Works of Reverend John Howe*, vol. 2, ed. Edmund Calamy (New York: John P. Haven, 1835), 1084-5

[63] J. Milton Smith, *The Stars of the Reformation* (London: S. W. Partridge & Co., 1878), 2

[64] Edwin Hall, *The Puritans and Their Principles* (New York: Baker and Scribner, 1846), 25

[65] Gotthard Victor Lechler, *John Wiclif and His English Precursors*, trans. by Peter Lorimer, (London: C. Kegan Paul & Co., 1878), 35

[66] Ezra Hall Gillett, *The Life and Time of John Huss* (Boston: Gould and Lincoln, 1863), 121

"In order that I may not make myself guilty by my silence, forsaking the truth for a piece of bread, or through fear of man, I avow it to be my purpose to defend the truth which God has enabled me to know, and especially the truth of the Holy Scriptures, even to death."[67] It was to this that Huss lived and was killed.

Bible—God's word

The classical scholar, Dr. E. V. Rieu, translated Homer into very modern English for the "Penguin Classics." Rieu was sixty, and a lifelong agnostic, when the same firm invited him to translate the gospels. As a result, he said, "It changed me. My work changed me. And I came to the conclusion, as I said, I think, in my Introduction, that these works bear the seal of the Son of Man and God. And they are the Magna Carta of the human spirit."[68]

Bible—hearing

In the early 1800s, the English preacher Rowland Hill paid a visit to an old friend, who said to him, "Mr. Hill, it is just sixty-five years since I first heard you preach, and I remember your text and part of your sermon."

"'Tis more than I do," was Hill's remark.

"You told us," his friend proceeded,

> that some people were very squeamish about the delivery of different ministers, who preached the same gospel. You said, suppose you were attending to hear a will read, where you expected a legacy to be left you, would you employ the time when it was reading, in criticizing the manner in which the lawyer read it? No, you would not; you would be giving all ear to hear if any thing was left to you, and how much it was. That is the way I would advise you to hear the gospel.[69]

---

67 Ibid., 151-152

68 "Translating the Gospels: A Discussion Between Dr. E.V. Rieu and the Rev. J.B. Phillips" in *The Bible Translator 6/4* (October 1955), 159

69 Edwin Sidney, *The Life of the Rev. Rowland Hill,* (London: Baldwin & Cradock, 1834), 190

Bible—hunger for

John Williams, the English missionary to the South Pacific in the early 1800s, was greeted one day by a native who shouted, "Welcome, servant of God, who brought light into this dark island; to you are we indebted for the word of salvation." The appearance of this person struck his attention, as the native's hands and feet had been eaten off by a disease, and he had to walk on his knees.

In reply to the greeting, Williams asked him what he knew of the word of salvation. He answered, "I know about Jesus Christ, who came into the world to save sinners." Williams then asked him what he knew about Jesus Christ. The man replied, "I know that he is the Son of God, and that he died painfully upon the cross to pay for the sins of men, in order that their souls might be saved, and go to happiness in the skies."

Williams did not remember him being at any of the services he taught, so he asked, "Where did you obtain your knowledge?"

The native answered, "As the people return from the services, I take my seat by the wayside, and beg a bit of the word of them as they pass by; one gives me one piece, another piece, and I collect them together in my heart, and by thinking over what I thus obtain, and praying to God to make me know, I understand a little about his word."[70]

Bible—love of

Dr. Claudius Buchanan was sharing with a friend the minute pains he had been taking with the proofs and revisions of a translation of the Syriac Testament in the early 1800s, every page of which passed under his eye five times before it was finally sent to press. He said he had expected beforehand that this process would have proved irksome to him, but that every fresh perusal of the sacred page seemed to unveil new beauties. Here he stopped and burst into tears. As soon as he recovered himself, he said to his friend, "I could not express the emotion I felt, as I recollected the delight it pleased God to afford me in the reading of his word."[71]

---

[70] John Williams, *A Narrative of Missionary Enterprises in the South Sea Islands* (London: Published for the Author, 1837), 209-10

[71] H. A. Downing, *Anecdotes for the Family, Or, Lessons of Truth and Duty for Every-day Life* (Hartford, Conn.: Case, Lockwood & Company, 1862), 43

Bible—love of

Mary Jones was a little Welsh girl, the daughter of a poor weaver. In 1794, at the age of ten, she began to lay by all the money she could possibly save, with her heart set upon buying a Bible. In 1800, after six years of carefully saving her pennies, she had the required amount. She had been directed to the Rev. Thomas Charles of Bala, who had acquired a number of Bibles for distribution. Mary walked barefoot twenty-five miles to his hometown.

That evening, as she had been instructed by her pastor, she came to the home of David Edwards, a Methodist pastor of Bala. As it was too late in the day to see Rev. Charles, she spent the night at Edward's home. Early the next morning, David Edwards and the little girl were in the street and on their way to the residence of Thomas Charles. They knocked and were received in. David Edward introduced Mary, and she told her story of longing for a Bible and the years of saving up for it. After hearing her story, Mr. Charles turned to David Edwards, and he sadly said,

> I am indeed grieved that this dear girl should have come all the way from Llanfihangel to buy a Bible, and that I should be unable to supply her with one. The consignment of Welsh Bibles that I received from London last year was all sold out months ago, excepting a few copies which I have kept for friends whom I must not disappoint. Unfortunately the Society which has hitherto supplied Wales with the Scriptures declines to print any more, and where to get Welsh Bibles to satisfy our country's need I know not.

Until now, Mary had been looking up into Mr. Charles's face with eyes full of hope and confidence, but as he spoke these words to David Edwards, and she noticed his overclouded face and began to understand the full import of his words, she buried her face in her hands and wept.

After a few moments, Mr. Charles rose from his seat and laid his hand on Mary's head. With his own voice broken and unsteady, he said to her, "My dear child, I see you *must* have a Bible, difficult as it is for me to spare you one. It is impossible, yes, simply impossible to refuse you." He turned to a cupboard behind him, and opening it, drew forth a Bible. Then, laying a hand once more on her head, he said to Mary, as she looked at him with inexpressible joy and thankfulness, "If you, my dear girl, are glad to receive this Bible, truly glad am I to be able to give it to you. Read it carefully, study it diligently, treasure up the sacred words in your memory, and act up to its teachings."

As Mary wept tears of delight and gratitude, Mr. Charles turned to his friend and said,

David Edwards, is not such a sight as this enough to melt the hardest heart? A girl, so young, so poor, so intelligent, so familiar with the Scripture, compelled to walk all the distance from Llanfihangel to Bala (about fifty miles there and back) to get a Bible! From this day I can never rest until I find out some means of supplying the pressing wants of my country that cries out for the Word of God.

It was out of Mary Jones's love for God's word and her savings and prayer that the British and Foreign Bible Society was formed in 1804.[72]

Bible—meditation on

Pastor and seminary professor James W. Alexander was, in many respects, a model Christian man and minister. One important secret of it lay in some of his habits. One of these was that of taking, every morning, a verse or passage from the Bible for his meditation during the day, and with the view, he said, of having his entire life filled with its spirit and influence.[73]

Bible—power of

Puritan John Flavel was minister of Dartmouth, in England. One day, he preached from these words: "If any man love not the Lord Jesus Christ, let him be anathema maranatha." The discourse was unusually solemn—particularly the explanation of the curse. At the conclusion, when Flavel rose to pronounce the blessing, he paused, and said: "How shall I bless this whole assembly, when every person in it who loves not the Lord Jesus is anathema maranatha?" The solemnity of this address deeply affected the audience—but

---

[72] Mary Emily Ropes, *The Story of Mary Jones and Her Bible* (New York: American Tract Society, 1892), i-108

[73] n.a. *Anecdotes Illustrative of Old Testament Texts* (New York: E. B. Treat & Company, 1899),146

not everyone. In the congregation was a lad named Luke Short, about fifteen years old, a native of Dartmouth. Shortly after, he went to sea and sailed to America, where he passed the rest of his life. His life was lengthened far beyond the usual term. When a hundred years old, he was able to work on his farm, and his mind was not at all impaired. He had lived all this time in carelessness and sin; he was a sinner a hundred years old and ready to die accursed. One day, as he sat in his field, he reflected on his past life and of the days of his youth. His memory recalled Flavel's sermon, a considerable part of which he remembered. The earnestness of the minister—the truths spoken —the effect on the people—all came fresh to his mind. He felt that he had not loved the Lord Jesus; he feared the dreadful anathema; he was deeply convinced of sin and was brought to faith in Christ. He lived to his one hundred and sixteenth year, giving every evidence of true faith.[74]

Bible—power of

In the days when George Whitefield was preaching, a young man named John Thorpe was a member of an infidel club that called themselves the "Hell Fire Club." Among their amusements was that of holding imitations of religious services and exhibiting mimicries of popular ministers. Young Thorpe went to hear Whitefield, that he might take him off before his profane associates; he heard him so carefully that he caught his tones and his manner, and something of his teaching. When the club met to see his caricature of the great preacher, Thorpe opened his Bible that he might take a text to preach from it after the manner of Whitefield; his eye fell on the passage, "Except ye repent, ye shall all likewise perish." As he spoke upon that text, he was carried beyond himself, lost all thought of mockery, spoke as one in earnest, and was the means of his own conversion.[75]

Bible—power of

Hermon Norton was the corresponding secretary of the American and Foreign Christian Union in the 1800s. In his missionary travel through the

[74] Robert Murray M'Cheyne, *Additional Remains of the Rev. Robert Murray M'Cheyne* (Edinburgh: John Johnstone, 1847), 77-8

[75] C. H. Spurgeon, *The Metropolitan Tabernacle Pulpit, Sermons Preached and Revised by C. H. Spurgeon during the Year 1870, vol. XVI* (London: Passmore & Alabaster, 1871) 508-509

western part of New York, he came to a village where there was a society of Universalists, whose preacher was a man of great zeal and earnestness. He tried various attempts to draw Mr. Norton into a debate, but the latter avoided him. One day, however, they met by accident, and were introduced to each other. The Universalist would not let the opportunity go by.

"Well, Mr. Norton," he said, "I am one of those who hold that all will be saved."

"I am aware of that," said Mr. Norton.

"And I think I can convince you that the doctrine is true," said the Universalist. He then entered upon the usual arguments in support of such views, receiving an attentive hearing from Mr. Norton, until he had said all that he wished to.

"I have but one answer to make to all that," said Mr. Norton, looking him steadily in the face.

"Well, sir, what is it?" asked the Universalist.

"Except you repent you will perish."

This reply greatly perplexed the other. He complained that Mr. Norton had not met the case; but being assured by the latter that he had nothing else to say, he rallied and put forth some other arguments, being determined if possible to draw him out.

Mr. Norton heard him quietly until he was through, and again said, "I have but one reply to make to all that." The other paused to hear what it would be, when Mr. Norton solemnly repeated the awful words, "Except you repent you will perish."

"Why," said the wounded man, for the word of the Spirit had pierced him deeply, "you will not argue at all."

"I have nothing more to say," Mr. Norton quietly replied. After a short pause, the Universalist turned to leave the room.

"Stop, my friend," said Mr. Norton. "I wish to say to you that there is one thing that you will not be able to forget."

"What is it, sir?" he asked.

"Except you repent, you will lose your soul." A bitter smile of incredulity was the only reply to this last remark. Mr. Norton saw nothing more of him that day.

On the following day, the Universalist called upon Mr. Norton, and expressed a desire to have more conversation.

"No," said Mr. Norton, "I do not wish any more conversation with you."

"Oh, sir," said the other, "I have not come to argue with you; you were right yesterday when you told me that there was one thing I would not be able to forget. I feel that it is true, that except I repent, I must perish, and I have come to ask you what I must do to be saved?"

"My dear friend, said Mr. Norton, "if that be the way, I shall be happy to talk with you as long as you please." And they did talk together, and prayed together, and the result was that the Universalist became a believer and a preacher of the truth which he had previously labored to divert and destroy.[76]

Bible—reveals God

As a young Christian, Harry Ironside visited an old, dying man named Andrew Fraser, who could barely speak above a whisper. After a few words of introduction, he said to Ironside, "Young man, you are trying to preach Christ; are you not?"

Ironside replied, "Yes, I am."

"Well," the older saint whispered, "sit down a little, and let us talk together about the Word of God." He opened his well-worn Bible, and until his strength was gone, simply, sweetly, and earnestly he opened up truth after truth as he turned from one passage to another, in a way that Ironside's own spirit had never entered into them.

Before he realized it, tears were running down his face, and Ironside asked, "Where did you get these things? Could you tell me where I could find a book that would open them to me? Did you learn these things is some seminary or college?"

Ironside said that he would never forget his answer. "My dear young man, I learned these things on my knees on the mud floor of a little sod cottage in the north of Ireland. There with my open Bible before me, I used to kneel for hours at a time, and ask the Spirit of God to reveal Christ to my soul and to open the Word to my heart, and He taught me more on my knees on that mud floor that I ever could have learned in all the seminaries or colleges in the world."[77]

---

[76]   C. Chamberlain, *The Layman's Assistant* (Hartford: Published by the author, 1862), 225-7

[77]   H. A. Ironside, *In the Heavenlies* (Neptune, New Jersey: Loizeaux Brothers, 1937), 86-87

Bible—truth of

William Tyndale was ordained as a Roman Catholic priest in England in 1521. In a day when the Scriptures were in Latin, he became convinced of the need for an English translation. He stated that "it was impossible to establish the lay people in any truth except the Scripture were plainly laid before their eyes in their mother tongue, that they might see the process, order, and meaning of the text."[78] He was refused permission for this from the bishop of London, so he traveled to Germany where he translated the New Testament from Greek to English. King Henry VIII and the religious authorities were furious. He continued his work, translating the first five books of the Old Testament, but was betrayed and arrested near Brussels in 1535. In 1536, Tyndale was condemned to death as a heretic, to be strangled and then burned. His last words were, "Lord, open the king of England's eyes."[79] Tyndale gave his life for God's Word, and his prayer was answered. After his death the king authorized the publishing of the Bible in English for public use.

Bible—truth of

Naimbanna was an African prince, who arrived in England from the Sierra Leone in 1791. He was given a Bible and told that it was the Word of God. When asked later how he was convinced that it was indeed, the Word of God, Naimbanna replied, "When I found all good men minding the Bible, and calling it the Word of God, and all bad men disregarding it, I then was sure that the Bible must be what good men call it, the Word of God."[80]

Bible—understanding

Queen Mary of Scotland once asked the Reformer John Knox, "You interpret the Scriptures in one way, they [the pope and cardinals] in another; whom shall I believe, and who shall be judge?"

---

[78] Thomas Russell, ed., *The Works of the English Reformers, William Tyndale and John Frith, vol. I* (London: Ebenezer Palmer, 1831), 3

[79] John Foxe, *Book of Martyrs* (Cincinnati, Ohio: A. B. Roff, 1831), 264

[80] James Cooper, ed., *The Evangelical Repository, vol. XVI* (Philadelphia: William S. Young, 1857) 540

Knox answered, "You shall believe God who plainly speaketh in his word, and farther than the word teacheth you, you shall believe neither the one or the other. The word of God is plain in itself; if there is any obscurity in one place, the Holy [Spirit], who is never contrary to himself, explains it more clearly in other places, so that there can remain no doubt, but unto such as are obstinately ignorant."[81]

Bible—understanding

John Newton was once approached by a man who said, "Sir, I have collated every word in the Hebrew Scriptures seventeen times; and it is very strange if the doctrine of atonement, which you hold, should not have been found by me." Newton responded, "I am not surprised at this: I once went to light my candle with the extinguisher on it; now, prejudices from education, learning, etc., often form an extinguisher. It is not enough that you bring the candle: you must remove the extinguisher."[82]

Bible—validation

Marco Mariani was an Italian evangelist in the 1800s. As he spoke with an owner of an orchard in northern Italy, the man replied, "You tell me that your book is the Word of God, but you have no proof of it."

Mariani suddenly changed the subject, and, looking out at his fruit trees, said, "What fine looking pears! But what a pity they are of such poor quality."

"What! What!" exclaimed the orchard owner. "Of poor quality! It is plain that you have not tasted them. Pick one or two, and try!" The evangelist did so, and began to eat.

"Yes, you are right," he said, smacking his lips, "the pears are excellent. But, sir, you must deal with my book as I have dealt with your fruit. Taste, and you will see that the Word of God is good."[83]

---

[81] Thomas M'Crie, *Lives of the Scottish Reformers* (Xenia, Ohio: The Board of the Calvinistic Book Concern, 1846), 93

[82] Richard Cecil, *Memoirs of the Rev. John Newton* (New York: Thomas A. Ronalds, 1809), 160-1

[83] n.a., *The Highway in the Wilderness, A Popular Illustrated Report of the British and Foreign Bible Society for the Year MDCCCCVII-VIII*, (London: Bible House, 1908), 59

Bible—value of

It is recorded of Robert Murray M'Cheyne that his family devotions were full of life, full of gladness, to the end. Indeed, his very manner of reading the chapter reminded one of a man poring into the sands for pieces of fine gold, and from time to time holding up to you what he delighted to have found. He said once, "One gem from that ocean is worth all the pebbles from earthly streams."[84]

Blessing

Andrew Fuller was an English pastor and one of the founders of the Baptist Missionary Society, which sent William Carey to India. He once said to a friend,

> There was a period in my ministry when most of my people were in a very desponding state of mind. The more I tried to comfort them, the more they complained of doubts and depressions. They dragged on heavily in the way toward heaven...I knew not what to do nor what to think. At this time our attention was directed to the claims of the perishing heathen in India. My people were aroused and interested. They set out with earnestness and zeal in this new department of Christian usefulness. They did what they could, and while thus engaged, their lamentations ceased. The sad became cheerful, the desponding calm, and I, instead of having to comfort my flock, was myself comforted by them. God blessed them when they tried to be a blessing.[85]

Blessing

Robert Chapman was an English pastor of the nineteenth century. One day he was asked how he was. He replied that he was burdened. With concern, his friend inquired, "Burdened, Mr. Chapman?"

"Yes," he replied, referring to Psalm 68:19, "he daily loadeth us with benefits."[86]

---

[84] G. S. Bowes, *Illustrative Gatherings for Preachers and Teachers* (London: Wertheim, Macintosh & Hunt, 1860), 406

[85] C. Chamberlain, *The Layman's Assistant* (Hartford: Published by the author, 1862), 225-7

[86] Frank Holmes, *Brother Indeed* (London: Victory Press, 1956), 74

Blessing

When Dwight L. Moody was a young boy, his father died and life was difficult. An old man met him, asked him about his home, and then, laying his trembling hand upon his head, told him that although he had no earthly father, his heavenly Father loved him, and gave him a bright new cent. As an adult, Moody reflected, "I do not remember what became of that cent, but that old man's blessing has followed me for over fifty years, and to my dying day I shall feel the kindly pressure of that hand upon my head. A loving deed costs very little, but done in the name of Christ it will be eternal."[87]

Boldness

In 370 A. D., Basil of Caesarea became the bishop of Caesarea. At this time, the emperor Valens was promoting the doctrine of Arianism, which denies the divinity of Jesus Christ. Valens commanded the praetorian to offer to Basil the alternative of conforming to the Arian Creed, or of resigning his bishopric. Modestus accordingly summoned Basil, who appeared before him with his customary composure and dignity. At first the prefect addressed him courteously, but, finding that he was inflexible, changed his tone, and angrily asked Basil what he meant by persisting in his obstinate disobedience to the emperor's will. Basil answered, "Because his will is inconsistent with that of my Sovereign Lord, and I cannot worship any human creature, being myself a subject of that Lord."

Modestus passionately inquired if Basil had no fear of the penalties that was in his power to inflict—confiscation, exile, torture, even death itself. Basil smiled as he replied,

> What are such threats to me? He who has nothing to lose can scarce fear confiscation, and I have no possessions save these mean garments, and some few books. Neither does he fear exile who counts no spot on earth his home, being here but a pilgrim and a sojourner, seeking a safer place of rest. Heaven is my home. Nor do I fear torture—my frail body would endure but little— you could strike but one blow and my pain is past—I should

---

[87] William R. Moody, *The Life of Dwight L. Moody by his Son* (New York: Fleming H. Revell, 1900), 32-35

but depart sooner to Him, for Whose service I am willing to live, and after Whom my soul yearns.

Modestus expressed his astonishment that Basil dared to speak thus freely. Basil answered,

> Perhaps you have not met a Christian bishop, or under such circumstances you would have found the same conduct. In matters of this world we would be the humblest and gentlest of all men, and would not exalt ourselves against a prince or any other man. But when God and the things concerning Him are involved, we overlook all else, and fix our eyes only on Him. And we rather glory in fire and sword, torture and prison, in such case. Therefore, threaten, and insult me as you will. Tell the emperor that nothing shall induce me to disobey my Master, or to assent to an heretical and impious creed.

Reporting his lack of success to the emperor, Modestus said, "We are conquered by this bishop, whom no threatenings can shake, no arguments move, no promises allure. Timorous or mean men may be wrought upon, but as for him, except by open force, we have no chance of conquering him."[88]

Boldness

Chrysostom was brought before the Roman emperor, who threatened him, saying, "I will slay thee."

Chrysostom replied, "Nay, thou canst not, for my life is his with Christ in God."

The emperor threatened, "I will take way thy treasures."

Chrysostom responded, "Nay, that thou canst do, for, in the first place, I have none thou knowest of. My treasure is in heaven, and my heart is there"

The emperor then warned, "But I will drive thee away from man, and thou shalt have no friend left.

"Nay," said Chrysostom, "and that thou can'st not, for I have a Friend in

---

[88]   William James E. Bennett, *Lives of Certain Fathers of the Church in the Fourth Century, vol. I* (London: W. J. Cleaver, 1847), 92-95

heaven from whom thou can'st not separate me. I defy thee; there is nothing thou can'st do to hurt me."[89]

Brevity of Life

Once when John Wesley was kept waiting, he looked at his watch and exclaimed, "I have lost ten minutes forever."[90]

Brevity of Life

Jonathan Burr was a pastor in the early 1600s who did not conform to the Church of England. He was suspended and not allowed to preach. In despair over this, he said, "My preaching is my life. If I be laid aside from that, I shall quickly die."[91] Burr decided to set sail with his three children and his wife, who was pregnant with their fourth, to New England.[92]

That next year he became ill with smallpox. But God spared his life, and after his recovery, he made this commitment to the Lord:

> I, Jonathan Burr, being brought in the arms of Almighty God over the vast ocean, with my family and friends, and graciously provided for in a wilderness; and being sensible of my own unworthiness and self-seeking; yet of infinite mercy, being called unto the tremendous work of feeding souls; and being late with my family delivered out of a great affliction of the small-pox; and having found the fruit of that affliction; God tempering, ordering, and mitigating the evil thereof, so as I have been graciously and speedily delivered; I do promise and vow to Him that hath done all things for me;
>
> 1. That I will aim only at his glory and the good of souls, and not my own glory.

---

[89] n. a., *Early Days, vol. IV* (London: John Mason), 153-4

[90] Thomas Brown, *A History of the Origin and Progress of the Doctrine of Universal Salvation* (Albany, New York: G. Wood, 1826) 335-6

[91] Benjamin Brook, *The Lives of the Puritans, vol. III* (London: James Black, 1813), 463-4

[92] Cotton Mather, *Magnalia Christi Americana, or, The Ecclesiastical History of New-England from its First planting in the Year 1620, Unto the Year of Our Lord 1698, vol. 1* (Hartford, Conn.: Silas Andrus & Son, 1855), 372-374

2. That I will walk humbly, with lower thoughts of myself, considering that I am a puff of breath sustained by the power of his grace alone.

3. That I will be more watchful over my heart, to keep it in a due frame of holy obedience, without running out so far after the creature; for I have seen that he is my only help in time of need.

4. That I will put more weight upon that firm promise, and sure truth, that he is a God hearing prayer.

5. That I will set up God more in my family, more in myself, wife, children, and servants, conversing with them in a more serious manner. For this God aimed at in sending his hand into my family. I will remember death. In myself I am nothing, in Christ all things.

God blessed his ministry, and after hearing him preach, puritan Thomas Hooker remarked, "Surely, this man will not be long out of heaven. He preaches as if he were there already."[93]

Character

Because of an awareness of real virtue, the English preacher Rowland Hill was indifferent to the remarks of his enemies. On a particular occasion, he was scurrilously attacked in one of the public journals, and was urged by a zealous friend, exasperated against the writer, to bring legal action in defense. To this Hill replied, with calm dignity—"I shall neither answer the libel, nor prosecute the writer, and that for two reasons—first, because, in attempting the former, I should probably be betrayed into unbecoming violence of temper and expression, to my own grief, and the wounding of my friends; and in the next place, I have learned by experience *that no man's character can be eventually injured but by his own acts.*"[94]

Character

When the famous missionary-explorer to Africa, David Livingstone, had not been heard from for many months, people all over the world became

---

[93]   Benjamin Brook, *The Lives of the Puritans, vol. III* (London: James Black, 1813), 463-5

[94]   Edwin Sidney, *The Life of the Rev. Rowland Hill,* (London: Baldwin & Cradock, 1834), 411

anxious for news. Henry Stanley, a reporter for the *New York Herald,* set out to look for Livingstone and finally found him at Ujiji in Central Africa. After spending four months with the doctor, Stanley wrote:

> I went to Africa as prejudiced as the biggest atheist in London. But there came a long time for reflection. I saw this solitary old man there and asked myself, 'How on earth does he stay here? What is it that inspires him?' For months I found myself wondering at the old man carrying out all that was said in the Bible, 'Leave all things and follow me.' But little by little my sympathy was aroused. Seeing his piety, his gentleness, his zeal, his earnestness, I was converted by him although he had not tried to do it! It was not Livingstone's preaching which converted me. It was Livingstone's living![95]

Character

Fred Shepard was an American medical missionary who served over thirty years in the Ottoman Empire at Aintab, central Turkey. He turned his mission station into a major medical relief center, where he treated Armenians, Kurds, and Turks. In 1915 he contracted typhus working among the victims of the Armenian Genocide, and died. Reflecting on his life, a poor Armenian declared, "I have never seen Jesus, but I have seen Dr. Shepard."[96]

Comfort

Puritan William Gouge suffered greatly with "sharp and bitter pains" because of urinary infections, asthma, and lung disease. When a friend sought to comfort him by mentioning the gifts that God had given him and the ministry he had done, he responded, "I dare not think of any such things for comfort. Jesus Christ, and what He hath done and endured, is the only ground of my sure comfort."[97]

---

[95]   Henry M. Stanley, *How I Found Livingstone in Central Africa* (London: Sampson, Low, Marston, Low and Searle, 1872), 434

[96]   Alice Shepard Riggs, *Shepard of Aintab* (New York: Interchurch Press, 1920), 196

[97]   James Reid, *Memoirs of the Lives and Writings of Those Eminent Divines, Who Covened in the Famous Assembly at Westminster, in the Seventeenth Century, vol. I* (Paisley, Great Britain:

Comfort

Martin Luther was well acquainted with grief, having lost his beloved daughter Magdalene when she was thirteen years old. When Luther's friend Justus Jonas lost his wife in 1542, he wrote to him with this letter of comfort,

> Grace and peace in Christ, who is our salvation and consolation, my dear Jonas! I have been so thoroughly prostrated by this unexpected calamity that I do not know what to write. We have all lost in her the dearest of friends. Her bright presence, her eye so full of trust, all drew forth our love, especially as we knew that she shared both our joys and sorrows as if they had been her own... The deep longing after one so distinguished by piety, propriety, and amiability makes me weep. Therefore I can easily imagine your feelings. Temporal consolation is of no avail here. One must look solely to the unseen and eternal... Mourn, therefore, as you have good cause to do, but at the same time comfort yourself with the thought of the common lot of humanity. Although according to the flesh the parting has been very bitter, nevertheless we shall be reunited in the life beyond, and enjoy the sweetest communion with the departed, as well as with Him who loved us so, that He purchased our life through His own blood and death. It is very true that God's mercy is better than life. What does it matter though we should suffer a little here, when there we shall partake of joy unspeakable? God, who has tried you, will comfort you now and for ever. Amen. Martin Luther.[98]

Compassion

In the mid-1800s, a young minister was discouraged. In spite of his diligent study and labor, his ministry was not flourishing. He had been reading about Robert Murray M'Cheyne, who recently died at the age of thirty, yet who

---

S. and A. Young, 1811), 358

[98]   *The Letters of Martin Luther*, trans. by Margaret A. Currie (London: MacMillan and Co., 1908), 419-20

had shook Scotland with tremendous spiritual force. This minister felt that he should like to visit Dundee where M'Cheyne served as pastor. The old sexton who served under M'Cheyne was still there and he agreed to take him through the church.[99] He led the young man into M'Cheyne's study. He said, "Sit down in that chair." The traveler hesitated a moment and then sat down. On the table in front of him was an open Bible.

The sexton said, "Drop your head in the book and weep. That is the way our minister always did before he preached."

Then he said, "Come with me." He took him into the pulpit before the open Bible. "Now," he said, "stand there and drop your head in your hands over the book and begin to weep. That is the way our minister did before he preached."[100]

Compassion

One Sunday, Robert Raikes, who was the owner and publisher of the *Gloucester Journal*, was talking with a woman. Their conversation was interrupted by a group of boys. In the 1700s, Sunday was the only day off for working children, which became a day, as the woman put it, of "noise and riot, playing and cursing and swearing in a manner so horrid as to convey to any serious mind an idea of hell rather than any other place."[101]

Raikes was motivated to do something about this. He hired four women to teach children reading and the Bible from ten o'clock to noon, then returning after lunch from one o'clock to five-thirty. Raikes later wrote, "It is now three years since we began; and I wish you were here, to make inquiry into the effect. A woman who lives in a lane where I had fixed a school, told me, some time ago, that the place was quite a heaven upon Sundays, compared to what it used to be. The numbers who have learned to read, and say their catechism, are so great that I am astonished at it. Upon the Sunday afternoon the mistresses take their scholars to church, a place into which neither they nor their ancestors ever entered with a view to the glory of God."[102]

---

[99]   F. W. Boreham, *The Heavenly Octave* (New York: Abingdon, 1936), 34

[100]   Cortland Myers, *How Do We Know?* (Philadelphia, The Judson Press, 1927), 46

[101]   William Henry Watson, *The History of the Sunday School Union* (London: Sunday School Union, 1853), 4

[102]   Ibid., 6

Compassion

When Colonial missionary John Eliot was eighty-five years old, his friends urged him that it was time to cease from his missionary toils among the Indians of New England. He replied, "My understanding leaves me, my strength fails me, but, thank God, my charity holds out."[103]

Compassion

In the late 1800s, Charles Spurgeon founded a children's orphanage, which his biographer called, "the greatest sermon Mr. Spurgeon ever preached." Once, when visiting the children there with a friend, Spurgeon asked, "Will you go to the infirmary? We have an infirmary and quarantine, for sometimes the poor creatures we take in need a good deal of purifying. We have one boy very ill with consumption; he cannot live, and I wish to see him, for he would be disappointed if he knew I had been here and had not seen him." His friend describes the visit, writing,

> We went into the cool and sweet chamber, and there lay the boy. He was very much excited when he saw Mr. Spurgeon. The great preacher sat by his side, and I cannot describe the scene. Holding the boy's hand in his, he said,
> "Well, my dear, you have some precious promises in sight all around the room. Now, dear son, you are going to die, and you are very tired lying here, and you will be free from all pain, and you will rest." "Nurse, did he rest last night?"
> "He coughed very much."
> "Ah, my dear boy, it seems very hard for you to lie here all day in pain, and cough all night. Do you love Jesus?"
> "Yes."
> "Jesus loves you. He bought you with His precious blood, and He knows what is best for you. It seems hard for you to lie here and listen to the shouts of the healthy boys outside at play. But soon Jesus will take you home, and then He will tell you the reason, and you will be so glad."

---

[103]   A. J. Gordon, *The Holy Spirit in Missions* (New York: Fleming H. Revell Company, 1893), 47-8

Then, laying his hand on the boy, without the formality of kneeling, he said, "O Jesus, Master, this dear child is reaching out his thin hand to Thine. Touch him, dear Savior, with Thy loving warm clasp. Lift him as he passes the cold river, that his feet be not chilled by the water of death; take him home in Thine own good time. Comfort and cherish him till the good time comes. Show him Thyself as he lies here, and let him see Thee and know Thee more and more as his loving Savior."

After a moment's pause he said, "Now, dear, is there anything you would like? Would you like a little canary in a cage, to hear him sing in the morning? Nurse, see that he has a canary tomorrow morning. God-bye [sic], my dear; you will see the Savior perhaps before I shall."

Then Spurgeon's friend concludes:

I have seen Mr. Spurgeon holding by his power sixty-five hundred persons in a breathless interest; I knew him as a great man universally esteemed and beloved; but as he sat by the bedside of a dying pauper child, whom his beneficence had rescued, he was to me a greater and grander man than when swaying the mighty multitude at his will.[104]

Compromise

Robert Robinson came to faith in Christ after hearing George Whitefield preach. In 1758, when he was twenty-three, he wrote the lyrics to the hymn, "Come Thou Fount of Every Blessing." In this beloved song, Robinson expresses the joy of the believer in light of God's grace and goodness. Yet as the hymn concludes, he confesses, "Prone to wander, Lord, I feel it, prone to leave the God I love." Sadly, this was the case in his own life, as Robinson lost his spiritual fervor and devotion. One day, he was traveling in a stagecoach with a lady who had just before happened to be reading this hymn. She asked his opinion of it, but he changed the subject and turned her attention to another topic. After a short period, she returned to

---

[104] John B. Gough, *Sunlight and Shadow; or, Gleanings from my Life Work* (London: R. D. Dickinson, 1881), 242-3

her question, and described the benefits she derived from the hymn, and her strong admiration of its sentiments. She observed that Robinson was greatly agitated, but she did not know why. Finally, overcome, he burst into tears, and said, "Madam, I am the poor unhappy man who composed that hymn many years ago; and I would give a thousand worlds, if I had them, to enjoy the feeling I then had."[105]

Compromise

When Mary came to the British throne in 1553, she arrested Thomas Cranmer, the Archbishop of Canterbury, on charges of heresy. He was imprisoned for two years. With the hope of receiving leniency, Cranmer recanted most of his Protestant views. Yet he was still condemned to die. He then publicly renounced his recantations and heroically met his death. When he was set to the stake to be burned, and the flame was kindled, he thrust his right hand into the fire and held it there with unflinching steadiness, exclaiming from time to time, "This hand hath offended—this unworthy hand! Lord Jesus, receive my spirit."[106]

Confidence

"I shall not die, but live, and declare the works of the Lord" (Psalm 118:17). This text was inscribed by Martin Luther upon his study wall, where he could always see it when at home. Many Reformers had been done to death—Huss, and others who preceded him, had been burnt at the stake; Luther was cheered by the firm conviction that he was perfectly safe until his work was done. In this full assurance he went bravely to meet his enemies at the Diet of Worms, and indeed, went courageously whenever duty called him. He felt that God had raised him up to declare the glorious doctrine of justification by faith, and all the other truths of what he believed to be the gospel of God; and therefore no fire could burn him, and no sword could kill him till that work was done. Thus he bravely wrote out his belief, and set it where many eyes would see it, "I shall not die, but live, and declare the works of the Lord."

---

[105] Joseph Belcher, *Historical Sketches of Hymns, Their Writers, and Their Influence* (Philadelphia: Lindsay & Blakiston, 1859) 229-230

[106] Charles Webb Le Bas, *The Life of Archbishop Cranmer, vol. II* (London: J. G. & F. Rivington, 1833), 248

It was no idle boast; but a calm and true conclusion from his faith in God and fellowship with him.[107]

Confidence

Martin Luther once spoke pointed words of wisdom to a man who was much depressed. He said to him,

> Man, what are you doing? Can you think of nothing else but your sins, and dying, and damnation? Turn your eyes away, and direct them to Christ. Cease to fear and lament. You really have no reason for it. If Christ were not here, and had not done this for you, you would then have reason to fear; but He is here, has suffered death for you, and has secured comfort and protection for you, and now sits at the right hand of His Heavenly Father to intercede for you.[108]

Confidence

When Scottish pastor Ebenezer Erskine was dying in 1754, a friend asked him, "Sir, you have given us much good advice as to our souls; pray tell me what are you now doing with your own?"

He replied, "I am doing just what I was doing forty years ago; I am resting on that word, 'I am the Lord thy God;' and resting on this, I mean to die."[109]

Confidence

Puritan William Perkins once encountered a young man, condemned to death, ascending the gallows. The prisoner looked upon the gathered crowd with such distress that he looked half dead already. Perkins said to him, "What man! What is the matter with thee? Art thou afraid of death?" The young man explained that he was afraid of something worse, of what would come after death.

---

[107]   C. H. Spurgeon, *The Metropolitan Tabernacle Pulpit, Sermons Preached and Revised by C. H. Spurgeon during the Year 1892, vol. XXXVIII* (London: Passmore & Alabaster, 1892), 2

[108]   James Macaulay, *Luther Anecdotes* (London: Religious Tract Society, 1894) 110

[109]   H. A. Downing, *Anecdotes for the Family, Or, Lessons of Truth and Duty for Every-day Life* (Hartford, Conn.: Case, Lockwood & Company, 1862), 348

Perkins replied, "Come down again man, and thou shalt see what God's grace will do to strengthen thee." When the prisoner came down, Perkins took his hand and they kneeled together for prayer. Perkins prayed such a fervent prayer of the confession of sins and its consequence of God's terrible and eternal judgment, that the man burst into an abundance of tears. Seeing this effect, Perkins began the second part of his prayer, showing Jesus Christ as the Savior, extending His hand of mercy, and His power to deliver him from God's condemnation. The prisoner's eyes were opened to "see how the black lines of all his sins were crossed, and cancelled with the red lines of his crucified Savior's precious blood, so graciously applying it to his wounded conscience, as made him break out with new showers of tears for joy for the consolation he found.

He gave such an expression of it to the onlookers, that they lifted their hands, and praised God to see such a blessed change in him. The man rose from his knees and went to the gallows with such cheerfulness and liveliness, being delivered from hell and heaven opening up to receive his soul, to the great rejoicing of the those who witnessed it.[110]

Contending for the faith

Athanasius lived at a crucial time, when Arianism was widely taught—the belief that Jesus was not equal to God, that He was created by God before time. Athanasius, who was the greatest theological opponent of Arianism, attended the Council of Nicea in 325, with 300 bishops to resolve this issue. It was a time when "the Christian world was divided into two parts, until at length, by the zeal and courage of Saint Athanasius, the Arians were condemned in a general council, and a creed formed upon the true faith, as Saint Athanasius hath settled it."[111]

Athanasius was fervent in his denunciation of Arianism. He accused the Arians of perverting Scripture,[112] called them Antichrists[113] and opposers of

---

[110]   Clarke, Samuel, *The Marrow of Ecclesiastical History* (London: Printed for T. U., 1654), 852-3

[111]   James Hamilton, *Our Christian Classics: Readings for the Best Divines*, (London: James Nisbet and Co., 1857), 157

[112]   John Henry Newman, *Select Treatises of S. Athanasius* (Oxford: John H. Parker, 1844), 19

[113]   Ibid., 75

Christ,[114] and compared their conduct to the serpent when he beguiled Eve.[115] By refusing to compromise with the powerful Arian party, Athanasius was exiled five times over a period of thirty years. But his courageous faithfulness resulted in Arianism being exiled from orthodox teaching and biblical truth protected.

Contending for the faith

On December 8, 1414, John Huss was imprisoned for his teaching, waiting his trial and execution. During this time he wrote a letter, saying, "O most faithful Christ, draw us weak ones after thee, for we cannot follow thee if thou dost not draw us. Give us a strong mind, that it may be prepared and ready. And if the flesh is weak, help us by thy grace, and accompany us, for without thee we can do nothing; and least of all, can we face a cruel death. Give us a ready and willing spirit, and undaunted heart, the right faith, a firm hope, and perfect love, that patiently and with joy we may for thy sake give up our life."[116]

Contending for the faith

In 1521, Martin Luther was ordered to appear before a formal deliberative assembly (The Diet of Worms) before Emperor Charles V to renounce or reaffirm his views. Copies of his writings were laid out on a table, and he was asked if they were his and whether he stood by their contents. Luther confirmed he was their author, but requested time to think about the answer to the second question. He prayed, consulted friends, and gave his response the next day: "*Since your most Serene majesty* and your High mightiness require from me a simple, clear and direct answer, I will give you one, and it is this: I can not submit my faith either to the pope or to the councils, because it is as clear as day they have erred and contradicted each other. Unless, therefore, I am convinced by the testimony of Scripture, or on plain and clear grounds of reason, so that conscience shall bind me to make acknowledgment of error, I neither can nor will retract; for it is neither safe nor wise to do anything contrary to conscience."

---

[114] Ibid., 77

[115] Ibid., 19

[116] E. H. Gillett, *The Life and Times of John Huss, vol. II*; (Boston: Gould and Lincoln, 1864) 33-4

And then, looking round on the assembly, he said, "Here I stand. I can do no other. May God help me. Amen."[117]

Unless I am convinced by the testimony of the Scriptures or by clear reason (for I do not trust either in the pope or in councils alone, since it is well known that they have often erred and contradicted themselves), I am bound by the Scriptures I have quoted and my conscience is captive to the Word of God. I cannot and will not recant anything, since it is neither safe nor right to go against conscience. May God help me. Amen."

Contentment

On July 8th, 1796, the Charles Simeon had a remarkable encounter as he came across a group of blind men weaving. Simeon wrote in his journal,

> May I never forget the following fact: One of the blind men... answered, "I never saw till I was blind, nor did I ever know contentment when I had my eye-sight, as I do now that I have lost it. I can truly affirm, though few know how to credit me, that I would on no account change my present situation and circumstances with any that I ever enjoyed before I was blind."[118]

Contentment

In the 1700s, an English pastor, Dr. Stonehouse, was passing through Salisbury Plain, England, fearful of the appearance of the sky. He came upon a shepherd named David Saunders, and asked him what sort of weather it would be the next day. The shepherd replied, "It will be such weather as pleases me." The pastor was surprised by that answer, and asked him how that could be.

"Because," replied the shepherd, "It will be such weather as shall please God, and whatever pleases him always pleases me."[119]

---

[117] J. A. Wylie, *The History of Protestantism*, vol. I (London: Cassell, Petter & Galpin) 344

[118] William Carus, ed., *Memoirs of the Life of the Rev. Charles Simeon* (London: Hatchard and Son, 1847), 124-125

[119] *The Scottish Herald, vol. III* ed. by James Glassford, et. al. (Edinburgh: John Johnstone, 1838), 208

Conviction

On February 8, 1555, the day before he was burned at the stake in front of his cathedral, John Hooper was visited in prison by his friend Sir Anthony Kingston. Sir Anthony urged him to change from his Protestant beliefs and accept the Roman Catholic doctrine which was being enforced by Queen Mary.

"Consult your safety," he said, "life is sweet and death is bitter, and your life hereafter may do good."

Hooper replied, "I thank you for your friendly counsel. True it is that death is bitter and life is sweet, but alas! Consider that death to come is more bitter and the life to come is more sweet. Therefore, for the desire and love I have to the one, and the terror and fear I have of the other, I do not so much regard this death nor esteem this life; but have settled myself, through the strength of God's Holy Spirit, patiently to pass through the torments and extremities of the fire now prepared for me, rather than to deny the truth of His Word."[120]

Conviction

When Puritan pastor Nathaniel Heywood was forced out of his church in 1662 for nonconformity, one of the men of his congregation came to him and said, "Ah! Mr. Heywood, we would gladly have you preach still in the church." Heywood responded, "Yes, I would as gladly preach as you can desire it, if I could do it with a safe conscience." The man replied, "Oh, sir, many a man now-a-days makes a great gash in his conscience; cannot you make a little nick in yours?"[121] Heywood answered, "No, I must follow Christ fully."[122]

Conviction

When the Scottish minister John Welsh, was banished to France in 1606, his wife Elizabeth, the daughter of John Knox was told by King James that he might return to Scotland if he would acknowledge the authority of bishops.

---

[120] n.a., *Writings of Dr. John Hooper* (Philadelphia: William S. Martien, 1842), 6-7

[121] Samuel Palmer, *The Nonconformist's Memorial: Being an Account of the Ministers, who Were Ejected Or Silenced after the Restoration, particularly by the Act of Uniformity, which took Place on Bartholomew-day, Aug. 24, 1662* (London: W. Harris, 1775), 102

[122] C. H. Spurgeon, *The Metropolitan Tabernacle Pulpit, Sermons Preached and Revised by C. H. Spurgeon during the Year 1875, vol. XXI* (London: Passmore & Alabaster, 1876) 114

Elizabeth knew that this would be a violation of conviction and conscience, and so in reply, she raised her apron and said, "Please your Majesty, I'd rather kep [catch] his head there."[123]

Conviction

Because of preaching, Puritan John Bunyan was imprisoned for twelve long years from 1660-1672. He expressed his feelings about this, saying,

> The parting with my wife and poor children hath often been to me in this place as the pulling of the flesh from my bones; and that not only because I am some what too fond of these great Mercies, but also because I should have often brought to my mind the many hardships, miseries and wants that my poor family was like to meet with should I be taken from them, especially my poor blind child, who lay nearer my heart than all I had besides.[124]

Bunyan could have left prison anytime by simply agreeing not to preach. But he stood firm, saying,

> If nothing will do unless I make of my conscience a continual butchery and slaughter-shop, unless putting out my own eyes, I commit me to the blind to lead me, as I doubt not is desired by some, I have determined, the Almighty God being my help and shield, yet to suffer, if frail life might continue so long, even till the moss shall grow on mine eyebrows, rather than thus to violate my faith and principles.[125]

Courage

John Rogers was an English preacher in the sixteenth century and the first martyr under the reign of Queen Mary. In January 1554, Bonner, the

---

[123] James Anthony Froude, *Thomas Carlyle: A History of the First Forty Years of His Life, 1795-1835, vol. I* (London: Longmans, Green, and Co., 1882) 108-9

[124] John Brown, *John Bunyan: His Life Times and Work* (Boston and New York: Houghton, Mifflin and Company, 1888), 189-90

[125] Ibid., 240

new Bishop of London, sent him to Newgate Prison, where he was remained for a year. On January 29, 1555 he was sentenced to death. Up to that day, no one could tell how the English reformers would act in the face of death, and could hardly believe that they would actually give their bodies to be burned for the faith. But on February 4, as a crowd gathered and saw John Rogers walking steadily and unflinchingly to his fiery grave, they erupted in enthusiastic applause. Count Noailles, the French Ambassador, wrote home a description of the scene, saying that Rogers went to death "as if he was walking to his wedding."[126]

Courage

When John Eliot preached to the Massachusetts Indians in the 1600s, some of the Indian chiefs opposed and threatened him. He replied, "I am about the work of the great God, and my God is with me, so that I neither fear you nor all the chiefs in the country. I will go on, and do you touch me if you dare."[127]

Death—a liberator

William Jenkyn was a Puritan pastor ejected from his ministry for nonconformity and sent to prison in 1684. Soon his health began to decline. A petition was presented to the King for his release, which was backed by an assurance from his physicians, that his life was in danger from close imprisonment. But no other answer could be obtained than this: "Jenkyn shall be a prisoner as long as he lives."

After his death, a nobleman said to the king, "May it please your Majesty, Jenkyn has got his liberty."

Upon which the king replied, "Aye, who gave it him?

The nobleman answered, "A greater than your majesty, the King of kings."[128]

---

[126] John Charles Ryle, *Facts and Men* (London: William Hunt and Company, 1882) 8

[127] *An Account of John Eliot: The Friend of the American Indians* (Dublin: Bentham & Hardy, 1826), 6

[128] Walter Wilson, *The History and Antiquities of Dissenting Churches and Meeting Houses, in London, Westminster, and Southwark, vol. III* (London: Printed for the author, 1810), 331-333

Death—is gain

Ignatius, student of the apostle John and Bishop of Antioch, lived and died for Christ as a martyr. He said, "I would rather die for Jesus Christ, than rule to the utmost ends of the earth."[129]

Death—peace in

When he was dying in 1690, Puritan Thomas Goodwin remarked, "Ah, is this dying? How I have dreaded as an enemy this smiling friend."[130]

Death—peace in

Colonial Puritan preacher Cotton Mather exclaimed on his death bed, "I am not afraid to die: if I was, I should disgrace my Savior. I am in his hand, where no ill can befall me."[131]

Death—peace in

When a friend visited pastor Benjamin Parsons as he was dying in 1855, he asked him, "How are you today, sir?"

Parsons replied, "My head is resting very sweetly on three pillows; infinite power, infinite love, and infinite wisdom."[132]

Death—perspective of

John Newton one day mentioned at his table the death of a lady. A young woman who sat opposite immediately said, "Oh, sir, how did she die?"

He replied, "There is a more important question than that, my dear, which you should have asked first."

---

[129] William Wake, ed., *The Genuine Epistles of the Apostolical Fathers* (London: Samuel Bagster, 1840), 188

[130] William Jay, *Morning Exercises for the Closet: For Every Day in the Year, vol. I* (London: Hamilton, Adams, and Co., 1829), 49

[131] Augustus Toplady, *The Works of Augustus M. Toplady, vol. IV* (London: Printed for the Proprietors and sold by W. Row, 1794), 179

[132] Paxton Hood, *Dark Sayings on a Harp* (London: Jackson, Walford, and Hodder, 1865), 170

"Sir," said she, "what question can be more important than 'How did she die'"?

Newton's answer was, "How did she live?" [133]

Death—perspective of

In 1799 the eminent British sculptor John Bacon died. In his will he ordered that the following words, on plain stone, be inscribed over his grave:

> What I was as an artist seemed to me of some importance while I lived BUT what I really was as a believer in Christ Jesus is the only thing of importance to me now. [134]

Death—result of sin

Martha Wesley was the sister of the Charles Wesley, who criticized most severely Charles's hymn which began

> Ah, lovely appearance of death
> What sight upon earth is so fair?

She did not believe at all in the lovely appearance of death, but thought it repulsive, and she never would look at a corpse, "Because," she said, "it was beholding sin upon its throne." [135]

Death—the entrance to heaven

John Owen, in his last hours, when on his dying bed, dictated a short letter to a friend. The secretary had written, "I am yet in the land of the living," when Owen at once arrested him. "Stop, alter that," he said. "Write, 'I am yet in the land of the dying, but I hope soon to be in the *land of the living*.'" [136]

---

[133] Harvey Buckland, *A Book for Spare Moments. The Urn and the Page.* (Edinburgh: James Hogg, 1856), 37

[134] Richard Cecil, *Memoirs of John Bacon* (London: F. and C. Rivington, 1801) 20-21

[135] J. B. Wakeley, *Anecdotes of the Wesleys: Illustrative of Their Character and Personal History* (London: Hodder & Stoughton, 1869), 6

[136] Emily Elizabeth Steele Elliott, *Northcote Memories* (London: Seeley, Jackson, & Halliday), 109

Death—without Christ

Colonel Ethan Allen, hero of the American Revolutionary War, was an unbeliever who wrote a book to deny the deity of Jesus Christ. A physician, Doctor Elliot, came to visit his home when his beloved daughter was dangerously sick. He was taken to the library, where Allen read to him some of his writings. While thus engaged, a messenger entered, informing Allen that his daughter was dying, and desired to speak with him. He immediately went to her chamber, followed by Doctor Elliot. The wife of Colonel Allen was a pious woman who had instructed her daughter in the principles of Christianity. As soon as her father appeared at her bedside, she said to him, "I am about to die; shall I believe in the principles you have taught me, or shall I believe in what my mother has taught me?"

Allen became extremely agitated; his chin quivered and his whole frame shook. After a few minutes, he replied, "Believe what your mother has taught you."[137]

Diligence

When Theodore Beza sought John Calvin to refrain at least during his sickness from dictating and writing, he answered, "Would you that the Lord should find me idle when he comes?"[138]

Diligence

In 1690, on the day of his death when he was eighty years old, John Eliot, "The Apostle of the Indians," was teaching the alphabet to an Indian child at his bedside. A friend asked him, "Why not rest from your labors now?"

Eliot replied, "Because, I have prayed to God to render me useful in my sphere, and now that I can no longer preach, he leaves me strength enough to teach this poor child his alphabet."[139]

---

[137] Charles Walter Brown, *Ethan Allen: Of Green Mountain Fame, a Hero of the Revolution* (Chicago: M.A. Donohue & Company, 1902) 212

[138] David N. Lord, *Theological and Literary Journal, vol. v* (New York: Franklin Knight, 1853), 582

[139] Joseph Belcher, *The Clergy of America* (Philadelphia: J. B. Lippincott & Co., 1849), 179-80

Diligence

George Whitfield once remarked to Colonial pastor William Tennent, "Brother Tennent, you are the oldest man amongst us, do you not rejoice to think that your time is so near at hand, when you will be called home?"

Tennent replied, "My business is to live as long as I can, as well as I can, and to serve my master as faithfully as I can, until he shall think proper to call me home."[140]

Discernment

A Quaker in the 1600s called upon the imprisoned John Bunyan with what he claimed was a message from the Lord. He declared, "After searching for thee in half the jails of England, I am glad to have found thee at last."

Bunyan replied sarcastically, "If the Lord sent thee, you would not have needed to take so much trouble to find me out, for He knows that I have been in Bedford jail these seven years past."[141]

Discernment

The eighteenth century English preacher William Grimshaw was speaking with a woman who had expressed her admiration of a certain minister, one who was gifted in talent but lacked grace. "Madam," said Grimshaw, "I am glad you never saw the devil." When asked why he made this remark, he said,

> Because he has greater talents than all the ministers in the world. I am fearful, if you were to see him, you would fall in love with him; as you seem to have so high a regard for talent without sanctity. Pray, do not be led away with the sound of talents. Let the ministry under which Providence has called you never be deserted under the influence of novelty. There dwell; and pray fervently that it may prove to you increasingly edifying, consolatory, and instructive.[142]

---

[140]   John Gillies, *Memoirs of the Life and Character of the Late Rev. George Whitefield*, ed. by Aaron C. Seymour (Philadelphia: Simon Probasco, 1820), 154

[141]   Robert Chambers, *The Book of Days*, vol. II (London, W. & R. Chambers, 1832), 289

[142]   R. Spence Hardy, *William Grimshaw, Incumbent of Haworth, 1742-63* (London: John Mason, 1860), 221-2

Encouragement

Colonial Puritan pastor John Eliot was known for encouraging others to seek God. When he was informed of any news of importance, he would say, "Brethren, let us turn all this into prayer." If he visited the house of a friend he would to say, "Come, let us not have a visit without prayer. Let us pray down the blessing of heaven on your family before we go."[143] One of Eliot's friends said of him, "I was never with him but I got, or might have got, some good from him"[144]

Encouragement

John Wesley, before his death, wrote a letter to William Wilberforce, the British legislator who worked for the abolition of the slave trade in England for twenty years. It was a monumental, challenging effort that at times seemed impossible, and Wesley wrote to encourage Wilberforce in his labor:

Feb. 24. 1791

My dear Sir,

Unless the Divine power has raised you up... I see not how you can go through your glorious enterprise, in opposing that execrable villany which is the scandal of religion, of England, and of human nature. Unless God has raised you up for this very thing, you will be worn out by the opposition of men and devils; but if God be for you who can be against you. Are *all* of them together stronger than God? Oh be not weary of well doing. Go on in the name of God, and in the power of his might, till even American slavery, the vilest that ever saw the sun, shall vanish away before it. That he who has guided you from your youth up may continue to strengthen you in this and all things, is the prayer of, dear sir,

Your affectionate servant,
John Wesley.[145]

---

[143] Benjamin Brook, *The Lives of the Puritans, vol. III* (London: James Black, 1813), 485

[144] John Wilson, *Life of John Eliot, the Apostle of the Indians* (Edinburgh: William Oliphant, 1828), 222

[145] Robert Isaac Wilberforce and Samuel Wilberforce, *The Life Of William Wilberforce, vol. I*

Eternity

Jonathan Edwards was used by God in an extraordinary way. One of the reasons for this was his perspective on living in light of eternity, seen in his diary entry from Monday, February 3, 1724: "Let every thing have the value now which it will have on a sick bed: and frequently, in my pursuits of whatever kind, let this question come into mind, 'How much shall I value this, on my death bed?'"[146]

Eternity

When Puritan Bishop John Hooper was condemned to be burned in 1555, Sir Anthony Kingston urged him to recant, saying that life was sweet, and death was bitter. Hooper replied,

> I thank you for your friendly counsel, although it be not so friendly as I could have wished it. True it is, that death is bitter, and life is sweet: but alas! Consider that the death to come is more bitter, and the life to come is more sweet. Therefore for the desire and love I have to the one, and the terror and fear of the other, I do not so much regard this death, nor esteem this life; but have settled myself, through the strength of God's Holy Spirit, patiently to pass through the torments and extremities of the fire now prepared for me, rather than to deny the truth of his word.[147]

Evangelism—commanded

At a dinner given in his honor, a lady asked medical missionary Wilfred Grenfell, "Is it true that you are a missionary?"

Grenfell replied, "Isn't it true that you are?"[148]

(London: John Murray, 1838), 297

[146] S. E. Dwight, *The Life of President Edwards* (New York: G. & C. Carvill, 1830), 102

[147] John Hooper, *Later Writings of Bishop Hooper: Together with His Letters and Other Pieces ed. by Charles Nevinson* (Cambridge: University Press, 1852), xxv

[148] James M. Gray, ed., *Christian Thought, vol. 20,* (Mount Morris, Ill.: The Moody Bible Institute, 1919), 572

Evangelism—commanded

In 1857, naval officer Andrew Foote commanded the *USS Portsmouth*. While in Siam, the King was received onboard for dinner. As they sat down, Commander Foote gave thanks to God for their meal, which surprised the King. He remarked that he thought only the missionaries did that. "True," replied Foote, "but every Christian is a missionary"[149]

Evangelism—commitment of

At the end of his missionary work in New Guinea and other South Sea islands in the 1800s, James Chalmers reflected back on his hardships and sacrifices and said this, "I have had twenty-one years experience amongst the natives... recall the twenty-one years, give me back all its experience, give me its shipwrecks, give me its standings in the face of death, give it me surrounded with savages with spears and clubs, give it me back again with spears flying about me, with the club knocking me to the ground, give it me back, and I will still be your missionary!"[150]

Evangelism—compassion of

An American preacher once preached in the pulpit of the Scottish preacher Robert Murray M'Cheyne, and asked if anyone knew him personally. He was met with no response—all had died or moved away since his day. At last in the doorway of the church, he met an old Scotsman of ninety years old who said that years ago he had heard Robert Murray M'Cheyne preach. He was asked to tell what his text was, but he could not remember. He was then asked to tell something about the sermon, but again, he could not remember. He was then asked to recount something about his manner in the pulpit, but he could not. "But," he said,

> There is one thing I can tell you. I will never forget when I was a mere lad by the roadside one day. M'Cheyne came by. He stopped by me, came over to the side of the fence where I stood and said,

---

[149]   Stephen Abbott Northrop, *A Cloud of Witnesses: The Greatest Men in the World for Christ and the Book* (Fort Wayne, Ind: M. Long, 1894), 153

[150]   Richard Lovett, *James Chalmers, His Autobiography and Letters* (London: Religious Tract Society, 1902), 276-7

"Jamie, I am going to see your sick sister. I am afraid she is not going to live." Then he put his hand on my head and said, as the tears ran down his face, "Jamie, lad, I am concerned about your soul. I want you to give your heart to Christ; I must have you saved.

The Scotsman then added, "I have forgotten everything else about M'Cheyne, but I can feel those fingers on my head yet."[151]

Evangelism—joy of

A Christian Armenian talking to Cyrus Hamlin, missionary to Turkey in the 1800s, was expressing his astonishment over people waking up to the truth of Christ. He said, "Yes, it is going forward; it will triumph, but, alas! I shall not live to see it. Alas that I am born an age too soon!"

Hamlin answered, "But do you remember what our Savior said, 'There shall be joy in the presence of God over one sinner that repenteth'? You may not live to see the truth triumphant in this empire, but should you reach the kingdom of heaven your joy over your whole nation will be infinitely greater than it could be on earth."

The Armenian seem surprised at this thought, but after examining the passage, he was enraptured at the thought that our interest in the Church of Christ and the progress of His kingdom on earth is something which death cannot touch, and which, instead of ceasing in this life, will only be increased and perfected in another. He replied, "O fool, and slow of heart, to read the gospel so many times without perceiving such a glorious truth."[152]

Evangelism—God's Word in

Ralph Norton, who was the Director of Personal Work for the Chapman-Alexander Missions in the early 1900s, was talking with some friends about evangelism, in which God used him so wonderfully. When they noticed the almost exclusive place he gave to the Bible in personal work, one asked him, "What do you do in cases where the unsaved man does not accept the Bible as having any authority?"

---

[151] Cortland Myers, *The New Evangelism* (Philadelphia: American Baptist Publication Society, 1903) 15-6

[152] *The Christian Witness and Church Members' Magazine*, vol. VII, ed. by John Campbell (London: John Snow, 1850), 56-57

Norton answered, "If I had a fine Damascus sword with a keen double-edged blade, I would not sheath it in a fight just because the other man said he did not believe in it."[153]

Evangelism—God's Word in

John Wesley was once stopped by a robber, who demanded his money or his life. Mr. Wesley, after giving him the money, said, "Let me speak one word to you; the time may come when you will regret the course of life in which you are now engaged." And then, quoting John 1:9 he said, "Remember this, 'The blood of Jesus Christ cleanseth from all sin.'"

No more was said, and they parted. Many years after, as Wesley was going out of a church building in which he had been preaching, a stranger introduced himself, and asked him if he remembered being waylaid at such a time. He said he recalled it. The stranger said, "I was that man, and that single verse you quoted on that occasion was the means of a total change in my life and habits. I have long since been in the practice of attending the house of God and of giving attention to his word, and trust that I am a Christian."[154]

Evangelism—hindrances

David Brainerd, missionary to the American Indians in the 1700s, was asked by one why he desired the Indians to become Christians, seeing the Christians were so much worse than the Indians are in their present state. The Christians, he said, would lie, steal, and drink, worse than the Indians. It was they who first taught the Indians to be drunk: and they stole from one another. He supposed that if the Indians should become Christians, they would then be as bad as these. Brainerd was grieved and joined with him in condemning the wicked conduct of some who are called Christians and told him that these were not Christians in heart; that he hated such wicked practices, and did not desire the Indians to become such as these.[155]

---

[153]   F. N. Peloubet, Amos R. Wells, *Peloubet's Select Notes on the International Sunday School Lessons* (Boston: W. A. Wilde, 1918), 271

[154]   J. B. Wakeley, *Anecdotes of the Wesleys: Illustrative of Their Character and Personal History* (London: Hodder & Stoughton, 1869), 175x

[155]   Jonathan Edwards, Sereno Edwards Dwight, *Memoirs of the Rev. David Brainerd; Missionary to the Indians* (New Haven, Conn.: S. Converse, 1822), 174

Evangelism—message of

When the men whom John Wesley sent out to preach returned, he would ask these questions: "Has anybody been converted? Has anybody been convicted of sin? Did you make anybody mad?" If the answer was no, he would say to them, "Well then, you need not go out to preach again."[156] Wesley understood that when God's Word is faithfully presented, people either become convicted, they become saved, or they become antagonistic.

Evangelism—obedience in

Amy Carmichael left England in 1895 for India. As she traveled and evangelized throughout that country, she realized that many young girls were offered by their parents as temple prostitutes. She began rescuing these young Indian girls from this horror, ministering the love and truth of Christ. She established a home and school for these rescued children, laboring in India for fifty-five years, not once returning to England. Exhorting Christians, she pleads for obedience to Christ's command to bring the gospel to the lost, writing

> But singing hymns from a distance will never save souls. By God's grace, coming and giving and praying will. Are we prepared for this? Or would we rather sing? Searcher of hearts, turn Thy search-light upon us! Are we coming, giving, praying *till it hurts*? Are we praying, yea agonizing in prayer? Or is prayer but "a pleasant exercise"—a holy relief for our feelings?[157]

Evangelism—obedience in

John Vassar, American preacher of the 1800s, once spoke to a lady in a hotel about her soul. Her husband came in a little later and found her weeping. Upon hearing the cause, he angrily exclaimed, "I will let that man know that he is to mind his own business!"

---

[156]   Charles Edward Locke, *A Man's Reach* (New York: Eaton & Mains, 1914), 258

[157]   Amy Wilson-Carmichael, *Things as They Are: Mission Work in Southern India* (London: Morgan and Scott, 1903), 271-2

"O husband," exclaimed the weeping woman, "if you had heard him you would have known that he was about his business."[158]

Evangelism—priority of

Before William Carey set off as a missionary to India, he was a shoe cobbler in England. He would tell everyone he could about the gospel of Jesus Christ. One day a friend came to him and said, "I want to speak to you very seriously."

"Well," said Carey, "What is it?"

His friend said, "By your going about to people as you do, you are neglecting your business. If you only attended to making shoes more than you do, you would be all right, and would soon get on and prosper; but as it is you are simply neglecting your business."

Carey replied, "Neglecting my business? My business is to extend the Kingdom of God and I only cobble shoes to pay expenses!"[159]

Evangelism—urgency of

Scottish pastor Thomas Chalmers, on a return from England, was a guest in the house of a nobleman near Edinburgh. He was the life of the conversation that evening, on the subject of the causes and cure of poverty. Among those present was an old Highland chieftain, who listened with intense interest. The conversation was kept up to a late hour. When the company broke up, they were shown upstairs into their apartments. The apartment of Chalmers was directly opposite to that of the old chieftain, who had already retired with his attendant. As Chalmers was undressing himself, he heard an unusual noise in the chieftain's room; the noise was succeeded by a heavy groan. He hastened into the apartment, which was in a few moments filled with the company who all rushed in to the relief of the old man. It was a sad sight which met their eyes; the white-headed chief had fallen into the arms of his attendant, in a stroke. He breathed for a few moments, and then expired. Chalmers stood in silence, with both hands

---

[158] Cortland Myers, *The New Evangelism* (Philadelphia: American Baptist Publication Society, 1903) 71-2

[159] *The Churchman, Volume 90, ed. by W. Livingston Larned* (New York: The Churchman Co., 1904), 935

stretched out, and bending over the deceased. He was the very picture of distress, and was the first to break silence. He exclaimed,

> Never in my life, did I see, or did I feel, before this moment, the meaning of that text, 'Preach the Word; be instant in season, and out of season; reprove, rebuke, exhort, with all long-suffering and doctrine.' Had I known that my venerable old friend was within a few minutes of eternity, I would not have dwelt on that subject which formed the topic of this evening's conversation. I would have addressed myself earnestly to him. I would have preached unto him, and you, Christ Jesus and Him crucified. I would have urged him and you, with all the earnestness befitting the subject, to prepare for eternity. You would have thought it, and you would have pronounced it out of season; but ah! It would have been in season, both as it respected him, and as it respects you.[160]

Evangelism—urgency of

When Bishop Phillips Brooks was recovering from an illness, he denied seeing all visitors. But when the famed agnostic Robert Ingersoll called, Brooks received him at once. Ingersoll said to him, "I appreciate this very much, but why do you see me when you deny yourself to your friends?"

Brooks replied, "Well, you see, I feel confident of seeing my friends in the next world, but this may be my last chance of seeing you."[161]

Evangelism—urgency of

When John Duncan, professor of Hebrew and Oriental languages at New College, Edinburgh, was dying in 1870, someone told him that there was a man in the hospital whose language no one could speak. "I will learn it," the dying scholar replied, "I will learn it, that I may tell him about the Saviour."[162]

---

[160] William C. Brownlee, ed., *The Magazine of the Reformed Dutch Church, vol. I* (New Brunswick, New Jersey: Rutgers Press, 1827), 33

[161] Seth Scott Bishop, ed., *Illinois Medical Bulletin*, vol. 6 (Chicago: Illinois Medical College, 1905) 671

[162] J. D. Jones, *The Glorious Company of the Apostles* (London: James Clarke & Co., Limited, 1800), 169-170

Evangelism—warning of

A Scottish lady heard George Whitefield preach from Matthew 25:10, "And the door was shut." He showed against whom the door would be shut, and from what the sinner would be excluded. There were two trifling young men sitting near the lady, and not far from the door of the church, who were full of hilarity and glee, and were making light of the solemn appeals of the preacher; and during the sermon she heard one of them say in a low tone to the other, "O, well, what if the door be shut? Another will open."

Whitefield had not proceeded far in his discourse when he said, "It is possible there many be some careless, trifling persons here today who may ward off the force of this impressive subject by lightly thinking, 'What if the door be shut? Another will open.'"

This repetition of their remark by the preacher came upon them like a sudden flash of lightning. It put an effectual stop to their trifling. The young men were sorely troubled under his pointed appeals. Whitefield went on to say with the utmost solemnity, "Yes, another door will open, and I will tell you what door it will be: it will be the door of the bottomless pit! The door of hell! The door that conceals from the eyes of angels the horrors of damnation!"[163]

Example

At the funeral of Nicholas Haussmann in 1522, Martin Luther gave this simple eulogy. He said, "What we preach, he lived."[164]

Example

Dr. Maltbie Babcock was pastor of the Brick Church in New York in the 1800s. A lady in his congregation once sent him tickets to the opera. Dr. Babcock was a gifted musician and composer, and a great lover of music, yet he returned the tickets with thanks, saying he could not use them.

The lady felt somewhat indignant, as if her practice of attending the opera had been condemned by her pastor, and went to see him about it. He quietly told her that he did not sit in judgment on anyone else. He then recounted

---

[163] Joseph Beaumont Wakeley, *Anecdotes of the Rev. George Whitefield, M.A., with Biographical Sketch,* (London: Hodder and Stoughton, 1872), 319

[164] F. B. Proctor, ed., *The Clergyman's Magazine,* (London: Hodder and Stoughton, 1880), 223

an operation at the hospital that he had witnessed recently, where the physicians and nurses had taken every possible precaution to be thoroughly clean, lest by the lightest contamination they might endanger the life of the patient. He asked her, "Do you think they did right to be so careful?"

She replied, "Most certainly! Anything less would have been criminal."

Then he gently said, "My dear fried, I am a surgeon of souls. If the conduct of the operators at the hospital is right, and anything less would have been criminal, you will quickly understand how I feel about doing the least thing that might influence a weak soul who might be looking to me for an example. I have thought of everything that people say to justify themselves in doing this or that, but as for myself, I cannot run the risk. For their sakes I sanctify myself, trying to do so in the spirit of my Master. That is all."

The lady was silent for a moment, then rose to go. There were tears in her eyes. She was thankful that she had that kind of a pastor."[165]

Example

Major General Oscar Westover was the fourth chief of the United States Army Air Corps. When he was a student at the United States Military Academy in the early 1900s, someone asked a group of men at the academy the question, "What is a Christian?" Immediately one of the men replied, "Oscar Westover."[166]

Faith

Augustine was confronted by a man who showed him his idol and exclaimed, "Here is my god; where is yours?" Again, the man pointed to the sun in the sky and said, "Behold, here is my god; where is yours?"

Augustine replied, "I did not show him my God, not because I did not have one to show him, but because he did not have eyes to see Him."[167]

---

[165] Howard Agnew Johnston, *Enlisting for Christ and the Church* (New York: Association Press, 1919), 115

[166] Clayton Sedgwick Cooper, *The Century Illustrated Monthly Magazine*, Vol. LXXX, New Series: Vol. LVII, May to October, 1910 (New York: The Century Co.), 150

[167] *The Christian Witness and Church Members' Magazine, vol. V,* ed. by John Campbell, (London: John Snow & Co., 1869), 266

Faith

Lord Congleton was an English nobleman and devout Christian who lived in the 1800s. He had a large number of people on his estate who were very poor. He tried in many ways to do them good, but found it hard to get them to believe the Bible and become Christians. He thought over the matter a long time. He said to himself, "What shall I do to show these people *how* they may be saved, and secure for themselves a share in all the blessings of the gospel?"

At last he hit upon a creative plan, and at once carried it out. He made up his mind to give public notice that on a particular day, from nine o'clock in the morning to twelve o'clock at noon, he would be in his office, with his steward; and that if any of his tenants, or the people who lived on his grounds, were troubled by debts which they could not pay, if they would bring their bills with them, and tell how much they owed, they should have their debts paid, and get a receipt for the same. This notice was written out, signed by own name, and posted up in different places. People read it, and talked about it, and wondered it over, but could not tell what to make of it.

At last the day appointed came. At nine o'clock precisely his carriage drove up to his office. He got out and entered the office, and sat there with his steward. A crowd of people gathered outside, and talked freely about this strange offer.

"It's all a hoax," said one man. "I don't believe a word of it."

"But there's his lordship's own signature," replied another, "and *he* never tries to hoax people. He always means what he says."

"There must be a mistake about it somewhere," said another. "I'm not going to be made a fool of in this way."

And thus they talked on, but no one went in. About eleven o'clock an old man who lived with his wife in the poor-house, came along. He owed some money which he could not pay, but which he greatly desired to have paid before his died. He had heard of this offer, and made up his mind to accept it. Some of his friends tried to persuade him not to go. But he pointed to the written notice against the wall. "I know," said he, "that *that's* his lordship's name, and I'm sure he would never put his name to anything intended to deceive."

So he went in. "Please your lordship, here's the bill for what I owe. I am living it's true in the poor-house; but I can't die happy while I'm in debt."

"And why should I pay your debts?" asked Lord Congleton.

"I can't tell, please your lordship," said the old man. "But I saw the promise signed by your lordship's own name. I had faith in your promise, and so I came."

"Right," said Lord Congleton. "Steward, write a check for his debts." The man received it. He examined it. He saw it was all right, and then said:

"Thank your lordship a thousand times for your kindness. Now I'll go out and tell my friends."

"No, no," said Lord Congleton. "They've got the same promise that you had. If they believe my promise and come in, they shall have all that was promised. If they can't trust my word they can have nothing."

He waited in this office till the clock struck twelve. Then he went out. Waving overhead the check that had been given to him, he exclaimed, "I've got all that was promised. Three cheers for Lord Congleton! Hurrah! Hurrah! Hurrah!"

As Congleton came out and stepped into his carriage, there was a rush of men towards him, with bills in their hands, crying, "Please, your lordship here's my bill–and mine–and mine."

But he quietly waved his hand, and said, "My friends, if you had believed my promise, and brought your bills in time they would all have been paid. But you would not trust me; and I can do nothing for you now."[168]

Faith—and feelings

Evangelist Dwight L. Moody recounts a night, when preaching in Philadelphia, a young lady's eyes were riveted on him, as if she were drinking in every word. After his message he spoke to her. "Are you a Christian?" he asked.

She answered, "No; I wish I was; I have been seeking Jesus for three years."

"There must be some mistake," Moody replied.

She looked strangely at him, and said, "Don't you believe me?"

"Well, no doubt you thought you were seeking Jesus," Moody responded, "but it doesn't take an anxious sinner three years to meet a willing Savior."

"What am I to do then?"

Moody answered, "The matter is, you are trying to *do* something; you must just believe on the Lord Jesus Christ."

---

[168] Richard Newton, *The Life of Jesus Christ for the Young* (Philadelphia: George Barrie, 1880) 44-49

She replied, "Oh, I am sick and tired of the word: 'Believe, believe, believe!' I don't know what it is."

"Well," he said, "we'll change the word; take 'trust.'"

She asked, "If I say, 'I'll trust Him,' will He save me?"

"*No*; I don't say that; you may *say* a thousand things, but He will if you *do* trust Him."

"Well," she said, "I do trust Him; "but," she added in the same breath, "I don't feel any better.""

"Ah, I've got it now!" exclaimed Moody. "You've been looking for feelings for three years, instead of for Jesus."[169]

Faith—dead faith

William Grimshaw entered the ministry in England in 1731. Every Sunday his duties as a clergyman were regularly performed; the prayers were read with seriousness and a sermon was preached. But he was not a believer. After the death of his wife he began to earnestly seek for power over sin and purity of heart, giving up pleasures and avoiding outward transgression. He fasted and kept a diary of his sins and prayed prayers of vows, confessions, and supplications. He was increasingly confronted with the vileness of his heart, the bitterness of sin, and his utter inability to set himself right with God. One day visiting a friend, he came across a book by John Owen on justification. He recounts, "I was now willing to renounce myself; every degree of fancied merit and ability; and to embrace Christ only, for my all in all. O, what light and comfort did I now enjoy in my own soul, and what a taste of the pardoning love of God!"[170]

Faithfulness

Artists in the early church were faced with the problem of making their living from the production of idols. Their argument was that this was their living and that they must live. Tertullian response was, "*Must* you live?"[171]

---

[169]   John Lobb, *Arrows and Anecdotes of Dwight L. Moody* (London: "Christian Age" Office, 1876), 118

[170]   R. Spence Hardy, *William Grimshaw, Incumbant of Haworth, 1742-63* (London: John Mason, 1860), 14-20

[171]   T. R. Glover, *The Conflict of Religions in the Early Roman Empire,* (London: Methuen & Co.,

Faithfulness

Girolamo Savonarola was an Italian preacher who spoke against the corruption of the Roman Catholic Church. Pope Alexander VI was counseled by one of his bishops to offer him the red hat, that is, the office of cardinal, on the condition that he would cease to preach and retract what he had said. The Pope sent Lodovico de Ferrara, Master of the Sacred Palace to Savonarola with the offer. Three days they spent in earnest discussion; but the preacher was firm as a rock. When unsuccessful in disputation, the Master threw the bait. He said, "Cease from these predictions, be quiet, and His Holiness authorizes me to offer you a red hat."

Savonarola replied, "God forbid that I should be unfaithful to the embassy of my Lord. But—be at sermon tomorrow, and you shall hear." In his sermon Savonarola launched forth astounding censures on all orders of the clergy, and closed with declaring, "Red hat! I wish for no other red hat than that of martyrdom, reddened with my own blood." He was burned to death on May 23, 1498.[172]

Faithfulness

George Smith arrived as a missionary to South Africa in 1737. He endured persecution by the Dutch colonists for seven years before being forced out. During that time he led one poor woman to Christ. One hundred years later, when they celebrated the founding of that mission, they sought to sum up his brief work and calculated that more than 13,000 believers had come from that endeavor that seemed such a failure.[173]

Faithfulness

In the 1800s, Pastor George Lorimer met a man who claimed to be a Christian. When he asked him if he was a member of a church, the man answered, "No, the dying thief never joined the church, and he went to heaven."

1909), 321

[172] William Harris Rule, *Dawn of the Reformation. Savonarola. With events of the reign of Pope Alexander VI* (London: John Mason, 1855) 183-185

[173] Max Wood Moorhead, ed., *The Student Missionary Enterprise: Addresses and Discussions of the Second International Convention of the Student Volunteer Movement for Foreign Missions* (Boston: Fleming H. Revell, 1894), 128-129

Lorimer then asked, "But you support the cause of missions?"

The man replied, "No, the dying thief never contributed to missions, and he went to heaven."

"Yes," said the pastor, "but he was a dying thief, and you are a living one."[174]

Father—influence of

John Paton went as a missionary in the 1800s to the New Hebrides (modern day Vanuatu), where previous missionaries were killed and eaten by cannibals and others were driven off. What was it that gave him the commitment and courage to brave this endeavor? In his autobiography he gives the answer—it was the influence of his father. Growing up, as he saw the godly example of his father, he asked himself, "He walked with God, why may not I?"[175]

His father's love and faith was evident as John left to attend seminary and become a city missionary. Paton remembered,

> My dear father walked with me the first six miles of the way. His counsels and tears and heavenly conversation on the parting journey are as fresh in my heart as if it had been but yesterday, and tears are on my cheeks as freely now as then, whenever memory steals me away to the scene. For the last half mile or so we walked on together in almost unbroken silence, my father, as was often his custom, carrying hat in hand while his long flowing yellow hair (then yellow, but in later years white as snow) streamed like a girl's down his shoulders. His lips kept moving in silent prayers for me, and his tears fell fast when our eyes met each other with looks for which all speech was vain. We halted upon reaching the appointed parting place; he grasped my hand firmly for a minute in silence, and then solemnly and affectionately said,
>
> "God bless you my son! Your father's God prosper you, and keep you from all evil!"

---

[174]   Charles G. Fisher, ed., *The Missionary Guardian,* vol. IV (Philadelphia: Reformed Church Publication House, 1894), 154

[175]   John Gibson Paton, *John G. Paton, Missionary to the New Hebrides* (New York: Fleming H. Revell, 1898), 11-12

Unable to say more, his lips kept moving in silent prayer. In tears we embraced and parted. I ran off as fast as I could, and when about to turn a corner in the road where he would lose sight of me, I looked back and saw him still standing with his head uncovered where I had left him. Waving my hat in adieu, I was around the corner and out of sight in an instant, but my heart was too full and sore to carry me further, so I darted into the side of the road and wept for a time. Then rising up cautiously, I climbed the dike to see if he yet stood where I left him, and just at that moment I caught a glimpse of him climbing the dike and looking out for me! He did not see me and after he had gazed eagerly in my direction for a while he got down, set his face toward home and began to return. His head still uncovered and his heart, I felt sure, still rising in prayers for me.

I watched through blinding tears till his form faded from my gaze and then hastening on my way, vowed deeply and oft, by the help of God to live and act so as to never grieve or dishonor such a father and mother as He had given me. The appearance of my father when we parted, his advice, prayers and tears, the road, the dike, the climbing up on it and walking away head uncovered, have often, often, all through life risen vividly before my mind... The scene, not only helped by God's grace to keep me pure from the prevailing sins, but also stimulated me in all my studies that I might not fall short of his hopes, and in all my Christian duties that I might faithfully follow his shining example.[176]

Fasting

Colonial pastor William Tennent, Jr. was passing through a town in the state of New Jersey, in which he was a stranger and had never preached. Stopping at a friend's house to dine, he was informed that it was a day of fasting and prayer in the congregation, on account of a very severe and threatening drought. His friend had just returned from church, and the

---

[176] Ibid., 40-42

intermission was but half an hour. Mr. Tennent was requested to preach, and with great difficulty consented, as he wished to proceed on his journey. At church, the people were surprised to see this unknown and unexpected preacher ascend the pulpit. His whole appearance was covered with dust, and engaged their curiosity. On his rising up, instead of beginning to pray, as was the usual practice, he looked around the congregation with a piercing eye and earnest attention, and after a minute's profound silence, he addressed them with great solemnity in the following words:

> My beloved brethren! I am told you have come here today to fast and pray; a very good work indeed, provided you have come with a sincere desire to glorify God thereby. But if your design is merely to comply with a customary practice, or with the wish of your church officers, you are guilty of the greatest folly imaginable, as you had much better have stayed at home and earned your three shillings and sixpence, (at that time the stated price for a day's labor) but if your minds are indeed impressed with the solemnity of the occasion, and you are really desirous of humbling yourselves before Almighty God, your Heavenly Father, come, join with me, and let us pray.

This had an effect so uncommon and extraordinary on the congregation that the utmost seriousness was universally manifested. The prayer and the sermon added greatly to the impressions already made, and tended to rouse the attention, influence the mind, command the affections, and increase the temper which had been so happily produced. Many had reason to bless God for his unexpected visit, and to reckon this day one of the happiest of their lives.[177]

Forgiveness—God's

When Donald Cargill was led to the scaffold in 1681 and approached the cord by which he was to be hanged, he declared that he went up the ladder with less fear and agitation of mind than ever he entered the pulpit to

---

[177]   Archibald Alexander, *Biographical Sketches of the Founder and Principal Alumni of the Log College* (Philadelphia: Presbyterian Board of Education, 1851), 121-2

preach the Word of God to sinners. He proclaimed, "I am no more terrified at death, nor afraid of hell, because of sin, than if I had never had sin; for all my sins are freely pardoned and washed away, through the precious blood and intercession of Jesus Christ."[178]

Forgiveness—God's

Puritan Thomas Fuller once said, "He that falls into sin is a man; [he] that grieves at it, is a saint; [he] that boasteth of it, is a devil.[179] Two centuries later, English pastor William Marsh agreed, adding, "Only one thing more, He that forgives it is God."[180]

Forgiveness—God's

Dr. J. Wilbur Chapman had in his church a professor of mathematics whose life had been ruined by sin and had come to Christ through Chapman's preaching. One Sunday, as he was speaking to a group of men, Chapman told his men, as Psalm 103:12 declares, that God removes our sins from us as far as the east is from the west. Turning to the professor, Dr. Chapman said, "Professor, that is a mathematical proposition for you; how far is the distance from east to west?"

The professor reached for his pencil and notebook to make the calculation. Then, suddenly he stopped and burst into tears, and facing the group said, "Men, you can't measure it, for if you put your stake here, and east be ahead of you and west behind you, you can go around the world and come back to your stake, and east will still be ahead of you and west will still be behind you. The distance is immeasurable, and thank God," he cried, "that is where my sins have gone."[181]

---

[178] J. H. Merle D'Aubinge, *Germany, England, and Scotland: Or, Recollections of a Swiss Minister* (London: Simpkin, Marshall, and Co., 1848), 353-4

[179] Thomas Fuller, "The Holy and Profane States," in n.a., *The Library of the Old English Prose Writers* (Cambridge: Hilliard and Brown, 1831), 156

[180] Catherine Marsh, *The Life of the Rev. William Marsh* (London: James Nisbet & Co., 1868), 190

[181] *The Expositor, vol. XX ed. By G. B. F. Hallock* (Cleveland, Ohio: F. M. Barton, 1918), 143

Forgiveness—man's

John Wesley was sailing to America with General James Oglethorpe, the founder of the colony of Georgia. Wesley, hearing an unusual noise in the general's cabin, stepped in to inquire the cause of it. The general explained that he had caught a servant who had drunk up his wine. He said, "But I will be revenged on him. I have ordered him to be tied hand and foot, and to be carried on board the man-of-war that sails with us. The rascal should have taken care how he used me, for I never forgive." Wesley, calmly looking at him, replied, "Then I hope, sir, you never sin." The General was stunned at the reproof; and set the servant free.[182]

Forgiveness—man's

During the American Revolutionary War, a Tory named Michael Wittman was captured, accused of having carried aid and information to the British in Philadelphia. He was tried by court-martial, pronounced guilty of being a spy, and sentenced to be hanged. On the evening of the day before that set for the execution, Peter Miller, a friend of General Washington, came to see Washington. He said, "General Washington, I have come to ask a great favor of you."

Washington answered him, "I shall be glad to grant you almost anything, for we surely are indebted to you for many favors. Tell me what it is."

Miller replied, "I hear that Michael Wittman has been found guilty of treason and that he is to be hanged at Turk's Head tomorrow. I have come to ask you to pardon him."

Washington started back, and a cloud came over his face. "That is impossible," he said. "Wittman is a bad man. He has done all in his power to betray us. He has even offered to join the British and aid them in destroying us. In these times, we dare not be lenient with traitors; and for that reason, I am sorry that I cannot pardon your friend."

"Friend!" cried Miller. "Why, he is no friend of mine. He is my bitterest enemy. He has persecuted me for years. He has even beaten me and spit in my face, knowing full well that I would not strike back. Michael Wittman is no friend of mine."

---

[182] Thaddeus Mason Harris, *Biographical Memorials of James Oglethorpe: Founder of the Colony of Georgia in North America* (Boston: Printed for the author, 1841), 124

Washington was puzzled. "And still you wish me to pardon him?" he asked.

"I do," answered Miller. "I ask it of you as a great personal favor."

"Tell me," said Washington, with hesitating voice, "why is it that you thus ask the pardon of your worst enemy?"

"I ask it because Jesus did as much for me," was the old man's brief answer.

Washington turned away and went into another room. Soon he returned with a paper on which was written the pardon of Michael Wittman.

"My dear friend," he said, as he placed it in the old man's hands, "I thank you for this example of Christian charity."

Miller traveled all night, running to arrive before the execution at sunrise. Peter Miller had saved the life of his enemy, perhaps of his only enemy. Michael Wittman, with his head bowed upon his breast, went forth a free man and a changed man, because of forgiveness.[183]

Forgiveness—man's

Corrie Ten Boom was a Dutch Christian who with her family, helped many Jews escape the Nazis during World War II. But they were betrayed and her entire family was arrested and imprisoned. Her father died 10 days later. Corrie and her sister Betsie were sent to a political concentration camp in the Netherlands, then to the Ravensbrück concentration camp, where Betsie died.

Following WWII, Corrie became famous for her book *The Hiding Place*, which gave her the opportunity to proclaim Christ to thousands of people on speaking tours. One evening in 1947, after she had spoken about the forgiveness of Christ at a church in Munich, she had a stunning encounter. This is what she writes:

> The solemn faces stared back at me, not quite daring to believe. And that's when I saw him, working his way forward against the others. One moment I saw the overcoat and the brown hat; the next, a blue uniform and a cap with skull and crossbones. It came back with a rush — the huge room with its harsh overhead lights, the pathetic pile of dresses and shoes

---

[183] James Baldwin, *An American Book of Golden Deeds* (New York: American Book Company, 1907), 102-109

in the center of the floor, the shame of walking naked past this man. I could see my sister's frail form ahead of me, ribs sharp beneath the parchment skin. Betsie, how thin you were! That place was Ravensbruck, and the man who was making his way forward had been a guard, one of the most cruel guards. Now he was in front of me, hand thrust out. "A fine message, Fraulein! How good it is to know that, as you say, all our sins are at the bottom of the sea!" And I, who had spoken so glibly of forgiveness, fumbled in my pocketbook rather than take that hand. He would not remember me, of course— how could he remember one prisoner among those thousands of women? But I remembered him. I was face-to-face with one of my captors and my blood seemed to freeze.

"You mentioned Ravensbruck in your talk," he was saying. "I was a guard there. But since that time," he went on, "I have become a Christian. I know that God has forgiven me for the cruel things I did there, but I would like to hear it from your lips as well. Fraulein," — again the hand came out — "will you forgive me?"

And I stood there—I whose sins had again and again to be forgiven — and could not forgive. Betsie had died in that place. Could he erase her slow terrible death simply for the asking? It could have been many seconds that he stood there—hand held out—but to me it seemed hours as I wrestled with the most difficult thing I had ever had to do. For I had to do it — I knew that. The message that God forgives has a prior condition: that we forgive those who have injured us. "If you do not forgive men their trespasses," Jesus says, "neither will your Father in heaven forgive your trespasses." And still I stood there with the coldness clutching my heart.

But forgiveness is not an emotion—I knew that too. Forgiveness is an act of the will, and the will can function regardless of the temperature of the heart. "Jesus, help me!" I prayed silently. "I can lift my hand. I can do that much. You supply the feeling." And so woodenly, mechanically, I thrust out my hand into the one stretched out to me. And as I did, an incredible thing took place. The current started in my shoulder, raced down my arm, sprang into our joined hands. And then this healing warmth seemed to flood my whole being, bringing tears to my eyes.

"I forgive you, brother!" I cried. "With all my heart!" For a long moment we grasped each other's hands, the former guard and the former prisoner. I had never known God's love so intensely, as I did then.[184]

Gentleness

Misjudged and criticized by a fellow missionary, and not wanting any scandal before unbelievers, David Livingstone gave up his house and garden at Mabotsa, with all the toil and money they had cost him, and went with his young bride to some other place, to begin anew the toil of house and school building, and ministry. His colleague was so struck with his generosity that he said had he known his intention he never would have spoken a word against him. Livingstone had spent all his money, and out of a salary of a hundred pounds it was not easy to build a house every other year. But he stuck to his resolution. Parting with his garden was very painful for him, especially when he thought of the hands into which it was to fall. "I like a garden," he wrote, "but paradise will make amends for all our privations and sorrows here."[185]

Gentleness

Puritan pastor John Deering was at a public dinner, sitting across from a young man who broke out into profane swearing. Deering reproved him and the young man taking this as an affront, immediately threw a glass of beer in his face. Mr. Deering took no notice of the insult, but wiped his face, and continued eating as before. The young gentleman renewed his profane conversation; and Mr. Deering reproved him as before. With more rage and violence, he flung another glass of beer in his face. Deering continued unmoved, still showing his zeal for the glory of God, by bearing the insult

---

[184] Corrie Ten Boom, *Tramp for the Lord* (Fort Washington, Penn.: Christian Literature Crusade and Old Tappan, New Jersey: Fleming H. Revell, 1974), 55-57

[185] William Garden Blaikie, *The Personal Life Of David Livingstone* (New York: Revel, 1880), 92

with meekness and humble silence. This so astonished the young man, that he rose from the table, fell on his knees, and asked Deering's pardon; and declared that if any of the company offered him similar insults, he would stab them with his sword.[186]

Gentleness

John Wesley one day remarked to his friend Adam Clarke,

> As I was walking through St. Paul's Churchyard I observed two women standing opposite to one another. One was speaking and gesticulating violently, while the other stood perfectly still and in silence. Just as I came up and was about to pass them, the virago [scolding woman], clenching her fist and stamping her foot at her imperturbable neighbor, exclaimed, "Speak, wretch, that I may have something to say."
>
> "Adam," said Wesley, "that was a lesson to me; silence is often the best answer to abuse."[187]

Gentleness

On one occasion, a nurse in one of the London hospitals complained to Taylor Smith, the Chaplain-General to the forces that she had been rudely treated by some patients. "Thank God for that," was his reply.

"What do you mean?" asked the astonished nurse.

Smith replied, "Why, if you are carrying a vessel and somebody knocks up against you, you can only spill out of the vessel what is inside. And when people misjudge and persecute us, we can only spill what is inside. In the case of a godless man, he will probably swear. But if you are filled with the Holy [Spirit], you will manifest the gentleness of Christ, and make men astonished. Count it all joy when the testing times come. What I pray for is not that you may have less trials, but that you may have more grace."[188]

---

[186] Benjamin Brook, *The Lives of the Puritans, vol. I* (London: James Black, 1813), 211

[187] J. B. Wakeley, *Anecdotes of the Wesley's: Illustrative of the Character and Personal History* (London: Hodder and Stoughton, 1869), 166

[188] *Expositor and Current Anecdotes, vol. 16, no. 1, ed. by Evan J. Lena* (Cleveland, Ohio: F. M. Barton, October, 1914) 842

Giving—and greed

A farmer went to hear John Wesley preach. He was not a believer, but his attention was soon riveted on Wesley's sermon, which was about money. His first point was, "Get all you can." The farmer nudged a neighbor, and said, "This is strange preaching! I never heard the like of this before! This is very good. Yon man has got things in him; it is admirable preaching." John talked about industry, activity, and purposeful living.

Then he came to his second point, which was, "Save all you can." The farmer became more excited. "Was there ever anything like this?" he asked. Wesley denounced thriftlessness, waste, and the love of luxury. The farmer rubbed his hands, and he thought, "All this have I done from my youth up." It truly seemed to the farmer that salvation had come to his house.

But then Wesley came to his third point, which was, "Give all you can." "Ay dear, ay dear," said the farmer, "he has gone and spoilt it all."[189]

Giving—consistent with beliefs

Nineteenth century pastor John Hall told of a man who, while in church, sang most piously the hymn,

> Were the whole realm of nature mine,
> That were a present far too small

and all the throughout his singing, was fumbling in his pocket to find the smallest coin for the offering.[190]

Giving—consistent with beliefs

In 1854, American statesman, politician, and soldier Sam Houston came to faith in Christ and was baptized. Afterward, he pledged to pay half the salary of the local pastor. When someone asked him why, he replied, "My pocketbook was baptized, too."[191]

---

[189] n.a., *The Preacher's Lantern, vol., 1* (London: Hodder & Stoughton, 1871), 649-50

[190] n.a., *Harper's New Monthly Magazine,* vol. XLII (New York: Harper & Brothers, 1871), 479

[191] Franklyn Thomas Fields, *Texas Sketchbook A Collection Of Historical Stories From The Humble Way* (Houston: Humble Oil & Refining Co., 1955), 33

Giving—generously

John Eliot was very generous, often giving more than he could afford. One day the parish treasurer, on paying his salary, intended that he should convey it all home without giving any of it away. He put the money into a handkerchief, and tied it in as many hard knots as he could. Eliot took his handkerchief and departed for home. On his way he called to see a poor, sick woman. On entering, he gave them his blessing, and told them that God had sent them some relief. The sufferers shed tears of gratitude as Eliot, with moistened eyes, began to untie the knots in his handkerchief. After many efforts to get at his money, and impatient at the perplexity and delay, he gave the handkerchief and all the money to the mother of the family, saying with a trembling voice, "Here, my dear, take it; I believe the Lord designs it all for you."[192]

Giving—generously

During his service as a missionary in Turkey in the nineteenth century, William Schauffler was repeatedly asked how, having so little, he was able to give away so much and yet did not exhaust his store. He replied, "I keep shoveling over to the Lord, and he keeps shoveling back to me, and his shovel is bigger than mine."[193]

Giving—obligation of

Puritan pastor John Foxe, author of "The Book of Martyrs," was very generous to the poor. As he was going one day from the house of the Bishop of London, be found many people begging at the gate. Having no money, he immediately returned to the bishop and borrowed five pounds, which he distributed among the poor people. After some time, the bishop asked him for the money.

Foxe said to him, "I have laid it out for you, and have paid it where you owed it, to the poor that lay at your gate." Hearing this, the bishop thanked Foxe for what he had done.[194]

---

[192] Martin Moore, *Memoir of Eliot: Apostle to the North American Indians* (Boston: Seth Goldsmith and Crocker & Brewster, 1842), 125-6

[193] H. C. Haydn, ed., *American Heroes on Mission Fields* (New York: American Tract Society, 1890), 26

[194] Benjamin Brook, *The Lives of the Puritans, vol. I* (London: James Black, 1813), 338

Giving—praying and

In the Newmarket church where Charles Spurgeon first served as pastor, there was an old saint by the name of Sewell. One day he could not avoid being late to a meeting to raise money for home missions that was being held, and arrived as the meeting was closing. As he entered, Spurgeon said, "Our brother who has just come in will, I am sure, close the meeting by offering prayer for God's blessing on the proceedings of this evening." He stood up, but instead of praying began to fumble around in his pockets.

Spurgeon remarked, "I am afraid that my brother did not understand me. Friend Sewell, I did not ask you to *give*, but to *pray*."

To which the straightforward, bluff old saint replied, "Ay, ay, but I could not pray till I had given; it would be hypocrisy to ask a blessing on that which I did not think worth giving to."[195]

Giving—to the Lord

Andrew Fuller asked for a gift of money from a friend for foreign missions. His friend responded, "Seeing it is *you*, Andrew, I will give five pounds."

Fuller promptly replied, "Seeing it is *me* to whom you propose to give five pounds, I will not accept your gift."

His friend replied, "You are right. And now seeing it is the Lord Jesus Christ, I will give ten pounds."[196]

Giving—while there is opportunity

In the 1700s there lived a Christian merchant named John Thornton. He was once approached for financial assistance by a minister whose family was greatly in need of food. Thornton listened to his story and immediately gave him a draft for fifteen pounds. While the grateful minister was still with him, his mail arrived, and Thornton begged him not to go until he should see if there was any news which might interest him. He began to read one of the letters, and after a considerable pause, said, "Here is a letter conveying very bad news indeed: I have lost a very valuable ship, and certainly my loss

---

[195] Susannah Spurgeon, W. J. Harrald, The *Autobiography of Charles H. Spurgeon* (Cincinnati, Ohio: Curts & Jennings, 1898) 257-258

[196] *The Baptist Missionary Magazine, vol. LV* (Boston: Franklin Press, 1875), 125

cannot be less than twenty thousand pounds. You must return to me that draft, my dear sir; and to prove that I do not deceive you, read the letter which I have just received."

What could the poor minister do? He recalled the condition of his starving and sickly wife and children, and anticipated the grievous disappointment of his returning without assistance. With heavy heart, he handed the draft to Mr. Thornton and began to read the letter as a way of concealing his distressed countenance. He soon perceived the loss was ever greater than Thornton had mentioned, and all his hopes died away.

In the meantime Thornton had been writing, and when the letter was returned to him, he said, "You see, my dear sir, how unpleasantly I am situated; however, here is another paper which I desire you will put in your pocket." The hopeless minister took it, and opening it, found a draft for fifty pounds. He looked at Thornton with incredulity, and Thornton replied, "My dear sir, as the Almighty seems determined to deprive me of the wealth which he gave, and which he has so good a right to take away, I must be speedy, therefore, to give while it is in my possession."[197]

Glorifying God

The eighteenth century Scottish preacher John Brown of Haddington was once approached by a lad of an excitable temperament. He informed him he wished to be a preacher of the gospel. John Brown, finding him as weak in intellect as he was strong in conceit, advised him to continue in his present vocation. The young man replied, "But I wish to preach and glorify God."

Brown answered him, "My young friend, a man may glorify God making [brooms]; stick to your trade, and glorify God by your walk and conversation."[198]

Glorifying God

In her diary, Lady Campbell recalls how she was seized with a fever which threatened her life. It was then, she recounted, "the first question of the

---

[197]   H. A. Downing, *Anecdotes for the Family, Or, Lessons of Truth and Duty for Every-day Life* (Hartford, Conn.: Case, Lockwood & Company, 1862), 34-5

[198]   John Brown, *Spare Hours* (Boston and New York: Houghton, Mifflin and Company, 1861), 181

Assembly's Catechism was brought to my mind: 'What is the chief end of man?'"
as if some one had asked it. When I considered the answer to it, "To glorify God,
and to enjoy Him for ever," I was struck with shame and confusion. I found
I had never sought to glorify God in my life, nor had I any idea of what was
meant by enjoying Him for ever. Death and judgment were set before me; my
past sins came to my remembrance; I saw no way to escape the punishment
due unto them, nor had I the least glimmering hope of obtaining the pardon
of them through the righteousness of another." This led to her searching the
Scriptures and believing on the Lord Jesus as her Savior.[199]

God—attributes

When the Westminster Assembly met in the 1640s to prepare the
Catechism, they came to the question, "What is God?" The men were so
impressed with the greatness of the subject, and with their own inability
to frame a suitable answer to so very solemn a question, that for a time no
one spoke a word. After long consideration, George Gillespie, the youngest
of the Scotch Commissioners, was asked to lead them in prayer, asking for
light from above.

His prayer began, "O God! Thou Spirit, infinite, eternal, and unchangeable,
in Thy being, wisdom, power, holiness, justice, goodness, and truth."

Some of those present wrote his words, and the Assembly received them
both as an answer to their prayer, and to the solemn question, "What is God?"
No one suggested a single alteration.[200]

God—care of

In 1662, the Act of Uniformity was enacted in England, requiring ministers
to publicly affirm, "I do here declare my unfeigned assent and consent to all
and everything contained and prescribed in and by the book entitled, *The
Book of Common Prayer, and Administration of the Sacraments, and other Rites
and Ceremonies of the Church of England.*"[201] Some two thousand Puritan

---

[199] T. S. Jones, *The Life of the Right Honourable Willielma, Viscountess Glenorchy* (Edinburgh:
Printed for William White and Co., 1822), 122-3

[200] Mary Thomson Symington, *Home Lessons on the Old Paths or Conversations on the Shorter
Catechism* (Paisley: J. and R. Parlane, 1878), 26

[201] T. W. Davids, *Annals of Evangelical Nonconformity in the County of Essex: from the time of*

ministers were forced to resign the positions in the Church of England. Philip Henry remarks, about the care of God, that during the persecution of the two thousand ejected ministers, although many were very poor, and had large families, he never heard of one arrested for debt.[202]

God—comfort of

Puritan pastor John Janeway had a friend who was experiencing perplexing fears about the state of his soul. He wrote him a letter, expressing these comforting thoughts of God's love:

> Oh! Stand still and wonder. Behold and admire his love! Consider what thou canst discover in this precious Jesus. Here is a sea; cast thyself into it, and thou shalt be compassed with the height, and depth, and breadth, and length of love, and be filled with all the fullness of God. Is not this enough? Wouldst thou have more? Fling away all excepting God. For God is a sufficient portion, and the only proper portion of the soul.[203]

God—comfort of

Horatio Spafford was an attorney in Chicago and an elder of his church, noted for his Christian character, and his many deeds of kindness to those in want. His family was taking a vacation to Europe, but as he was delayed because of business, he sent his wife and four children ahead on a French ocean liner. In the blackness of a November night in 1873, the steamship collided with another ship, and in twelve minutes went down, carrying to death two hundred and thirty souls, among them Spafford's four daughters. Mrs. Spafford sank with the ship, but was rescued. When she was ashore, she sent a message to her husband in Chicago: "Saved, but saved alone. What shall I do?" Mr. Spafford left for Europe, and returned with her to Chicago. In his great sorrow, there came from his heart a song of trust in God and His care:

Wycliffe to the Restoration (London: Jackson, Walford, and Hodder, 1863), 332

[202] G. S. Bowes, *Illustrative Gatherings for Preachers and Teachers* (London: Wertheim, Macintosh & Hunt, 1860), 98

[203] Benjamin Brook, *The Lives of the Puritans, vol. III* (London: James Black, 1813), 280

When peace, like a river, attendeth my way,
When sorrows like sea billows roll;
Whatever my lot,
Thou hast taught me to know,
"It is well, it is well with my soul"[204]

God—Creator

William Robinson was the son of a wealthy Quaker in England. In the early 1700s, he came to America and taught in a school in New Jersey. One night, as he was riding, the moon and stars shone with unusual brightness. As he was meditating upon on the beauty and grandeur of the scene, he said to himself, "How transcendently glorious must be the Author of all this beauty and grandeur be!" But then a thought struck him with the suddenness and force of lightning, "But what do I know of this God? Have I ever sought His favor, or made Him my friend?" This impression never left him till he took refuge in Christ, as the hope and life of his soul.[205]

God—Creator

Pastor Henry Ward Beecher was friends with the renowned agnostic orator of the late 1800s, Robert G. Ingersol. Beecher had a celestial globe in his study, a present from a manufacturer. On it was an excellent representation of the constellations and the stars which compose them. Ingersol was delighted with the globe. He examined it closely and turned it round and round. He exclaimed, "It's just what I wanted—who made it?"

Beecher repeated, "Who made it? Oh, nobody, Colonel—it just happened!"[206]

God—discipline of

In 1873 Hudson Taylor wrote a letter to a young worker who had recently joined the mission in China. In it, he said,

---

[204] Nicholas Smith, *Hymns Historically Famous* (Chicago: Advance Publishing Company, 1901), 209-11

[205] Richard Webster, *A History of the Presbyterian Church in America* (Philadelphia: Joseph M. Wilson, 1857), 474

[206] Edward Garstin Smith, *The Life and Reminiscences of Robert G. Ingersoll* (New York: The National Weekly Publishing Company, 1904), 11

May God make this year a year of much blessing to you. Do not be afraid of His training school. He both knows His scholars, as to what they are, and He knows for what service they are to be fitted. A jeweller will take more pains over a gem than over a piece of glass; but the one he takes most pains over is longest under discipline and most severely dealt with. Once finished, however, the burnish never tarnishes, the brightness never dims. So with us. If we are purified, at times, as in a furnace, it is not merely for earthly service, it is for eternity. May you so appreciate the plans of the Master that you can triumphantly glory in the love that subjects you to such discipline, though the discipline itself be sharp and to the flesh hard to bear...[207]

God—faithfulness of

In 1874, when funds at the China Inland Mission were about depleted, Hudson Taylor wrote to his wife saying, "The balance in hand yesterday was sixty-seven cents! The Lord reigns: herein is our joy and confidence." And when the balance was still lower, he wrote to a friend, saying, "We have this, and all the promises of God."[208]

God—fear of

Andrew Fuller was traveling with two young men and was disturbed by their profane conversation. After a time, one of them, observing his seriousness, accosted him with an air of impertinence, inquiring in rude and indelicate language, whether, on his arrival to Portsmouth, he should not indulge himself in a manner corresponding with their own evil intentions. Fuller, looking the inquirer full in the face, replied in a measured and solemn tone, "Sir, I fear God." Scarcely a word was spoken during the remainder of the journey.[209]

---

[207] Dr. and Mrs. Howard Taylor, *Hudson Taylor and the China Inland Mission* (London: China Inland Mission, 1918), 235

[208] Dr. and Mrs. Howard Taylor, *Hudson Taylor and the China Inland Mission* (London: China Inland Mission, 1918), 235

[209] n.a., *The Scottish Christian Herald, vol. II, January 7-December 30, 1837* (Edinburgh: John Johnstone, 1837) 624

God—glory of

On the morning of the day on which John Owen died, Thomas Payne, who had been entrusted with the publication of the doctor's work, entitled, "Meditations on the Glory of Christ," called to inform him that he had just been giving it to the printer.

"I am glad to hear it," said the doctor; and, lifting up his hands and eyes, exclaimed, "but, O brother Payne, the long-wished for day is come at last, in which I shall see that glory in another manner than I have ever done, or was capable of doing in this world!"[210]

God—glory of

Early in the summer of 1765, when she was in her twenties, Lady Glenorchy was seized with a violent fever, which threatened to prove fatal. She was thus exposed with the danger of eternal ruin. She records this instance in her journal:

> During the course of the fever, the first question of the Assembly's Catechism was brought to my mind, "What is the chief end of man?" as if someone had asked it. When I considered the answer to it, "To glorify God, and enjoy him for ever," I was struck with shame and confusion. I found I had never sought to glorify God in my life, nor had any idea of what was meant by enjoying him forever. Death and judgment were before me—my past sins came to my remembrance. I saw no way to escape the punishment due unto them, nor had I the least glimmering hope of obtaining the pardon of them through the righteousness of another.

Upon the direction of a friend, she turned to the book of Romans. She said, "I saw that God could be just, and justify the ungodly. The Lord Jesus now appeared to me as the city of refuge, and I was glad to flee to him as my only hope."[211]

---

[210] Walter Wilson, *The History and Antiquities of Dissenting Churches and Meeting Houses, in London, Westminster, and Southwark* (London : Printed for the author, 1808), 277

[211] James A. Huie, *Records of Female Piety* (Edinburgh, Oliver & Boyd, 1841), 187-9

God—goodness of

Martin Luther had eyes to see the abundance of God's goodness in observing the birds, the leaves, the flowers, and the common gifts of God. At the table, a plate of fruit would open to him a whole volume of God's bounty, on which he would discourse. Taking a rose in his hand, he would say, "A man who could make one rose like this would be accounted most wonderful; and God scatters countless such flowers around us! But the very infinity of his gifts makes us blind to them."[212]

God—goodness of

The English pastor John Condor was born in 1714. His grandfather, Richard, fearful of the circumstances of the times, kissed him, and, with tears in his eyes, said, "Who knows what sad days these little eyes are likely to see?" At the end of his life, Condor reflected on that incident and remarked, "These eyes have, for more than sixty years, seen nothing but goodness and mercy follow me and the churches of Christ, even to this day."[213]

God—grace of

When John Bradford saw someone taken out to be hanged, tears would come to his eyes. When others asked him why, he said, "There goes John Bradford, but for the grace of God."[214]

God—grace of

The English evangelist Rodney "Gipsy" Smith attended a meeting in his church in which people were giving testimonies to God's salvation. One man stood and spoke of how the Lord saved him after being in prison for many years for burglary. When he sat down, his friend stood and with a trembling voice and tears, said that in 1881 he was before the grand jury for murder, and that God saved him from hanging and saved him from his sins.

---

[212] Elizabeth Charles, *Chronicles of the Schonberg-cotta Family* (London: T. Nelson and Sons, 1864), 420

[213] C. H. Spurgeon, *Feathers for Arrows* (New York: Sheldon & Company, 1870), 83

[214] C. H. Spurgeon, *The Metropolitan Tabernacle Pulpit, Sermons Preached and Revised by C. H. Spurgeon during the Year 1871, vol. XVIII* (London: Passmore & Alabaster, 1872), 184

When he sat down, another man stood and shared, "I had been a drunkard for twenty years, and the Lord saved me."

Then another man stood and said, "I have been a coiner of base [counterfeit] money, and the Lord has saved me."

Yet another man stood and said, "I have had a checkered career. I have ridden about Manchester with the present Prime Minister, and I have ridden in the police van. I have been a publican, and I have swept the floors for other publicans. I have been drunk on champagne, and I have begged a penny for a drink. I have dined with aldermen, and I have begged a crust in the street." And then he spoke of how Jesus saved him.

As they went on, Gipsy Smith could not sit still any longer. He got up and said, "Men, listen. God has done wonders for you, but don't forget he did more for this gipsy boy than for all of you put together. He saved me before I got there."[215]

God—help of

On June 14, 1645, the Battle of Naseby was fought. It was the key battle of the first English Civil War, as the forces of King Charles I fought the army of Sir Thomas Fairfax. Oliver Cromwell fought as Lieutenant General, and as a man of faith he gave God the credit for the victory. He wrote the dispatch announcing the result of this battle to the Speaker of the House of Commons, saying, "He [the king] drew out to meet us. Both armies engaged. We, after three hours' fight very doubtful, at last routed his army... Sir, this is none other but the hand of God; and to Him alone give the glory, wherein none are to share with Him."[216]

God—holiness of

Early Puritans were scornfully called "Precisians" because of their precise concern to please and obey the Lord.[217] A gentleman once said to Puritan

---

[215] Gipsy Smith, *As Jesus Passed By: And Other Addresses* (New York, Fleming H. Revell Company, 1905), 53-55

[216] Charles Knight, *The Popular History of England, vol. IV* (Boston, Estes and Lauriat, 1874), 42

[217] Richard Baxter, *A Call to the Unconverted: Now Or Never; and Fifty Reasons Why a Sinner Ought to Turn to God this Day without Delay* (Glasgow: Printed for Chalmers and Collins, 1825) 259

pastor Richard Rogers, "Mr. Rogers, I like you, and your company very well, only you are too precise."

To this Rogers replied, "Oh sir, I serve a precise God."[218]

God—incomprehensible

American statesman Daniel Webster was once asked, "Mr. Webster, can you comprehend how Jesus Christ can be both God and man?"

Webster, fixing his eyes on the man with a keen look, replied: "No, sir, I cannot comprehend it. If I could comprehend Jesus Christ, He would be no greater than myself; and such is my conviction of accountability to God, and such my sense of sinfulness before Him, and such is my knowledge of my incapacity to recover myself, that I feel and know that I need a superhuman Almighty Savior."[219]

God—joy of

Amy Carmichael wrote a letter to comfort a friend who was very ill. In it she said,

> Life can be difficult. Sometimes the enemy comes like a flood. But then is the time to prove our faith and live our songs. A day or two ago when everything was feeling more than usually impossible I opened on Psalm 40 with its new song. 'He hath put a new song in my mouth, even praise.' How like Him it is to 'put' it there. We couldn't find it for ourselves, so He puts it. And when He puts it we can sing it.[220]

God—justice of

Over a hundred seventy-five years ago, Scottish pastor William Innes was called to the bedside of an unbeliever who told him, when he was taken ill, that he thought he would rely on the general mercy of God. He said that as he never had done anything very bad, he hoped all would be well. "But," he

[218] A. W. M'Clure, *Lives of the Chief Fathers of New England, Vol. II* (Boston: n.p., 1870), 13

[219] Elwin L. House, *The Mind of God* (New York: Revel, 1917), 108

[220] Amy Carmichael, *Candles in the Dark* (Fort Washington, Penn.: Christian Literature Crusade, 1982), 51

added, "as my weakness increased, I began to think, Is not God a just being as well as merciful? Now, what reason have I to think he will treat me with mercy, and not with justice? And if I am treated with justice," he exclaimed with much emotion, "where am I?"

"I showed him," said Innes, "that this was the very difficulty the gospel met and removed, as it showed how mercy could be exercised in perfect consistency with the strictest demands of justice, while it was bestowed through the atonement made by Jesus Christ."

After explaining this truth, the man understood and accepted it. One of the last things he said to Innes before he left was, "Well, I believe it must come to this. I confess I here see a solid footing to rest on, which on my former principles, I could never find.[221]

God—justice of

Before his appointment as a Supreme Court Justice, Horace Gray once presided over a case where a man was justly charged. Through a technicality, Gray was obligated to release him, but as he did so he addressed him, saying, "I believe you are guilty and would wish to condemn you severely, but through a petty technicality, I am obliged to discharge you. I know you are guilty, and so do you, and I wish you to remember that one day you will pass before a better and wiser Judge, when you will be dealt with according to justice and not according to law."[222]

God–love of

Charles Spurgeon once went to visit a friend who had built a new barn. On top of the barn was a weather vane with the words, "God is love." Spurgeon asked his friend, "What do you mean by that? Do you mean that God's love is as changeable as the wind?" His friend answered, "No, I believe that God is love whichever way the wind blows."[223]

---

[221] William Innes, *The Church in the Army* (Edinburgh: Waugh and Innes, 1835), 211-2

[222] J. L. Nye, *Anecdotes on Bible Texts, The Epistles of Paul the Apostle to the Corinthians and the Galatians* (London: Sunday School Union, 1882), 22

[223] Charles F. Goss, *Echoes from the Pulpit and Platform* (Hartford, Conn.: A. D. Worthington & Co., 1900), 259

God–mercy of

About one hundred fifty years ago the Scottish pastor Alexander Whyte had an appointment once with a member of his church, Doctor Carmen, a physician of Edinburgh. As their time came to an end, Dr. Carmen looked at Dr. Whyte with an earnest look and asked, "Now, ha'e ye any word for an old sinner?"

"It took my breath away," said Dr. Whyte. "He was an old saint! But it is the paradox of grace that the greatest saints feel they are the greatest sinners. So I just rose up and held out my hand to him, and I said to him [quoting Micah 7:18]. "He delighteth in mercy." I had nothing else to say, and escaped out of the room.

The next morning Dr. Whyte received a letter. Opening it, he found these words, written by Dr. Carmen:

> Dear friend, I will never doubt Him again—the sins of my youth. I was near the gates of hell, but that word of God comforted me, and I will never doubt Him again. I will never despair again. If the devil casts my sin in my teeth, I will say, 'Yes, it is all true, and you cannot tell the half of it, but I have to do with the One who delighteth in mercy.'"[224]

God—power of

The Scottish missionary to Africa, Mary Slessor, was told by a tribal chief that his war-loving people would be unlikely to be helped by a woman. She replied, "In measuring the woman's power you have evidently forgotten to take into account the woman's God."[225]

God—providence of

Hans Egede was the first missionary to Greenland in 1721. With his wife, he labored there for fourteen years amid indescribable privations and bitter disappointments. In 1735 his wife died, and dejected in spirit and broken in

[224] *The Sunday School Journal, vol. xlvii,* ed. *by Henry H. Meyer, et. al.* (Cincinnati, Ohio: The Methodist Book Concern, 1915), 454

[225] William Pringle Livingstone, *Mary Slessor of Calabar: Pioneer Missionary* (London: Hodder and Stoughton, 1916), 108

health, he bade farewell to Greenland. His farewell sermon was from Isaiah 49; I said... I have spent my strength for nought, and in vain: yet surely my judgment is with the Lord, and my work with my God."

But Count Zinzendorf was stirred by the sight of two Eskimo boys whom Egede had baptized and sent to Europe. This, together with the news of the slave trade in the West Indies, motivated Zinzendorf to apply himself to missionary work, and two men volunteered for Greenland, and two for the island of St. Thomas, and the Moravian Missions began, which sent forth two thousand missionaries around the world.[226]

God—providence of

When Bonner, the Bishop of London had secured a royal warrant for the arrest of Bernard Gilpin in 1558, he promised that he would be at the stake in a fortnight. Gilpin laid his hand on his house-steward, he said, "At length they have prevailed against me. I am accused to the Bishop of London, from whom there will be no escaping. God forgive their malice, and give me strength to undergo the trial."

As soon as he was apprehended he set out for London, in expectation of death by fire. But on the journey he broke his leg, which unavoidably detained him some time on the road. Those conducting him maliciously threw at Gilpin one of his frequent sayings, "That nothing happens to us but what is intended for our good."

When they asked him whether he thought his broken leg was so intended, he meekly replied that he had not doubt of it. He was proved right; before he was able to travel, Queen Mary died, and he was set free.[227]

God—sovereignty of

On the day before his death, Puritan John Owen wrote, "I am leaving the ship of the church in a storm; but whilst the great Pilot is in it, the loss of a poor under-rower will be inconsiderable."[228]

---

[226] Eugene Stock, *The History of the Church Missionary Society: Its Environment, Its Men and Its Work* (London: The Society, 1899), 26-7

[227] Benjamin Brook, *The Lives of the Puritans, vol. I* (London: James Black, 1813), 253

[228] Andrew Thomson, *Life of John Owen, D.D.* (Edinburgh: Johnstone and Hunter, 1853) 164-5

God—sovereignty of

On the fourteenth day of April, 1865, President Lincoln was assassinated. The following morning, New York City presented a scene of the most perilous excitement. Placards were pasted up in New York, Brooklyn, and Jersey City, calling upon loyal citizens to meet around Wall Street Exchange at eleven o'clock. Thousands came, armed with revolvers and knives, ready to avenge the death of the martyred President. Fifty thousand men gathered there, their blood boiling with the fires of patriotism. A portable gallows was carried through the crowd, lifted above their heads, the bearers muttering, "Vengeance" as they went. The prospect was that the office of the *World*, a disloyal journal, and some prominent sympathizers with the rebellious south, would be swallowed in the raging sea of passion. The wave of popular indignation was swollen by the harangues of public speakers. For an instant, vengeance and death upon every paper and every man opposed to Lincoln seemed to move the mighty crowd. Possibly the scene of the French revolution would have been reproduced in the streets of New York had not General James A. Garfield, the future President of the United States, stepped forward and beckoned to the excited throng. "Another telegram from Washington!" cried hundreds of voices. It was the silence of death that followed. It seemed as if every listener held his breath to hear.

Lifting his right arm toward heaven, in a clear, distinct, steady, ponderous voice, that the multitude could hear, the speaker said:

> Fellow citizens: Clouds and darkness are round about Him! His pavilion is dark waters and thick clouds of the skies! Justice and judgment are the habitation of His throne! Mercy and truth shall go before His face! Fellow citizens; God reigns, and the Government at Washington still lives!

The effect of his remarkable effort was miraculous. One said of it:

> As the boiling wave subsides and settles to the sea when some strong wind beats it down, so the tumult of the people sank and became still. As the rod draws the electricity from the air, and conducts it safely to the ground, so this man had drawn the fury

from that frantic crowd, and guided it to more tranquil thoughts than vengeance.[229]

God—sovereignty of

When William Schauffler went to Constantinople to preach the gospel in the 1800s, he was warned by the Russian ambassador, who said, "My imperial master, the Czar, will never allow Protestantism to set foot in Turkey."

Dr. Schauffler calmly answered him, "The kingdom of Christ, who is my Master, will never ask the Emperor of Russia where it may set its foot."[230]

God—sufficiency of

To someone who was in need of encouragement, Hudson Taylor wrote this in 1898, "Go forward in the strength of the Lord, and in the sufficiency that comes from Him alone, and thank Him for your conscious insufficiency, for when you are weak, then He can be strong in you."[231]

God—sufficiency of

In 1903, Booth Tucker was conducting evangelistic meetings in Chicago. One night, after Tucker had preached on the sympathy of Jesus, a man approached him and said, "You can talk like that, how Christ is dear to you and helps you; but if your wife was dead, as is my wife, and you had [your] babies crying for their mother who would never come back, you could not say what you are saying."

Just a few days later, Tucker's wife was killed in a train accident. Her body was brought to Chicago for the funeral. After the service, Tucker looked down on the body of his wife and then said, "the other day when I was here, a man said I could not say Christ was sufficient, if my wife were dead and my children were crying for their mother. If that man is here, I tell him that Christ is sufficient. My heart is all crushed. My heart is all bleeding. My heart

[229] William M. Thayer, *From Log-Cabin to White House: The Story of President Garfield's Life* (London: Hodder and Stoughton, 1881), 337-9

[230] n.a., *Almanac for 1887 issued by American Board of Commissioners for Foreign Missions* (Boston: The American Board, 1887), 19

[231] Dr. and Mrs. Howard Taylor, *Hudson Taylor and the China Inland Mission* (London: China Inland Mission , 1918), 574

is all broken. But there is a song in my heart, and Christ put it there, and if that man is here, I tell him that though my wife is gone and my children are motherless, Christ speaks comfort to me today."

The man was there, and came down the aisle, and fell down beside the casket, saying, "If Christ can help like that, I will surrender to Him."[232]

God—Trinity

A Unitarian once asked the American statesman Daniel Webster regarding the Trinity, if he believed that one and three are the same thing. Webster replied, "Sir, I believe you and I do not understand the arithmetic of heaven."[233]

Gospel—good news

In 1899, Dwight L. Moody went to speak to the Penitentiary in Canon City, Colorado on Thanksgiving Day. The governor of the state wrote him, enclosing a pardon for a woman imprisoned there. The woman was unaware of this and Mr. Moody was greatly pleased to be the bearer of the message.

At the close of the address, Mr. Moody produced the document, saying, "I have a pardon in my hands for one of the prisoners before me." He had intended to make some further remarks, but immediately he saw the excitement caused by the announcement was so severe that he dared not go on. Calling her name, he said, "Will you come forward and accept the Governor's Thanksgiving gift?"

The woman hesitated a moment, then arose, gave a shriek, and, crossing her arms over her breast, fell sobbing and laughing across the lap of the woman next her. Again she arose, staggered a short distance, and again fell at the feet of the matron of the prison, burying her head in the matron's lap. The excitement was so intense that Mr. Moody would not do more than make a very brief application of the scene to illustrate God's offer of pardon and peace. Afterward he said that should such interest or excitement be manifest in connection with any of his meetings—when men and women accepted the pardon offered for all sin—he would be accused of extreme fanaticism

---

[232] George W. Truett, *A Quest for Souls* (Dallas: Texas Baptist Book House, 1917), 311-2

[233] Joseph Banvard, *The American Statesman* (Boston, Gould and Lincoln, 1856), 20

and undue working on the emotions. Strange that men prize more highly the pardon of a fellow-man than the forgiveness of their God![234]

Gospel—its power

John Welsh was the great-grandson of John Knox, and a preacher in Scotland. After ejection from his parish of Irongray, he engaged for nineteen years in field preaching. The Government offered five hundred pounds for his apprehension. On one occasion, being pursued with unrelenting rigor, he was quite at a loss where to flee, but depending on Scottish hospitality, he called at the house of a gentleman of known hostility to field-preachers in general, and to himself in particular, though he had never seen Mr. Welsh before. He was kindly received. In the course of conversation Welsh was mentioned, and the difficulty of getting hold of him.

Welsh replied, "I am sent to *apprehend rebels*; I know where he is to preach to-morrow, and will give you the rebel by the hand."

The gentleman, overjoyed at this news, agreed to accompany his informant next morning. When they arrived, the congregation made way for the minister and his host. He desired the gentleman to sit down on the chair, at which, to his utter astonishment, his guest of the previous night stood and preached. During the sermon, the gentleman seemed much affected; and at the close, Mr. Welsh, according to his promise, gave him his hand.

But the gentleman exclaimed, "You said you were sent to apprehend rebels, and I, a rebellious sinner, have been apprehended this day."[235]

Gospel—uncompromised

Sir Monier Monier-Williams was a linguistic scholar who studied, documented, and taught Asian languages at Oxford University in the 1800s. He wrote a Sanskrit-English dictionary that is still in print. Addressing a company of missionaries, he gave them this exhortation:

> Go forth, then, ye missionaries, in your Master's name; go forth
> into all the world, and, after studying all its false religions and

---

[234] William R. Moody, *The Life of Dwight L. Moody by his Son* (New York: Fleming H Revell, 1900), 32-35

[235] Thomas M'Crie, *Sketches of Scottish Church History: Embracing the Period from the Reformation to the Revolution* (Edinburgh: John Johnstone, 1841), 496-497

philosophies, go forth and fearlessly proclaim to suffering humanity the plain, the unchangeable, the eternal facts of the gospel—nay, I might almost say the stubborn, the unyielding, the inexorable facts of the gospel. Dare to be downright with all the uncompromising courage of your own Bible, while with it your watchwords are love, joy, peace, reconciliation. Be fair, be charitable, be Christlike, but let there be no mistake. Let it be made absolutely clear that Christianity cannot, must not, be watered down to suit the palate of either Hindu, Parsee, Confusianist, Buddhist, or Mohammedan, and that whosoever wishes to pass from the false religion to the true can never hope to do so by the rickety planks of compromise, or by the help of faltering hands held out by half-hearted Christians.[236]

Grace

John Newton, the composer of the hymn "Amazing Grace," was once asked his opinion on some topic. He replied, "When I was young I was sure of many things; there are only two things of which I am sure now: one is that I am a miserable sinner; and the other that Jesus Christ is an all-sufficient Savior."[237]

Grace

Henry Venn was once addressed by a neighboring clergyman, "Mr. Venn, I don't know how it is, but I should really think your doctrines of *grace* and *faith* were calculated to make all your hearers live in *sin,* and yet I must own that there is an astonishing reformation wrought in your parish; whereas I don't believe I ever made one soul the better, though I have been telling them their duty for many years." Venn smiled at his honest confession, and frankly told him, he would do well to burn all his old sermons, and to see what preaching Christ would do.[238]

---

[236] George Claude Lorimer, *The Argument for Christianity* (Philadelphia: American Baptist Society, 1894), 445

[237] William Walters, *Rays of Gold from the Sun of Righteousness* (Halifax: Milner and Sowerby, 1861), 150

[238] n.a., *The Christian Magazine, vol. III,* (Boston: T. R. Marvin, 1826), 121

Grace

Charles Spurgeon was riding home one evening after a heavy day's work. He felt very wearied and depressed, when suddenly as a lightning flash, the Scripture came to his mind, "My grace is sufficient for thee." He writes,

> I reached home and looked it up in the original, and at last it came to me in this way, "MY grace is sufficient for THEE"; and I said, "I should think it is, Lord," and burst out laughing. I never fully understood what the holy laughter of Abraham was until then. It seemed to make unbelief so absurd. It was as though some little fish, being very thirsty, was troubled about drinking the river dry, and Father Thames said, "Drink away, little fish, my stream is sufficient for thee." Or, it seemed a mouse in the granaries of Egypt, after the seven years of plenty, fearing it might die of famine. Joseph might say, "Cheer up, little mouse, my granaries are sufficient for thee." Again, I imagined a man away up yonder, in a lofty mountain saying to himself, "I breathe so many cubic feet of air every year, I fear I shall exhaust the oxygen in the atmosphere," but the earth might say, "Breathe away, O man, and fill thy lungs ever, my atmosphere is sufficient for thee." Oh, brethren, be great believers! Little faith will bring your souls to heaven, but great faith will bring heaven to your souls.[239]

Gratitude

Gilbert Burnett was appointed the Bishop of Salisbury in 1689. He made it his practice to yearly visit its various parishes. On one of those visits, he came across a habitation more wretched than any he had ever seen. As he walked toward it, to his surprise he heard a voice of great and joyous praise. Drawing nearer, he looked in the window, and discovered a poor woman in extreme poverty. She had on a little stool before her a piece of black bread

---

[239] William Williams, *Personal Reminiscences of Charles Haddon Spurgeon* (The Religious Tract Society, 1895) 19

and a cup of cold water. With her eyes and hands lifted up to heaven, she repeatedly exclaimed, "What! All this and Jesus Christ too?"[240]

Gratitude

Henry Boehm, who served with Francis Asbury, writes of his experience with the early American bishop who rode an average of six thousand miles a years on horseback, preaching nearly every day,

> As Bishop Asbury and I were traveling through the woods, we would often stop to refresh both man and beast. The bishop would sit down by a spring of water, take a crust of bread from his pocket, and ask a blessing over it with as much solemnity and gratitude as he would over a table spread with the richest and most plentiful provision. Blessed man! Many a time it drew tears from my eyes when I witnessed it; and often, since the good bishop has gone to feast in Paradise, I have wept as I have thought upon it.[241]

Gratitude—a testimony to God

Henry Dorsey Gough was an American plantation owner in the 1700s. One day, as he rode over to one of his plantations, he was under "sore distress of soul," where he heard the voice of prayer and thanksgiving. He discovered that it came from a poor slave that had come from a near plantation. He was praying with his slaves; and thanking God most fervently for his goodness to his soul and body. The thankful prayer impacted Gough greatly, and he exclaimed, "Alas! O Lord, I have my thousands and tens of thousands, and yet, ungrateful wretch that I am, I never thanked thee as this poor slave does, who has scarcely clothes to put on or food to satisfy his hunger." God used this prayer of gratitude to draw Gough to faith.[242]

---

[240] Aaron Crossley Hobart Seymour, *The Life and Times of Selina, Countess of Huntingdon, vol. I,* (London: Simpkin, Marshall, and Co., 1839), 40

[241] J. B. Wakeley, *The Heroes of Methodism* (New York: Carlton & Porter, 1857), 52

[242] John Lednum, *A History of the Rise of Methodism in America: Containing Sketches of Methodist Itinerant, from 1736-1785* (Philadelphia: Published by the author, 1859), 154

Gratitude—difference between grateful and ungrateful hearts

The life and ministry of Henry Ward Beecher abounded in thankfulness to God. In one of his prayers, he prayed, "Accept the thanksgiving of hearts that this morning are laden with gratitude. O Lord, how much have we to be thankful for! How many of us have great joys unutterable![243] Beecher once explained the difference between a grateful and ungrateful heart in a vivid way. He said:

> If one should give me a dish of sand, and tell me there were particles of iron in it, I might look for them with my eyes, and search for them with my clumsy fingers, and be unable to detect them; but let me take a magnet and sweep through it, and how would it draw to itself the almost invisible particles, by the mere power of attraction! The unthankful heart, like my finger in the sand, discovers no mercies; but let the thankful heart sweep through the day, and as the magnet finds the iron, so it will find in every hour some heavenly blessings; only the iron in God's sand is gold.[244]

Gratitude—in affliction

Martin Rinkart was a German pastor who ministered during war and disease and devastating famine. In 1637 the plague ravaged his city, and in one year alone eight thousand people died. He personally buried four thousand, four hundred and eighty bodies. Yet through it all he looked to God, who gave him the grace and strength to live and to serve. Near the close of the Thirty Year's War in 1648, he wrote the hymn, "Now Thank We All Our God," in which he expresses his gratitude to God amid such great affliction:[245]

> Now thank we all our God,
> With heart and hands and voices
> Who wondrous things hath done

243 Henry Ward Beecher, *Prayers in the Congregation* (London: Strahan & Co., 1868)

244 Henry Ward Beecher, *Life Thoughts: Gathered from the Extemporaneous Discourses of Henry Ward Beecher ed. by Edna Dean Proctor* (Boston: Philipps, Samson, and Company, 1858), 116

245 Samuel Willoughby Duffield, *English Hymns: Their Authors and History* (New York and London: Funk & Wagnalls, 1886), 393-4

In whom His world rejoices
Who from our mother's arms
Hath blessed us on our way
With countless gifts of love
And still is ours today

Oh, may this bounteous God
Through all our life be near us
With ever joyful hearts
And blessed peace to cheer us
And keep us in His grace.
And guide us when perplexed
And free us from all ills
In this world and the next

Gratitude—in affliction

Allen Gardiner entered service in the Royal Navy in 1810 and came to Christ during one of his voyages. After his retirement, he made the commitment at the bedside of his dying wife to "seek out openings for the introduction of the gospel in any region where no attempt has been made." Through difficulties, he took the gospel to Africa, remarried, then went to New Zealand, and South America, where he brought his family. Traveling throughout the continent, he sailed with his fellow workers to Picton Island. Here they met with a series of disasters. The first day they lost an anchor and both their dingeys. Their boats grew leaky, and one of them was wrecked. The natives were threatening and sought to steal their supplies. Two of the men showed signs of scurvy. Provisions grew scarce. Want, disease, and severe weather led to death. One by one Allen Gardiner watched his friends die.

When his body was found, his diary was discovered recording the difficulties, hunger, thirst, and disease they suffered. In his last entry, away from his wife and children, with no food or water or hope for earthly survival he wrote, "Great and marvellous are the loving-kindnesses of the Lord!"[246]

---

[246] Sarah A. Myers, *Self-Sacrifice, Or the Pioneers of Fuegia* (Philadelphia: Presbyterian Board of Publication, 1861), 287

Gratitude—in affliction

J. Wilbur Chapman and his singing partner Charles Alexander conducted evangelistic campaigns in the early 1900s. At one meeting, a paralytic was wheeled down the aisle and placed before the platform. Alexander came up to him and asked, "What is your favorite hymn?"

The man immediately answered, "Count your blessings!"[247]

Gratitude—in everything

Bradford wonderfully fulfilled the command "In everything give thanks (1 Thessalonians 5:18). Immediately before his execution, he declared, "If the queen will give me life, I will thank her; if she will banish me, I will thank her; if she will burn me, I will thank her; if she will condemn me to perpetual imprisonment, I will thank her."[248]

Gratitude—to God

A lady applied to the benevolent Richard Reynolds of Bristol, England, on behalf of an orphan. After he had given generously she said, "When he is old enough, I will teach him to name and thank his benefactor."

Reynolds replied, "Stop—we do not thank the clouds for rain. Teach him to look higher, and thank Him who giveth both the clouds and the rain."[249]

Growth

German reformer Phillipp Melancthon was reproached by someone for changing his views on a certain subject. He replied, "Do you think, sir, that I have been studying assiduously for thirty years, without having learned anything?"[250]

---

[247]   *The Expositor, vol. XX* ed. By G. B. F. Hallock (Cleveland, Ohio: F. M. Barton, 1918), 142

[248]   John Fox, *Fox's Book of Martyrs: The Acts and Monuments of the Church* (London: G. Virtue, 1844), 212

[249]   Mary S. Wood, *Social Hours with Friends* (Philadelphia: Henry Longstreth, 1867), 73

[250]   H. A. Downing, *Anecdotes for the Family, Or, Lessons of Truth and Duty for Every-day Life* (Hartford, Conn.: Case, Lockwood & Company, 1862), 65

Growth

The English preacher Rowland Hill once entered the home of one of his congregation, and saw a child on a rocking horse. He remarked, "Dear me, how wondrously like some Christians! There is motion, but no progress."[251]

Growth

The rule which governs my life is this: anything that dims my vision of Christ, or takes away my taste for Bible study, or cramps me in my prayer life, or makes Christian work difficult, is wrong for me, and I must, as a Christian, turn away from it."[252]

Heart—wicked

I am more afraid of my own heart than of the pope and all his cardinals. I have within me the great pope, self."[253]

Heaven—anticipation of

As the hour of his death was approaching for the Reformer Philipp Melanchthon, the lectures at the University were intermitted and the whole body of the students were invited to join in prayer. Melanchthon, on being asked by one of them if there was anything he desired, replied, "Nothing but heaven."[254]

Heaven—appreciation of

Sometime after his miserable imprisonment as a missionary in Burma, Adoniram Judson gathered with several other persons one evening. The conversation turned to anecdotes of what different men in different ages had regarded as the highest type of sensuous enjoyment; that is, enjoyment

---

[251] Vernon John Charlesworth, *Rowland Hill: His Life, Anecdotes, And Pulpit Sayings* (London: Hodder and Stoughton, 1876), 118

[252] Ford C. Ottman, *J. Wilbur Chapman: A Biography* (New York: Doubleday, Page & Company, 1920), 322

[253] Louis Klopsch, *Many Thoughts from Many Lands* (New York: The Christian Herald), 52

[254] K. R. Hagenbach, *History of the Reformation in Germany and Switzerland Chiefly*, vol. II trans. Evelina Moore (Edinburgh: T. & T. Clark, 1879) 354

derived from outward circumstances. Judson exclaimed that these men were not qualified to judge. He said,

> I know of a much higher pleasure than that. What do you think of floating down the Irrawadi, on a cool, moonlight evening, with your wife by your side, and your baby in your arms, free—all free? But *you* cannot understand it, either; it needs a twenty-one months' qualification; and I can never regret my twenty-one months of misery, when I recall that one delicious thrill. I think I have had a better appreciation of what heaven may be ever since.[255]

Heaven—longing for

Henry Venn, as he once went to preach, was riding on the road, and came into company with another traveler. After riding together for some time, conversing on different subjects, the stranger, looking in his face, said, "Sir, I think you are on the wrong side of fifty?" "On the wrong side of fifty!" answered Venn. "No, sir, I am on the right side of fifty." "Surely," the stranger replied, "you must be turned fifty?" "Yes, sir," added Mr. Venn, "but I am on the right side of fifty, for every year I live I am nearer my crown of glory."[256]

Heaven— perfection of

When the Scottish pastor and professor Thomas Halyburton was dying in 1712, he requested a reading of Psalm 84, and a singing the latter part of it, and prayer. He joined in singing, and after prayer, said, "I had always a mistuned voice, a bad ear but, which is worse of all, I had a mistuned heart; but shortly, when I join the temple-service above, there shall not be, world without end, one string of the affections out of tune."[257]

---

[255] Francis Wayland, *A Memoir of the Life and Labors of the Rev. Adoniram Judson, Vol. I* (Boston: Phillips, Sampson, and Company, 1853), 395

[256] Aaron Crossley Hobart Seymour, Jacob Kirkman Foster, *The Life and Times of Selina, Countess of Huntingdon, Vol. I* (London: W. E. Painter, 1840), 487

[257] Thomas Halyburton, *Memoirs of the Life of the Reverend, Learned and Pious Mr. Thomas Halyburton* (Glasgow: Archibald McLean, 1756), 256

Heaven—wonder of

John Newton once said, "When I get to heaven, I shall see three wonders there; the first will be to see many people there that I did not expect to see; the second, to miss many that I did expect to see; and the third, and greatest wonder of all, will be to find myself there."[258]

Holiness

In 1840, Dan Edwards was ordained as a missionary to the Jews. After his ordination, he received the following letter of exhortation from Scottish pastor Robert Murray M'Cheyne:

> I trust you will have a pleasant and profitable time in Germany. I know you will apply hard to German; but do not forget the culture of the inner man—I mean of the heart. How diligently the cavalry officer keeps his sabre clean and sharp; every stain he rubs off with the greatest care. Remember you are God's sword—his instrument—I trust a chosen vessel unto him to bear his name. In great measure, according to the purity and perfections of the instrument, will be the success. It is not great talents God blesses so much as great likeness to Jesus. A holy minister is an awful weapon in the hand of God.[259]

Holiness

A young man was scoffing at Christianity because of the lack of holiness of some of its professors. English physician John Mason Good asked him, "Did you ever know an uproar made because an infidel went astray from the path of morality?"

The man admitted he had not. "Then," said the Doctor, "don't you see that you admit Christianity to be a holy religion, by expecting its professors to be holy, and that you pay it the highest compliment in your power?[260]

---

[258] H. A. Downing, *Anecdotes for the Family, Or, Lessons of Truth and Duty for Every-day Life* (Hartford, Conn.: Case, Lockwood & Company, 1862), 145

[259] Andrew A. Bonar, *Life and Remains: Letters. Lectures and Poems of the Rev. Robert Murray M'Cheyne* (New York: Robert Carter, 1848), 211

[260] James Gallaher, Frederick A Ross, David Nelson, ed., *The Calvinistic Magazine, vol. v*

Holiness

President Woodrow Wilson once had an encounter that he never forgot. He said,

> I remember once that I was in a very [common place]. I was in a barber shop, lying in a chair, and I was presently aware that a personality had entered the room. A man had come quietly in upon the same errand as myself, to have his hair cut, and sat in the chair next to me. Every word the man uttered, though it was not in the least didactic, showed a personal and vital interest in the man who was serving him. Before I got through with what was being done to me, I was aware that I had attended an evangelistic service, because Mr. Moody was in the next chair. I purposely lingered in the room after he had left and noted the singular effect that his visit had upon the barbers in that shop. They talked in undertones. They did not know his name. They did not know who had been there, but they knew that something had elevated their thought. I felt that I left that place as I should have left a place of worship.[261]

Hope

As a Sabbath School Superintendent in the early 1800s, Harlan Page took a sincere interest in the spiritual condition of his teachers. He tenderly asked one of his teachers, a young merchant, whether he had a well-grounded hope in Christ or not. The teacher answered, "No, sir." Page replied, "Well, I will write down your name as having no hope." The young man reflected on his answer and was troubled, which led to his coming to Christ and receiving the great hope of salvation in Him.[262]

(August 1831): 260

[261] Woodrow Wilson, *Historical Celebration in Recognition of the Eightieth year of the Origin of the Seminary the Fiftieth Year of its location in Chicago and the One Hundredth year of the Birth of Cyrus H. McCormick* (Chicago: McCormick Theological Seminary, 1910), 168-9

[262] William Allen Hallock, *Memoir of Harlan Page* (New York: American Tract Society, 1835), 196

Hope

In 1829, Alexander Campbell engaged in a debate over the evidences of Christianity with Robert Owen, a notorious infidel of that time. Owen visited Campbell to make the arrangements. In one of their travels about the farm they came to Campbell's family burial ground. Owen stopped, and said to Campbell, "There is one advantage I have over Christians: I am not afraid to die. Most Christians have fear in death, but if some few items of my business were settled, I should be perfectly willing to die at any moment."

"Well," answered Campbell, "you say you have no fear of death; have you any hope in death?"

After a pause, Owen replied, "No."

Campbell pointed to an ox standing near and replied, "Then you are on a level with that brute. He has fed until he is satisfied, and stands in the shade, whisking off the flies, and has neither hope nor fear in death."[263]

Heavenly mindedness

When visited the house of a merchant, he saw only books of business on the table, and all his books of devotion on the shelf. said to him, "Sir, here is earth on the table, and heaven on the shelf; pray do not sit so much at the table as to forget the shelf. Let not earth by any means thrust heaven out of your mind."[264]

Humility

Augustine was once asked what was the first step to heaven. He replied, "Humility." He was then asked what the second step was. He replied, "Humility." And when asked what the third step was, he replied, "Humility."[265]

---

[263] *The Sword and the Trowel ed. by C. H. Spurgeon*, (London: Passmore & Alabaster, July, 1882), 359

[264] Cotton Mather, *Magnalia Christi Americana, or, The Ecclesiastical History of New-England from its First planting in the Year 1620, Unto the Year of Our Lord 1698, vol. 1* (Hartford, Conn.: Silas Andrus & Son, 1855), 490-1

[265] Samuel Eales, *Sermons Ancient and Modern*, (London: Skeffington & Son, 1882),135

Humility

George Whitefield and John Wesley differed upon some theological points and in some of their methods of work. One of Whitefield's young followers was not so gracious, and one expressed his doubt concerning the salvation of Wesley. He asked, "Mr. Whitefield, when *we* get to heaven do you think we shall see Mr. Wesley?"

Whitefield replied, "I fear not, for he will be so near the throne, and we shall be at such a distance, we shall hardly get sight of him."[266]

Humility

At a social engagement in India attended by missionary William Carey, a general asked his aide if the missionary had not once been a shoemaker. Carey overheard the question and replied, "No sir; only a cobbler."[267]

Humility

When William Carey, the great missionary pioneer to India, was on his deathbed, he was visited by a missionary named Alexander Duff. He spent some time talking primarily about Carey's missionary life, until finally the dying man whispered, "Pray." Duff knelt down and prayed, and then said goodbye. As he passed from the room, he heard a feeble voice calling him back. Carey said to him, "Mr. Duff, you have been speaking about Dr. Carey. When I am gone, say nothing about Dr. Carey—speak about Dr. Carey's Savior."[268]

Humility

In 1784, Benjamin Franklin wrote a letter to the son of Cotton Mather, sharing an incident he had with his father when he was eighteen years old. He writes,

---

[266] W. H. Bidwell, *The National Preacher and Village Pulpit, vol. VIII* (New York: W. H. Bidwell, 1865), 53

[267] John Clark Marshman, *The Story of Carey, Marshman & Ward: the Serampore Missionaries* (London: Alexander Strahan & Co., 1864), 6

[268] Robert E. Speer, *Some Great Leaders in the World Movement* (New York: Fleming H. Revell, 1911), 58

He received me in his library, and, on my taking leave, showed me a shorter way out of the house through a narrow passage, which was crossed by a beam overhead. We were still talking as I withdrew, he accompanying me behind, and I turning partly towards him, when he said, hastily, "*Stoop, stoop!*" I did not understand him till I felt my head hit against the beam. He was a man that never missed an occasion of giving instruction, and upon this he said to me, "You are young, and have the world before you: STOOP as you go through it, and you may miss many hard thumps."

Franklin then adds,

This advice, thus beat into my head, has frequently been of use to me; and I often think of it, when I see pride mortified, and misfortunes brought upon people, by their carrying their heads too high.[269]

Humility

Joseph Parker was once asked, "Why did Jesus choose Judas?" Dr. Parker replied, "I do not know, but I have a harder question: Why did He choose me?"[270]

Humility

The twentieth president of the United States, James A. Garfield, was a devout Christian and a humble man. After his election, on taking up his residence at the White House, he said to his pastor, "In my church relations I am plain and simple James A. Garfield."[271]

---

[269] Benjamin Franklin, Epes Sargent, *The Select Works of Benjamin Franklin; Including His Autobiography* (Boston: Phillips, Sampson and Company, 1853), 469

[270] Malcolm James McLeod, *The Unsearchable Riches* (New York: Fleming H. Revell, 1911), 18

[271] William M. Thayer, *From Log-Cabin to White House: The Story of President Garfield's Life* (London: Hodder and Stoughton, 1881), 348

Humility

In 1890 Hudson Taylor was scheduled to speak at a large church in Melbourne, Australia. To a crowded audience, the moderator spoke in eloquent, well-chosen phrases of what had been accomplished in China through Taylor's efforts, finally introducing him to the audience as "our illustrious guest."

When Taylor stepped into the pulpit, he was quiet for a moment, and then said, "Dear friends, I am the little servant of an illustrious Master."[272]

Idolatry

Johann von Dannecker, the German sculptor, spent eight years in producing a face of Christ, and at last wrought out one in which the emotions of love and sorrow were so perfectly blended that beholders wept as they looked upon it. Afterwards, being solicited to employ his great talent on a statue of Venus, he replied, "After gazing so long into the face of Christ, think you that I can now turn my attention to a heathen goddess?"[273]

Idolatry

A lady once said to the English puritan preacher William Romaine, "Sir, I like the doctrine you preach, and I think I can give up everything but one."

Romaine replied, "What is that, Madam?"

She said, "Cards, sir."

Romaine asked, "You think you could not be happy without them?"

She answered, "No, sir, I could not."

Romaine said to her, "Then, madam, they are your God, and to them you must look for salvation."

This pointed and faithful reply led to her conversion.[274]

Jesus Christ—Deity of

In the 4th century, Emperor Theodosius denied the deity of Christ. When his son Arcadius was about sixteen, he made him an equal partner in the rule

---

Dr. and Mrs. Howard Taylor, *Hudson Taylor and the China Inland Mission* (London: China Inland Mission , 1918), 492-3

273 Adoniram Judson Gordon, *The Twofold Life* (New York: Revell, 1883), 125

274 J. B. Johnstone, ed., *The Christian Treasury,* (Edinburgh, Johnstone and Hunter, 1850), 96

of the empire. Among the noblemen who assembled to congratulate him on this occasion was a bishop named Amphilocus. He made a splendid address to the Emperor and was about to leave when Theodosius exclaimed, "What! Do you take no notice of my son?" The bishop then went up to Arcadius and putting his hands upon his head said, "The Lord bless you, my son." The Emperor, roused to fury by this slight, exclaimed, "What! Is this all the respect you pay to a prince that I have made of equal dignity with myself?"

Amphilocus replied, "Sir, you do so highly resent my apparent neglect of your son, because I do not give him equal honors with yourself? Then what must the eternal God think of you who has allowed His coequal and coeternal Son degraded in His proper divinity in every part of your empire?"[275]

Jesus Christ—His coming

Horatius Bonar was a Scottish preacher in the 1800s. At night, his last action as he retired for the night was to draw aside the curtain in his room and, gazing up into the starry heavens, and say, "Perhaps tonight, Lord?" And every morning, as he arose, his first movement was to raise the blind, and looking out upon the breaking dawn say, "Perhaps today, Lord?"[276]

Jesus Christ—His righteousness

Martin Luther once visited a dying student, and asked the young man what he should take to God. The young man replied, "Everything that is good, dear father—everything that is good!"

Luther, rather surprised, said, "But how can you bring Him everything that is good, seeing you are but a poor sinner?"

The student replied, "Dear father, I will take to my God in heaven a [repentant], humble heart, sprinkled with the blood of Christ."

Luther exclaimed, "Truly, this is everything good. Then go, dear son; you will be a welcome guest to God."[277]

---

[275] Chester Field, *Scripture Illustrated by Interesting Facts, Incidents, and Anecdotes* (New York: Harper & Brothers, 1847) 44-45

[276] *The Walther League Messenger, Volumes 53-54, ed. by Walter A. Maier* (Milwaukie, Wis.: Lutheran Synodical Conference, 1944), 321

[277] James Macaulay, *Luther Anecdotes* (London: Religious Tract Society, 1894) 104

Jesus Christ—His righteousness

Walter Marshall was an English preacher used greatly by God in pastoral ministry and in the writing of his book, *The Gospel Mystery of Sanctification.* In his earlier years, he had been greatly distressed about the state of his soul. The consciousness of guilt, and a dread of the divine displeasure, filled his heart with bitter anguish. At last, he turned to Puritan Thomas Goodwin, who told him, "You have forgotten the greatest of sin all, the sin of unbelief, in refusing to believe in Christ, and rely on his atonement and righteousness for your acceptance with God." Turning to Christ in faith, he was filled with joy and peace in believing.[278]

Jesus Christ—prizing

Ignatius, student of the apostle John and Bishop of Antioch in the first century and early second century, said this as he faced suffering and death: "Let fire, and the cross, let the companions of wild beasts, let breakings of bones and tearing of members, let the shattering in pieces of the whole body, and all the wicked torments of the Devil come upon me, only let me enjoy Jesus Christ."[279]

Jesus Christ— prizing

In 1562, a Dutch schoolmaster named Geleyn de Muler, of Audenarde, was apprehended by an inquisitor named Peter Titelmann for being "addicted to reading the Bible." The schoolmaster replied that if he were guilty of any crime, he should be tried before the judges of his town.

Titlemann answered, "You are my prisoner, and are to answer me and none other." The inquisitor proceeded accordingly to question him, and was soon satisfied of the schoolmaster's heresy. He commanded him to make immediate recantation. The schoolmaster refused.

Titlemann asked, "Do you not love your wife and children?

---

[278] David Bogue and James Bennett, *History of Dissenters, from the Revolution in 1688, to the Year 1808, vol. II* (London: Printed for the authors and sold by Williams and Smith, 1809) 238-9

[279] Ignatius, Polycarp, *The Martyrdom of Ignatius, Bishop of Antioch in the Year 109; and of Polycarp, Bishop of Smyrna, in the Middle of the Second Century* (Lexington, Kentucky: J. Clarke & Co., 1835), 42

"God knows," answered the schoolmaster, "that if the whole world were of gold, and my own, I would give it all only to have them with me, even had I to live on bread and water and in bondage."

The inquisitor replied, "You have, then, only to renounce the error of your opinions."

He responded, "Neither for wife, children, nor all the world, can I renounce my God and religious truth." He was then sentenced to the stake, strangled, and thrown into the flames.[280]

Jesus Christ—resurrected

In a moment of peril and fear, Martin Luther was once found tracing with his finger on a table the words, "Vivit, vivit," "He lives, He lives!"[281]

Jesus Christ—Savior

In the last months of his life on earth, pastor John Newton, the author of the hymn, "Amazing Grace," held to the truths he had preached in his ministry. Barely able to speak, he said, "My memory is nearly gone; but I remember two things: That I am a great sinner, and that Christ is a great Savior."[282]

Jesus Christ—Savior

Archibald Alexander was the first professor of Princeton Theological Seminary when it was established in 1812. After a lifetime of ministry, on his deathbed, he was heard to say to a friend, "All my theology is reduced to this narrow compass—Jesus Christ came into the world to save sinners."[283]

Jesus Christ—Savior

In 1857, Charles Spurgeon was scheduled to preach at the Royal Surrey Gardens. A day or two before the event, he visited the building to test

---

[280] John Lothrop Motley, *The Rise of the Dutch Republic* (London: George Routledge and Co., 1858), 290

[281] Alexander Maclaren, *A Year's Ministry* (London: Hodder and Stoughton, 1884), 68

[282] George Redford and John Angell James, ed., *The Autobiography of the Rev. William Jay ,vol. 1* (New York: Robert Carter & Brothers, 1855), 316

[283] C. H. Spurgeon, *Feathers for Arrows* (New York: Sheldon & Company, 1870), 29

its acoustic properties. Standing at the pulpit, he cried in a loud voice, "Behold the Lamb of God, which taketh away the sin of the world." Nearby was a workman, who knew nothing of what was being done. Hearing the words—which he said later came like a message from heaven—he was struck with conviction on account of sin. He put down his tools, went home, and afterward found salvation from his sin by beholding the Lamb of God.[284]

Jesus Christ—Savior

Dwight L. Moody once preached a message on the subject "Christ as a Deliverer." Afterwards, as he walked away, he commented to a Scotchman, "I didn't finish the subject."

The Scotchman replied, "Ah, man! You didn't expect to finish, did ye? It'll take all eternity to finish telling what Christ has done for man."[285]

Jesus Christ—Savior

At the close of a service in Philadelphia a century ago, a man approached the preacher, Daniel Stearns, and said, "I don't like your preaching. I do not care for the cross. I think that instead of preaching the death of Christ on the cross, it would be far better to preach Jesus, the teacher and example."

Dr. Stearns replied, "Would you be willing to follow Him if I preach Christ as the example?"

The man answered, "I would—I would follow him."

"Then," said Dr. Stearns, "let us take the first step. He did no sin. Can you take this step?"

The man looked confused. He replied, "No. I do sin and acknowledge it."

"Well, then," said Dr. Stearns, "your first need of Christ is not as an example, but as a savior."[286]

---

[284] Susannah Spurgeon and Mrs. W. J. Harrald, *The Autobiography of Charles H. Spurgeon: compiled from his diary, letters, and records, vol. II* (Cincinnati, Ohio: Curts & Jennings, 1899), 239

[285] *Northwestern Christian Advocate, vol. 51 ed. by David D. Thompson* (Chicago: Methodist Episcopal Church, 1903), 1

[286] n.a., *The Lutheran Witness, vol. 48, The Christian Advocate, vol. IV,* (St. Louis: Concordia Publishing House, 1929), 412

Jesus Christ—the resurrection and the life

Dwight L. Moody said that when he was a young man, he was called upon suddenly, in Chicago, to preach a funeral sermon. A good many Chicago businessmen were to be there, and he said to himself, "Now, it will be a good chance for me to preach the gospel to those men, and I will get one of Christ's funeral sermons." He recounts,

> I hunted all through the four Gospels trying to find one of Christ's funeral sermons, but I couldn't find any. I found He broke up every funeral He ever attended! He never preached a funeral sermon in the world. Death couldn't exist where He was. When the dead heard His voice they sprang to life. He will smash up the undertaking business when He comes to reign. "I am the resurrection and the life: he that believeth in Me, though he were dead, yet shall he live."[287]

Joy—a result of holiness

The English Puritan preacher Philip Henry's usual blessing to his newly married friends, was, "Others wish you all happiness, I wish you all holiness, and then there is no doubt but you will have all happiness."[288]

Joy—a testimony to others

A young girl, on a brief railway journey, met Frances Ridley Havergal, author of hymn "Take My Life and Let it Be." Long afterward, the girl said "I am so glad that I saw, just once, that God-satisfied face!"[289]

Joy—eternal

John Newton visited a Christian family that had suffered the loss by fire of all that they possessed. He greeted the mother of the family with these words, "I give you joy, madam!"

---

[287] Dwight Lyman Moody, *Moody's Latest Sermons,* (Chicago: The Bible Institute Colportage Association, 1900), 20

[288] Matthew Henry, *The Life of the Rev. Philip Henry* (London: William Ball, 1839), 111

[289] Louis Albert Banks, *The Sunday-Night Evangel* (New York & London: Funk & Wagnells Company, 1911), 286

Surprised, she exclaimed, "What! Joy that all my property is consumed?"

"Oh no," he answered, "but joy that you have so much property that no fire can touch."

This reminder checked her grief, and wiping her tears, she smiled like the sun shining after an April shower.[290]

Joy—from God's word

William Tyndale understood the life-giving treasure that Scripture is, and gave his life to translate it into the English language in the 1500s. He understood the gospel to be "good, merry, glad and joyful tidings, that maketh a man's heart glad, and maketh him sing, dance and leap for joy.[291]

Joy—God's gift

After a hard day's work in serious discussions, Charles Spurgeon and his friend, Theodore Cuyler, went out into the country together for a holiday. They roamed the fields in high spirits like boys let loose from school, chatting and laughing and free from care. Dr. Cuyler had just told a story at which Pastor Spurgeon laughed uproariously. Then suddenly he turned to Dr. Cuyler and exclaimed: "Theodore, let's kneel down and thank God for laughter!"[292]

Joy—in Christ alone

St John's College, Cambridge, receiving academic honors and success. But these did not bring him true satisfaction. He wrote in his journal, "I obtained my highest wishes but was surprised to find I had grasped a shadow."[293]

Martyn came to faith in Christ and turned his back on worldly pleasures to become a missionary. While ministering in India in 1807, he wrote of finding the satisfaction that he lacked before coming to Christ,

---

[290] Joseph T. Cooper, ed., *The Evangelical Repository, vol. V* (Philadelphia: William S. Young, 1846), 569

[291] Brooks Foss Westcott, *A General View of the History of the English Bible* (London: MacMillan and Co., 1872), 152

[292] n.a., "The Gift of Laughter," *The Sabbath Recorder, vol. 78,* (January 4, 1915): 157

[293] George Smith, *Henry Martyn: Saint and Scholar, First Modern Missionary to the Mohammedans 1781-1812* (London: The Religious Tract Society, 1892), 21

My heart at various times filled with a sense of Divine love,
frequently in prayer was blessed in the bringing of my soul near
to God. After dinner in my walk found sweet devotion ; and
the ruling thoughts were, that true happiness does not consist
in the gratifying of self in case or individual pleasure, but in
conformity to God, in obeying and pleasing Him.[294]

Martyn found his life as he gave it away to Christ and His ministry, dying
at the age of 31.

Joy—in persecution

William Romaine ministered in England in the 1700s amid opposition and
trials. When his fervent preaching brought a crowd of people to St. George's,
the rector removed him from ministry there. He was popularly elected to the
Evening Lectureship of St. Dunstan's, but the rector there took possession of
the pulpit in the time of prayer, so as to exclude him from preaching. Finally
it was decided after seven in the evening Romaine could have use of the
church. Until the clock struck seven, the church-wardens kept the doors firm
shut, and by drenching the people in rain and freezing them in frost, hoped
to weary out the crowd. Failing in this, they refused to light the church, and
Romaine often preached with no light except the solitary candle which he
held in his hand.[295] But despite these mistreatments and other persecution,
Romaine persevered with joy. He speaks of this abounding joy when he writes,

O my soul, what a rich provision thy God has made for the joy
of the heart. Admire and adore him for his great salvation,
for delivering thee from sin and sorrow, and for the free gift of
righteousness and life eternal... What a subject is here before
thee for delightful praise! Look at it in any true light, thou hast
reason to be glad with exceeding great joy. God, the infinite
fountain of good, is thy God. He rejoices in thee, therefore thou
shouldst rejoice in him. He loves thee freely, how canst thou

---

[294]   Ibid., 557

[295]   W. H. Bidwell, ed., "Simeon and His Predecessors," *The Eclectic Magazine of Foreign
Literature* (September to December 1847): 219

be sensible of this without loving him? His love hath blessed thee with all spiritual blessing in Christ Jesus: whilst thou are receiving them out of his fulness, how canst thou refuse to thank him with joyful lips? He says that he rejoices over thee to do thee good: the belief of this should fill thy heart with joy and gladness. Indeed, there is nothing in God but what should be to thee matter of rejoicing. His faithfulness and justice are on thy side, as well as his never-failing compassions: for he is thy God, thy covenant God; he has given his Son for thee, and his Spirit to thee; by his grace thou has been called to enjoy fellowship with the Father and the Son, and to partake of their covenant blessings. It is thy privilege to be improving this fellowship, and even upon earth to be tasting of the joys of heaven. May thy faith bring thee in a rich feast, yea a fullness of joy, till thy cup run over with the rivers of pleasure which are at God's right hand for evermore.[296]

Joy—in sorrow

English Puritan pastor Richard Baxter experienced much affliction in the 1600s with persecution, war, the death of his wife, imprisonment for eighteen months, and deteriorating health. But he looked to the Lord for joy and strength. He declared, "O what a life might men live if they were but willing and diligent! God would have our joys to be far more than our sorrows, yea, he would have us to have no sorrow but what tendeth to joy."[297]

Joy—in sorrow

Missionary Amy Carmichael was well acquainted with sorrow—she was badly injured in a fall in 1931, which left her bedridden, and for the last twenty years of her life until her death, she was confined to her room, in constant pain. Yet, to a friend who was sad, she wrote,

---

[296] William Romaine, *Treatises on the Life, Walk, and Triumph of Faith* (Glasgow: William Collins, 1830), 341-342

[297] Richard Baxter, *The Saint's Everlasting Rest* (Philadelphia: Presbyterian Board of Education, 1847), 351

Don't let your mind dwell on sadness as it saps the soul of strength. There is more blue sky overhead than clouds. The clouds will pass. I often think how sad we shall be at the end, if we have failed in joy. I don't want to fail[298]

Joy—of a godly life

The sons of the 18th and 19th century English legislator William Wilberforce wrote his biography. In it, they share an encounter toward the end of his life which highlights the joy and satisfaction of a godly life in contrast with the dissatisfaction of a life lived apart from Christ:

> The pages of his later Journal are full of bursts of joy and thankfulness; and with his children, and his chosen friends, his full heart welled out ever in the same blessed strains; he seemed too happy not to express his happiness; his "song was ever of the loving-kindness of the Lord." An occasional meeting at this time with some who had entered life with him, and were now drawing wearily to its close with spirits jaded and tempers worn in the service of pleasure or ambition, brought out strongly the proof of his better "choice."
>
> "This session," he says, "I met again Lord—— , whom I had known when we were both young, but of whom I had lost sight for many years. He was just again returned to parliament, and we were locked up together in a committee room during a division. I saw that he felt awkward about speaking to me, and went therefore up to him.
>
> "You and I, my Lord, were pretty well acquainted formerly."
>
> "Ah, Mr. Wilberforce," he said cordially; and then added with a deep sigh, "you and I are a great many years older now."
>
> "Yes, we are, and for my part I can truly say that I do not regret it."

---

298 Amy Carmichael, *Candles in the Dark* (Fort Washington, Penn.: Christian Literature Crusade, 1982), 94

"Don't you!" he said, with an eager and almost in-credulous voice, and a look of wondering dejection, which I never can forget.[299]

Judgment

Dwight L. Moody survived the devastating Great Chicago fire in 1871. Afterwards, he spoke of the dreadful scene:

> It was my sad lot to be in the Chicago fire. As the flames rolled down our streets, destroying every tiling in their onward march, I saw the great and the honorable, the learned and the wise, fleeing before the fire with the beggar and the thief and the harlot. All were alike. As the flames swept through the city, it was like the judgment day. Neither the mayor, nor the mighty men, nor the wise men, could stop these flames. They were all on a level then, and many who were worth hundreds of thousands were left paupers that night. When the day of judgment comes, there will be no difference: all sinners will suffer.[300]

Judging others

John Wesley warned against judging others, speaking of a time in his life when he said to a man, "Sir, I am afraid you are covetous."

The man replied, "What is the reason for your fear?"

Wesley explained, "A year ago, when I made a collection for the expense of repairing the foundery, you subscribed five guineas. At the subscription made this year, you subscribed only half a guinea."

The man made no reply, but later in the conversation said, "I know a man that goes to the market at the beginning of every week. There he buys a pennyworth of parsnips, which he boils in a large quantity of water. The parsnips serve him for food and the water for drink the ensuing week. So his meat and drink together cost him only a penny a week. This he constantly

[299] Robert Isaac Wilberforce and Samuel Wilberforce, *The Life Of William Wilberforce, vol. IV* (London: John Murray, 1838), 339-40

[300] Elias Nason, *The American Evangelists, Dwight L. Moody and Ira D. Sankey* (Boston: D. Lothrop & Co.,1877), 89

did, though he had then two hundred pounds a year, to pay the debts which he had contracted before he knew God!" Wesley then came to realize that he was humbly speaking of himself and he was convicted for judging the man as covetous.[301]

Judging others

The great British preacher, Joseph Parker, was preaching away from his church in the north of England. After the service, someone came up to him and criticized him for a certain unusual mannerism. Dr. Parker's only response, which left the man speechless, was, "And what else of the sermon can you remember?"[302]

Kindness

When someone mentioned the faults of another in the presence of John Fletcher, the Swiss and English preacher of the eighteenth century, he had a wonderful way of dealing with it. He would respond with kindness, saying, "Let us pray for him."[303]

Kindness

In the 1800s, Pastor Henry Ward Beecher was speaking to a man who was imprisoned for counterfeiting, and was released after serving his time. Coming back to New York, he did not attempt to hide his history and was willing to do anything. But everybody treated him as though he had a loathsome disease. No one was willing to trust him. After trying for a year to find employment, he was discouraged and heartbroken. He shared with Beecher that the strongest temptations were held out to him by his old confederates who were kind to him, enticing him to enter again into a life of dishonesty. He said, "I receive sympathy, Mr. Beecher, from none but the

---

[301] John Wesley, *The Works of the Reverend John Wesley, vol. II* (New York: J. Emory and B. Waugh, 1831), 487

[302] Albert Dawson, *Joseph Parker, D.D.: His Life and Ministry* (London: S. W. Partridge & Co., 1901), 142

[303] Davis W. Clark, *The Methodist Episcopal Pulpit, ed. by George Peck* (New York: Lane & Tippett, 1848), 281

worst folks. I receive nothing but unkindness and suspicion from the best folks. What am I going to do?"[304]

Kindness

George Herbert, walking to Salisbury to join in a musical party, saw a poor man with a poorer horse that was fallen under his load. They were both in distress and needed present help, which Mr. Herbert perceiving, put off his canonical coat, and helped the poor man to unload, and afterwards load his horse. The poor man blessed him for it, and he blessed the poor man, and was so like the good Samaritan, that he gave him money to refresh both himself and his horse. Thus he left the poor man; and at his coming to his musical friends at Salisbury they began to wonder that Mr. George Herbert, who used to be trim and clean came into that company so soiled and discomposed. But he told them of the reason, to which one of his company told him "he had disparaged himself by so dirty an employment."

Herbert answered that "the thought of what he had done would prove music to him at midnight."[305]

Knowing God

In 1873, Hudson Taylor wrote a letter to a fellow-worker going through a difficult trial. He encouraged him with these words:

> The one thing we need is to *know* God better. Not in ourselves, not in our prospects, not in heaven itself are we to rejoice, but in the Lord. If we *know* Him, then we rejoice in what He gives not because we like it, if pleasing, not because we think it will work good, if trying, but because it is *His* gift, *His* ordering; and the like in what He withholds or takes away. Oh, to know Him! Well might Paul, who had caught a glimpse of His glory, count "all things" as dung and dross compared with this most precious knowledge! *This* makes the weak strong, the poor rich,

---

[304] Henry Ward Beecher, *The original Plymouth Pulpit*, B. Waugh. *III* (Boston: The Pilgrim Press, 1870), 223

[305] William Walters, *Rays of Gold from the Sun of Righteousness* (Halifax: Milner and Sowerby, 1861), 256

the empty full; this makes suffering happiness, and turns tears into diamonds like the sunshine turns dew into pearls. This makes us fearless, invincible.

If we *know* God, then when full of joy we can thank our Heavenly Father, the Giver of all; when we feel no joy we can thank Him for that, for it is our Father's ordering. When we are with those we love, we can thank Him; when we yearn for those we love, we can thank Him. The hunger that helps us to feel our need, the thirst that helps us to drink, we can thank Him for; for what are food or drink without appetite, or Christ to a self-contented, circumstance-contented soul? Oh to *know* Him! How good, how great, how glorious—our God and Father, our God and Saviour, our God and Sanctifier—to know Him![306]

Lord's supper

The Duke of Wellington was once worshipping at his parish church and had remained to take the Lord's Supper. A very poor old man came up and knelt down close by the side of the Duke. Some one came and touched the poor man on his shoulder, and whispered to him to move further away, or to wait until the Duke had received the bread and the wine. But the keen eye and quick ear of the great commander caught the meaning of the touch and whisper. He took hold of the poor man's hand, and held him, to prevent him moving, and, in a reverential but distinct voice, said to him, "Do not move; we are all equal here."[307]

Lord's supper

At the coronation of King George III of Great Britain, after the crown was put upon his head, with great shouting, the two archbishops came to administer the Lord's supper. King George told them he would not take the Lord's supper with the crown upon his head, desiring to appear before the King of kings in no other character than in that of a humble Christian.[308]

---

[306] Dr. and Mrs. Howard Taylor, *Hudson Taylor and the China Inland Mission* (London: China Inland Mission , 1918), 236-7

[307] John Bate, *Objections to the Methodist Class-Meeting Answered: A Book for Hearers and Members* (London: Hamilton, Adams, and Co., 1866), 63

[308] Ingram Cobbin, *Georgiana: or, Anecdotes of George the Third* (London: John Hill, 1820), 58

Lord's supper

In preparing the Lord's table, Scottish preacher William Gregor conveyed this assurance to believers, "If you cannot come *with* assurance, come *for* assurance; if you cannot come with the strong confidence of him who said, 'Though He slay me, yet I will trust in Him,' at least come with the trembling faith of the afflicted parent who cried, 'Lord, I believe, help Thou mine unbelief.'"[309]

Lord's supper

Before his death in 1830, King George IV wished to take the Lord's supper and sent for the Bishop of Winchester. The royal messenger loitered on his way, and a considerable time elapsed before the Bishop's arrival. Upon learning the cause of so unusual a delay, King George rebuked his servant sharply, and dismissed him from his service. He then turned to the Bishop, and said he was now ready for the Lord's supper. The Bishop of Winchester calmly replied that while any irritation remained towards a fellow-creature, he must decline to administer the ordinance. The King, suddenly recollecting himself, sent for the offending party, and cordially pardoned him, saying to the Bishop, "My Lord, you are right!"[310]

Lord's supper

In the 1800s, pastor Edward Taylor faced his church in Boston, and said, "I have got something for you, children, it is a present from Jesus, something which He has sent to remember Him by." He held the cup of the Lord's supper under his outer coat, pressed to his heart, as if he would suddenly surprise them by bringing the precious gift out before their eyes. He then looked up and burst into tears as he pronounced His name. "He sends it to you, children, and tells me to say to you, 'Drink of this in memory of me.'"[311]

---

[309] William Wilson, *Memorials of Robert Smith Candlish* (Edinburgh: Adam and Charles Black, 1880), 43

[310] Catherine Sinclair, *The Kaleidoscope of Anecdotes and Aphorisms* (London: Richard Bently, 1851), 11

[311] Gilbert Haven, Thomas Russell, *Father Taylor, The Sailor Preacher* (San Francisco: B. B. Russell, 1872), 295

Love—for God means love for sinners

A man once testified in one of Dwight L. Moody's meetings of his experience with the Lord, that he had lived "on the Mount of Transfiguration" for five years. Moody quickly asked him, "How many souls did you win to Christ last year?"

"Well I don't know," was the astonished reply.

"Have you saved *any*?" Moody persisted.

"I don't know that I have," the man admitted.

"Well," said Moody, "we don't want that kind of mountaintop experience. When a man gets up so high that he cannot reach down and save poor sinners, there is something wrong."[312]

Love—its power

John Selwyn was a missionary to the South Sea Islands in the 1800s. There was a boy who had been brought from one of the rougher and wilder islands, and was consequently rebellious and difficult to manage. One day Selwyn spoke to him about something he had refused to do, and the boy, flying into a passion, struck him in the face. Selwyn, not trusting himself to speak, turned and walked away. The boy was punished for the offence, and, being still unsatisfactory, was sent back to his own island and there relapsed into godless ways. Many years afterwards the missionary who worked on that island, was sent for to a sick person who wanted him. He found this very man in a dying state and begging to be baptized. He told him how often he thought of the teaching he had received, and, when asked him by what name he should baptize him, he said, "Call me John Selwyn, because he taught me what Christ was like that day when I struck him, and I saw the colour mount in his face, but he never said a word except of love afterwards."[313]

Love—its power

English pastor Robert Chapman exemplified love that believers are to have for one another in every circumstance. He once came upon a man who had come under church discipline and excluded from church fellowship.

---

[312]   William R. Moody, *The Life of Dwight L. Moody* (New York: Fleming H. Revell, 1900), 367

[313]   F. D. How, *Bishop John Selwyn, A Memoir* (London: Isbister and Company, 1899), 175-6

This man had declared that he would never again have anything to do with Chapman. On no condition, he said, would he speak to him. One day they found themselves walking towards each other on the same street. When they met, Chapman, knowing all that the other had said about him, put his arms around him, and said, "Dear brother, God loves you, Christ loves you, and I love you." This simple, loving action broke down the man's hatred, and led him to repentance.[314]

Love—its power

In the 1800s Dwight L. Moody led a Sunday School for children. There was a child in his class whose family moved away to another part of the city. The little boy kept coming, even though it meant a long walk of five miles each way. Every Sunday he walked past forty churches with Sunday Schools—he walked past them all to the one he attended. One Sunday he was asked why he went so far, past so many others. He replied, "Because they love a fellow over there."[315]

Love—of enemies

In 1545, King Henry VIII revealed to Thomas Cranmer, the Archbishop of Canterbury, a plot against his life and commanded him to investigate it. Cranmer discovered that Thornden, the bishop of Dover, and Dr. Barber, his legal advisor, had been corrupted against him by Bishop Stephen Gardiner, and were collecting evidence against him. Informed of their treachery, he led Thornden and Barber into his garden and told them that some whom he had trusted had disclosed his secrets and accused him of heresy. He asked them how they thought such persons ought to be treated. They were loud in expressing their indignation, and declared that such traitors deserved to die. Cranmer replied, "Know ye these letters, my masters?" and showed them the proof of their own falsehood. The two offenders fell upon their knees to implore forgiveness, for it was evident that their lives were in his power. Cranmer simply bade them to ask forgiveness of God. His love and

---

[314] Frank Holmes, *Brother Indeed* (London: Victory Press, 1956), 63

[315] J. B. McClure, *Anecdotes and Illustrations of D. L. Moody* (Chicago: Rhodes & McClure, 1877), 50

forbearance on this and other similar occasions were such that it became a proverb among those who knew him: "Do my lord of Canterbury an ill turn, and he is your friend forever."[316]

Love—of enemies

In Holland in 1569 Dirk Willemzoon, was condemned to death because of his Christian beliefs. He had made his escape, closely pursued by an officer of justice, across a frozen lake. It was late in the winter, and the ice had become unsound. It trembled and cracked beneath his footsteps, but he reached the shore in safety. The officer was not so fortunate. The ice gave way beneath him, and he sank into the lake, uttering a cry for help. There were none to hear him, except the fugitive whom he had been hunting. Willemzoon returned, crossed the quaking and dangerous ice, at the peril of his life, extended his hand to his enemy, and saved him from certain death. The officer was desirous of avoiding the responsibility of sacrificing the preserver of his life, but was commanded to arrest him. On May 16th, he was burned to death under the most lingering torture.[317]

Love—of enemies

Alexander Duff was the first missionary from Scotland, sailing for Calcutta, India in 1829. He established a school for youth, reading the Scriptures in all the classes. As he read "The Sermon on The Mount," he found that it made a profound impression on the students, especially from the passage, "I say unto you, love your enemies; bless them that curse you; do good to them that hate you; and pray for them who despitefully use you and persecute you."

One of the Indian youths cried out, "Oh! How beautiful—how divine; surely, this is the truth, this is the truth, this is the truth," and for days and weeks afterwards was heard to exclaim, "How beautiful! Surely this is the truth!"[318]

---

[316] Francis Charles Massingberd, *The English Reformation* (London: Longmans, Green, and Co., 1866) 324-5

[317] John Lothrop Motley, *The Rise of the Dutch Republic* (London: George Routledge and Co., 1858), 241-2

[318] John William Kaye, *Christianity in India: An Historical Narrative* (London: Smith, Elder & Co., 1859), 502-503

Love—of enemies

Charles Spurgeon once sent a short letter of encouragement to someone who was having problems with a deacon in his church. He simply wrote,

> Bear. Bear. Bear. Forbear. Forbear. Forbear. In yielding is victory. Fight the devil and love the deacon—Love him till he is loveable.[319]

Marriage

In the 1600s, when Philip Henry sought to marry Katherine Matthews, the daughter of wealthy man, her friends objected in consideration of his social standing. They said that although he was a gentleman, and a scholar, and an excellent preacher, they did not even know where he came from.

"True," replied Miss Matthews, "but I know where he is going and I should like to go with him."[320]

Marriage—husbands loving wives

A newly married young man came to see Pastor Harry Ironside one day, exclaiming, "I want your help. I am in an awful state. I am drifting into idolatry."

Ironside asked, "What is the trouble?"

The man answered, "Well, I am afraid that I am putting my wife on too high a plane; I am afraid I love her too much, and I am displeasing the Lord."

Ironside responded, "Are you indeed? Do you love here more than Christ loved the Church?"

The man replied, "I don't think so."

Ironside told him, "Well, that is the limit, for we read, 'Husbands, love your wives even as Christ also loved he Church and gave Himself up for it (Ephesians 5:25)."[321]

---

[319] Iain H. Murray, *Letters of Charles Haddon Spurgeon* (Edinburgh: The Banner of Truth Trust, 1992), 77

[320] Matthew Henry, *The Miscellaneous Works of the Rev. Matthew Henry, vol. I* (London: Joseph Ogle Robinson, 1833), 41

[321] H. A. Ironside, *In the Heavenlies* (Neptune, New Jersey: Loizeaux Brothers, 1937), 170-1

Materialism

When Lawrence, one of the seven deacons of Rome in the fourth century, was ordered by the prefect of Rome in 258[322] to turn over the riches of the church, he promised that he would bring them. On the following day, he brought the poor together. When asked where the treasures were which he had promised, pointed to the poor saying, "These are the treasures of the Church."[323]

Materialism

English pastor Robert Hall ministered in the late 1700s and the early 1800s. On one occasion he was discussing the necessity of church reform with another clergyman, who enjoyed a lucrative living with the established church in England. When driven hard by the arguments of Hall, the clergyman responded, "I can't see it," "I don't see it," and "I can't see that at all."

At last, Hall took a letter from his pocket, and wrote on the back of it with his pencil the word "God." He asked, "Do you see that?"

The clergyman responded, "Yes."

Hall then covered it with a gold coin and asked, "Do you see it now?"

The clergyman responded, "No."

Hall replied, "I must wish you a good morning, sir," and left him to his thoughts.[324]

Meekness

Puritan John Cotton was a man of great humility, and though he was often insulted, he never expressed anger or resentment. Once after a sermon he was followed home by a conceited, ignorant man who with frowns told him his ministry had become either dark or flat. Cotton meekly replied, "Both, brother; it may be both. Let me have your prayers that it may be otherwise."

---

[322] Henry Walter, ed., *Expositions and Notes on Sundry Portions of the Holy Scriptures: Together with The Practice of Prelates by William Tyndale* (Cambridge, The University Press, 1846), 254

[323] Philip Schaff and Henry Wace, *A Select Library of the Nicene and Post-Nicene Fathers of the Christian Church, vol. X, St. Ambrose* (New York: The Christian Literature Company, 1896), 65

[324] Jacob Larwood, *The Book of Clerical Anecdotes* (London: John Camden Hotten, 1871), 57

At another time, Cotton was rudely insulted by a man in the street, who called him an old fool. Cotton replied, "I confess I am so. The Lord make thee and me wiser than we are, even wise unto salvation."[325]

Meekness

Puritan Matthew Henry was the object of much persecution in his time, but when maligned and reproached, he showed great meekness and patience, and instead of rendering evil for evil, returned it with good, ever seeking to improve such occurrences for his own advancement in Christian virtue. He would say, "How pleasant is it to have the bird in the bosom sing sweetly!"[326]

Ministry

On August 15, 1641, Puritan pastor Thomas Shepard wrote the following in his diary:

> I saw four evils attending my ministry.—
>
> 1. The devil treads me down by shame, discouragement, and an apprehension of the unsavory spirits of the people.
>
> 2. I am become too careless, because I have done well, and have been enlarged and respected.
>
> 3. Weakness and infirmities: as the want of light, life, and spirit.
>
> 4. The want of success.—I saw these things, and have cause to be humbled for them. I have this day found my heart heavy, depressed, end untoward, by musing upon the many evils to come. But I was comforted by recollecting, that though in myself I am a dying, condemned sinner, I am alive and reconciled by Christ; that I am unable to do any thing of myself, yet by Christ I can do all things; and that though I enjoy all these only in part in this world, I shall shortly have them in perfection in heaven.[327]

---

[325] Benjamin Brook, *The Lives of the Puritans, vol. III* (London: James Black, 1813), 159

[326] George Cheever, *A Cyclopaedia of Religious and Moral Anecdotes* (London: Charles Griffin and Company, 1848), 180

[327] Benjamin Brook, *The Lives of the Puritans, vol. III* (London: James Black, 1813), 105

Ministry

A man named Thomas Scott once shared with John Newton a call to God's service that seemed to conflict with his personal interests. Newton recounted the story of a nobleman who was selected as ambassador by his queen, but excused himself because of his family and urgent concerns at home. The queen responded, "You must go; only do you mind my concerns heartily, and I will take care of yours."

"Thus," says Newton, "God, as it were, says to you."[328]

Ministry

A distinguished stranger once had the opportunity to hear Thomas Chalmers, the leader of the free church in Scotland in the 1800s. One of his ardent admirers asked the man afterwards, "What do you think of Dr. Chalmers?"

The stranger replied, "Think of him? Why he has made me think so much of *Jesus* that I had no time to think of *him!*"[329]

Ministry

On September 8, 1796 John Newton wrote a letter to Hannah More, whom he led to Christ. More ministered to the poor in the area of Mendip, England, teaching them the Bible. Newton wrote to her, "I cannot wonder that a sense of the love of Jesus to *you* should constrain you as it does to devote all your time, and talents, and influence to your service. Nor do I wonder at the success and encouragement he gives you in your department."

More wrote Newton back with words of humility, saying, "God is sometimes pleased to work by the most unpromising and unworthy instruments; I suppose to take away every shadow of doubt that it is his own doing. It always gives me the idea of a great author writing with a very bad pen."[330]

---

[328] John Scott, *Letters and Papers of the Late Rev. Thomas Scott* (Boston: Samuel T. Armstrong, and Crocker, & Brewster, 1825), 197

[329] Ashbel Green, ed., *The Christian Advocate, vol. IV,* (Philadelphia: A. Finley, 1826) 163

[330] William Roberts, *Memoirs of the Life and Correspondence of Mrs. Hannah More, vol. I* (New York: Harper & Brothers, 1837) 474-6

Ministry

In 1871 Dwight L. Moody passed through a terrible struggle of soul concerning himself and his work. He would weep and pray in private agony, then, with a sorrowful face, go out to minister. He held meetings in Brooklyn, but they dragged heavily. Few people attended and none were spiritually moved. At last, when the congregation had fallen to eighteen people, an unnamed woman said to him, "Mr. Moody, we have plenty of preaching in Brooklyn; but if you would tell us something about the Bible, perhaps it would be blessed to us."

Moody accepted the suggestion, and set about preparing a study of the Bible. Telling the people to bring their Bibles, he set a study for the following afternoon. It is recorded that "at once the power of God came down." Day after day the meetings increased. A great revival broke out and many came to faith in Christ.[331]

Ministry—faithfulness in

Dwight L. Moody noticed a lady at the services whom he knew to be a Sunday school teacher. After the service he asked her where her class was. "O," said she, "I went to the school and found only a little boy, and so I came away."

He replied, "Only a little boy! Think of the value of one such soul! The fires of a reformation may be slumbering in that tow-headed boy; there may be a young Knox, or a Wesley, or a Whitefield in your class."[332]

Ministry—pastoral

In 1825, Edward Payson was asked what message he would send to the young men who were studying for the ministry. He replied,

> What if God should place in your hand a diamond, and tell you to inscribe on it a sentence which should be read at the last day, and shown there as an index of your own thoughts and feelings? What care, what caution would you exercise in the

---

[331] William Haven Daniels, *D.L. Moody and His Work* (Hartford, Conn.: American Publishing Company, 1875) 190-1

[332] *D.L. Moody's Child Stories: Related by Him in His Revival Work in Europe and America*, ed. by J. B. McClure (Chicago: Rhodes & McClure, 1877), 104

selection! Now this is what God has done. He has placed before you immortal minds, more imperishable than the diamond, on which you are about to inscribe every day and every hour by your instructions, by your spirit, or by your example, something which will remain and be exhibited, for or against you, at the judgment day."[333]

Missions

In the 1800s Pastor Phillips Brooks was once asked this question: "What is the first thing you would do if you had accepted a call to become the rector of a small, discouraged congregation that is not even meeting its current expenses?"

Brooks replied, "The first thing I would do would be to preach a sermon on, and ask the congregation to make an offering for, foreign missions."[334]

Missions

Grafton Burke was a missionary doctor at the hospital in Fort Yukon, Alaska in the early 1900s. One winter month an Eskimo runner came to him with word that a foreigner was lying in the snow about fifty miles away. Dr. Burke at once harnessed his dog team and set forth. He found the famous Canadian Arctic explorer Vilhjalmur Stefansson near death from pneumonia. The explorer recovered and was leaving the hospital, he said to the doctor, "Money cannot repay what you have done for me. You have saved my life. But I should like to make one criticism. You would accomplish more if you did not spend so much time in religious work and in prayer."[335]

The doctor replied, "If it had not been for prayer, I should not be here; this hospital would not have been here, and you would be lying dead in the snow."

---

[333] Edward Payson, *A Memoir of the Rev. Edward Payson*, ed. by A. L. Payson (London: R. B. Seeley and W. Burnside, 1830), 440

[334] n.a., *The Spirit of Missions: vol. LXXVIII* (New York: Episcopal Church, Board of Missions, 1913), 121

[335] *The Spirit of Missions, vol 98* ed. by G. Warfield (Burlington, New Jersey: Episcopal Church Domestic and Foreign Missionary Society, 1933), 429

Money

Andrew Fuller was examining an ingot of gold in the Bank of England. He said to his friend, "How much better to have this in the hand than in the heart!"[336]

Money

On March 8, 1713, Matthew Henry was returning to preach an evening sermon in London and was robbed. The thieves took about ten or eleven shillings. He wrote in his diary:

1.   What reason have I to be thankful to God, who have travelled so much, and yet was never robbed before.

2.   What a deal of evil the love of money is the root of, that four men would venture their lives and souls for about half-a-crown a-piece.

3.   See the power of Satan in the children of disobedience.

4.   See the vanity of worldly wealth; how soon we may be stripped of it. How loose, therefore, we should sit to it.[337]

Mother—influence of

Harvey Goodwin was the Bishop of Carlisle in England from 1869-91. At a meeting of mothers and daughters, he shared what had been the greatest impact on his life, as he said,

> I am one of those who lost their mothers at a very early age. I was very little over six years old when my dear mother was suddenly taken from me... Now, then, when I look back to the teaching of my mother, what do I think of it? I say deliberately, and without any amount of exaggeration, that though I have since that time been at school, been under tutors, been at college, and had all

---

[336]   Alexander Carson, *Baptism in Its Mode and Subjects* (Philadelphia: American Baptist Publication Society, 1857), 309

[337]   James Hamilton, *Our Christian Classics: Readings from the Best Divines, with Notices Biographical and Critical, vol. III* (London: James Nisbet and Co., 1858), 244

the experience of life, I do not believe that all the lessons that I have received since that time put together amount in value and in importance to the lessons which I learned from my mother before I was seven years old.[338]

Mother—influence of

English preacher Richard Cecil wasyouth, he hardened his conscience by reading books of infidelity, till he became a professed infidel himself.[339] What did God use to turn his life around? Cecil said that he was proud of his arguments against Christianity, but he admitted, "There was one argument I never could get over—the influence and life of a holy mother."[340]

Mother—influence of

In a humble cottage in a little town in Germany, just about the close of the seventeenth century, a Christian mother gathered her children about her death-bed to bid them farewell. Her family was the poorest, but the dying mother astonished her children by saying, "I have laid up a treasure for you—a very great treasure."

Eager to possess it, one of her little ones asked, "And where is it, mother?"

She replied, "Seek it in the Bible, my children, and you will find it; there is not a page which I have not wet with my tears." Among the children was a boy whom that mother's tears and prayers were the beginning of his spiritual birth. His name was Bartholomew Ziegenbalg, the first Protestant missionary to India.[341]

Mysticism

Andrew Bonar was speaking with a man whom he knew to be very excitable. The man told him that during his illness he had had a vision of

---

[338] Charles Bullock, ed., *Home Words for Heart and Heart* (London: "Home Words" Publishing Office, 1885), 40

[339] Josiah Pratt, *The Works of the Rev. Richard Cecil, M. A., with a Memoir of His Life*, vol. I (London: L. B. Seeley, 1816), 6

[340] W. Meynell Whittemore, *Pressing Onward; or, Earnest Counsels for Holy Living* (London: William Macintosh, 1875), 206

[341] A. J. Gordon, *The Holy Spirit in Missions* (New York: Fleming H. Revell Company, 1893), 47-8

angels, and had felt one of them touch him as he lay in bed. Dr. Bonar quietly remarked, "Have you a cat in the house? Don't you think it may have been the cat?"[342]

New Nature

Augustine, before his conversion, had been in the habit of associating with an immoral woman. After his conversion, she passed him in the street and said to him, "Augustine, it is I!"

As he could not go by without giving her some answer, he replied, "Yes, but it is not I!"[343]

New Nature

Harry Ironside had a Christian friend who would at times fly off and lose his temper. But his anger was always checked if someone looked at him and quietly said, "Is that old George or new George talking?"

In a moment the tears would come and he would say, "That's old George; new George would never behave that way."[344]

Obedience

When the English preacher Richard Cecil was a little boy, his father went on business to the India House, and took him along. While he was transacting his business, his son was dismissed, and directed to wait for him at the India House door. His father, on finishing his business, went out at another door, and entirely forgot that he had ordered his son to wait for him. In the evening, his mother, missing the child, inquired where he was.

His father, recollecting his directions, said, "You may depend on it, he is still waiting where I appointed him." He immediately returned to the India House, and found him on the spot where he had been ordered to wait.[345]

---

[342] Marjory A. Bonar, ed., *Reminiscences of Andrew A. Bonar* (London: Hodder and Stoughton, 1895), 87

[343] C. H. Spurgeon, *The Metropolitan Tabernacle Pulpit, Sermons Preached and Revised by C. H. Spurgeon during the Year 1895, vol. XLI* (London: Passmore & Alabaster, 1895) 452

[344] H. A. Ironside, *In the Heavenlies* (Neptune, New Jersey: Loizeaux Brothers, 1937), 170-1

[345] Josiah Pratt, *The Works of the Rev. Richard Cecil: With a Memoir of His Life, vol. I* (New York: John P. Haven, 1825), 69

Obedience

William Mompesson was an English pastor in 1665-6 when the plague killed 267 of his 350 parishioners, including his wife.[346] Faced with the brevity of life in a profuse way, on September 1, 1666 he wrote a letter to his patron, exhorting him to obedience, with these words:

> Dear Sir, let your dying Chaplain recommend this truth to you and your family, that no happiness nor solid comfort can be found in this vale of tears like living a pious life; and pray ever to retain this rule—never to do anything upon which you dare not first ask the blessing of God upon the success thereof.[347]

Obedience

On October 18, 1633, King Charles I issued the "Book of Sports," which authorized Sunday sports, viewed by the Puritans as violation of the Christian Sabbath. King Charles commanded his declaration to be read in churches.[348] Pastor George Newton of Taunton obeyed the command and read it to his congregation, immediately saying "These are the commandments of men." He then read the twentieth chapter of Exodus, saying, "These are the commandments of God; but whereas in this case the laws of God and the laws of man are at variance, choose ye which ye will obey."[349]

Opportunities, Seizing

James Hervey made the most of even small opportunities that God gave him. In the afternoon, when he was called down to tea, he would bring his Hebrew Bible or Greek New Testament, and would either speak upon one verse or upon several verses, as the occasion offered. At his funeral, William

---

[346] *Transactions of the Sanitary Institute of Great Britain, vol. IX, ed. by W. H. Cornfield, et. al.* (London: Offices of the Sanitary Institute, 1888), 122

[347] n.a., *Anecdotes of Distinguished Persons, vol. II* (London: T. Cadell Jun. and W. Davies, 1798), 121

[348] Joshua Toulmin Revised and Enlarged by James Savage, *The History of Taunton, in the County of Somerset* (Taunton: John Poole, 1822), 137-8

[349] Charles Stanford, *Joseph Alleine: His Companions & Times,* (London: Jackson, Walford, and Hodder, 1861), 69

Romaine commented, "The glory of God is seldom promoted at the tea table, but it was at Mr. Hervey's. Drinking tea with him was like being at an ordinance, for it was sanctified by the Word of God, and prayer."[350]

Parenting

On the day of his execution on August 22, 1651, Puritan pastor Christopher Love wrote this letter to his wife Mary. It is overflowing with love and wise counsel that is insightful and relevant for parents, single mothers, and other believers:

> My most gracious beloved,
>
> I am now going from a prison to a palace... I have finished my work; I am now to receive my wages. I am going to heaven, where there are two of my children; and leaving thee on earth, where there are, three of my babes; those two above need not any care; but the three below need thine. It comforts me to think two of my children are in the bosom of Abraham, and three of them will be in the arms and care of so tender and godly a mother! I know thou art a woman of a sorrowful spirit, yet be comforted. Though thy sorrows be great for thy husband's going out of the world, yet thy pains shall be the less in bringing thy child into the world: thou shalt be a joyful mother, though thou art a sad widow! God hath many mercies in store for thee: the prayers of a dying husband will not be lost. To my shame I speak it, I never prayed so much for thee at liberty, as I have done in prison. I cannot write more; but I have a few practical counsels to leave with thee, viz.
>
> 1. Keep under a sound, orthodox, and soul-searching ministry. Oh, there are many deceivers gone out into the world; but Christ's sheep know his voice, and a stranger will they not follow. Attend on that ministry which teaches the way of God in truth, and follow Solomon's advice: *Cease to hear the instruction that causeth to err from the way of knowledge.*

---

[350] James Hervey, *The Life of the Reverend Mr. James Hervey* (Berwick, England: Printed for R. Taylor, 1772) 109-10

2. Bring up thy children in the knowledge and admonition of the Lord. The mother ought to be the teacher in the father's absence. *The words which his mother taught him.* Timothy was instructed by his grandmother Lois, and his mother Eunice.

3. Pray in thy family daily, that thy dwelling may be in the number of the families that do call upon God.

4. Labor for a meek and quiet spirit, which is in the sight of God of great price.

5. Pore not on the comforts thou wantest; but on the mercies thou hast.

6. Look rather to God's end in afflicting, than at the measure and degree of thy afflictions.

7. Labor to clear up thy evidences for heaven, when God takes from thee the comforts of earth, that, as thy sufferings do abound, so thy consolations in Christ may much more abound.

8. Though it is good to maintain a holy jealousy of the deceitfulness of thy heart, yet it is evil for thee to cherish fears and doubts about the truth of thy graces. If ever I had confidence touching the graces of another, I have confidence of grace in thee. I can say of thee, as Peter did of Sylvanus, *I am persuaded that this is the grace of God wherein thou standest.* Oh, my dear soul, wherefore dost thou doubt, whose heart hath been upright, whose walkings have been holy! I could venture my soul in thy soul's stead. Such confidence have I in thee!

9. When thou findest thy heart secure, presumptuous and proud, then pore upon corruption more than upon grace: but when thou findest thy heart doubting and unbelieving, then look on thy graces, not on thy infirmities.

10. Study the covenant of grace and merits of Christ, and then be troubled if thou canst. Thou art interested in such a covenant that accepts purposes for performances, desires for deeds, sincerity for perfection, the righteousness of another, viz. that of Jesus Christ, as if it were our own. Oh, my love, rest, rest then in the love of God, in the bosom of Christ!

11. Swallow up thy will in the will of God. It is a bitter cup we are to drink, but it is the cup our Father hath put into our hands. When Paul was to go to suffer at Jerusalem, the Christians could say. *The will of the Lord be done.* O say thou, when I go to Tower-hill, *The will of the Lord be done.*

12. Rejoice in my joy. To mourn for me inordinately, argues that either thou enviest or suspectest my happiness. *The joy of the Lord is my strength.* O, let it be thine also! Dear wife, farewell![351]

Parenting

When the parishoners of Samuel Wesley's church set his house on fire, everyone of his children escaped the flames, with his six year old son John barely escaping before the whole roof fell in. When the child was carried out to his parents, Samuel cried out, "Come, neighbours, let us kneel down; let us give thanks to God! He has given me all my eight children; let the house go, I am rich enough."[352]

Parenting

The great English poet Samuel Taylor Coleridge was once talking with a man who thought it very unfair to influence a child's mind with any opinions before the child should come to the age to choose for itself. Coleridge then showed him his garden, and told him it was his botanical garden.

His friend exclaimed, "How so? It is covered with weeds!"

Coleridge replied, "Oh, *that* is only because it has not yet come to the age of discretion and choice. The weeds, you see, have taken the liberty to grow, and I thought it unfair in me to prejudice the soil towards roses and strawberries."[353]

---

[351] Benjamin Brook, *The Lives of the Puritans,* vol. *III* (London: James Black, 1813), 130-2

[352] Charles Buck, *A Theological Dictionary, Containing Definitions of All Religious and Ecclesiastical Terms, enlarged by E. Henderson* (London: Thomas Tegg, 1841), 770

[353] Samuel Taylor Coleridge, *Specimens of the Table Talk of the Late Samuel Taylor Coleridge* (New York: Harper & Brothers, 1835), 129

Parenting

John Penry was martyred on May 29, 1593, at the age of thirty four, leaving a widow and four daughters, the oldest who was not yet four years old. In prison before his death, he wrote a letter for when they would be old enough to understand. As he concludes his lengthy exhortation and encouragement, he writes

> ...my dear children, learn to read, that you may be conversant, day and night, in the word of the Lord. If your mother be able to keep you together, I doubt not but you shall learn both to write and read by her means. I have left you four Bibles, each of you one; being the sole and only patrimony or dowry that I have for you. I beseech you, and charge you, not only to keep them, but to read in them day and night; and before you read, and also, after reading, be earnest in prayer and meditation, that you may understand and perform the good way of your God... Finally, my daughters—grow in all graces of knowledge and godliness in Christ Jesus. Believe and hope firmly in that salvation which is to be had by Him. Suffer affliction with Him in this poor church. Continue in holy fear unto the end; then shall you and I have a blessed meeting in the great day of His appearance...
>
> From close prison, with many tears, and yet in much joy of the Holy Ghost, this 10th of 4th month of April, 1593, your poor father here upon earth, most careful to be joined with you for evermore in the kingdom of Jesus Christ,
> John Penry.[354]

Parenting

In talking with a poor man's daughter, Lady Huntingdon asked her whether she took any thought for her soul. The young woman answered, "I never knew that I had a soul."

Lady Huntingdon replied, "Bid your mother call on me today."

---

[354] John Waddington, *John Penry, The Pilgrim Martyr, 1559-1593* (London: W. & F. G. Cash, 1854), 136-45

When the old woman came, she said to her, "How is it that your daughter is sixteen years of age, and does not know that she has a soul?"

The woman answered, "In truth, my lady, I have so much care upon me, to find my daughter in food and clothes for her body, that I have no time to talk to her about her soul."[355]

Parenting

Horace Mann was asked, after a memorable commencement address, if he had not exaggerated in saying that no possible amount of time, thought and treasure could be too much to expend if it would save one boy from ignorance and evil and train him for life. He promptly replied, "Not if he were my boy!"[356]

Pastoral Ministry—opposition to

Martin Luther said that a good preacher should have these properties and virtues:

> *First*, to preach orderly [systematically].
> *Secondly*, he should have a ready wit.
> *Thirdly*, he should be eloquent
> *Fourthly*, He should have a good voice.
> *Fifthly*, A good remembrance.
> *Sixthly*, He should know where to make an end.
> *Seventhly*, He should be sure of his things [doctrine]
> *Eighthly*, He should venture and engage body and blood, wealth and honor, by the word.
> *Ninthly*, He should suffer himself to be mocked and buffeted of every one.[357]

---

[355] Augustus Toplady, *The Works of Augustus M. Toplady, vol. IV* (London: Printed for the Proprietors and sold by W. Row, 1794), 190

[356] Clarence Frank Birdseye, *Individual Training in Our Colleges*, (Norwood, Mass.: J. S. Cushing & Co., 1907), 196

[357] Martin Luther, *Luther's Table Talk* (London: Longman, Rees, Orme, Brown, and Green, 1832), 232-233

Pastoral Ministry—purity in

A friend asked George Whitfield why he was so particular to always have his clothes scrupulously clean. Whitfield answered, "No, no, these are not trifles—a minister must be without spot, even in his garments."[358]

Pastoral Ministry—priorities of

In 1900 G. Campbell Morgan once wrote a letter to a fellow preacher. In it, he said,

> Nothing is more needed among preachers today than that we should have the courage to shake ourselves free from the thousand and one trivialities in which we are asked to waste our time and strength, and resolutely return to the apostolic ideal which made necessary the office of the diaconate. [We must resolve that] "we will continue steadfastly in prayer, and in the ministry of the Word."[359]

Pastoral Ministry—seriousness of

When John Knox preached a series of messages at the Castle of St. Andrews in 1547, the men who heard him were greatly impressed, and seeing his fitness for pastoral ministry, they earnestly entreated Knox to enter at once upon the office of the ministry. But he declared that "he would not run where God had not called him," and refused their request. Upon this they took counsel, and ultimately agreed that John Rough, who was the preacher to the congregation within the castle, without giving any formal warning that he was about to do anything of the kind, should address to Knox a special public call in the name and before the face of the congregation.

Accordingly, in the presence of the people, and after having preached a sermon on the election of ministers, Rough turned to Knox and said,

---

[358] Orison Swett Marden, George Raywood Devitt, eds., *The Consolidated Encyclopedic Library, vol. XVI* (New York: The Emerson Press, 1903), 4692

[359] Jill Morgan, ed., *This Was His Faith: The Expository Letters of G. Campbell Morgan* (Westwood, New Jersey: Fleming H. Revell, 1952), 15

Brother, ye shall not be offended, albeit that I speak unto you that which I have in charge even from all those that are here present, which is this: In the name of God and of His Son Jesus Christ, and in the name of these that presently call you by my mouth, I charge you that ye refuse not this holy vocation, but that, as ye tender the glory of God, the increase of Christ's kingdom, the edification of your brethren, and the comfort of me whom you understand well enough to be oppressed by the multitude of labors, that ye take upon you the public office and charge of preaching even as ye look to avoid God's heavy displeasure, and desire that He shall multiply His graces with you.

Then turning to the congregation, he said, "Was not this your charge to me?"

They answered, "It was, and we approve it."

The combined suddenness and solemnity of this appeal completely unnerved Knox. He burst into tears and hastened to his closet, where we may well believe that he sought wisdom from God; and the result was that he was led to take up that ministry which he laid down only with his life."[360]

Patience

John Wesley recounts of his mother, Susanna Wesley, "I remember to have heard my father asking my mother, 'How could you have the patience to tell that blockhead the same thing, twenty times over?"

She answered, "Why, if I had told him but nineteen times, I should have lost all my labor."[361]

Patience

In the 1700s, someone behaved very rudely to James Boswell. He went to Samuel Johnson, his friend, and spoke of it as a serious distress. Johnson

---

[360] Wm. M. Taylor, *John Knox* (New York: A. C. Armstrong & Son, 1885), 14-16

[361] John Wesley, *The Works of the Rev. John Wesley, vol. VI* (London: Printed at the Conference-Office by Thomas Cordeux, 1810), 355

laughed and said, "Consider, sir, how insignificant this will appear twelve months hence."[362]

Patience

In the late 1700s in Scotland, a young lady gathered a class of poor, rough boys into Sunday School. Among them was a boy named Bob, the most wretched and unpromising of the group. The superintendent of the school told these boys to come to his house during the week and he would give them a new suit of clothes. They came and received the clothes as promised. After a Sunday or two, Bob failed to appear, but the teacher went after him and found the clothes in rags and Bob playing in the dirt with other boys. She begged him to come back and promised him another suit of clothes. This was repeated for a third time, and Bob came to faith in Christ. In a short time he felt a call to the ministry, and was granted a license to preach. Robert Morrison became the first missionary to China, the man who translated the Bible into Chinese.[363]

Peace

In 1653, Bulstrode Whitelock was embarking as Cromwell's ambassador for Sweden. He was much disturbed in his mind, as he rested on the preceding night, while he reflected on the state of Great Britain. It happened that a confidential servant slept in an adjacent bed, who, finding that his master could not sleep, said, "Pray, sir, will you give me leave to ask you a question?"

Whitelock replied, "Certainly."

The servant continued, "Pray, sir, don't you think God governed the world very well before you came into it?"

Whitelock answered, "Undoubtedly."

"And pray, sir, don't you think that He will govern it quite as well when you are gone out of it?"

Again, Whitelock answered, "Certainly."

---

[362] Charles Buck, *Works of the Rev. Charles Buck, vol. V* (Philadelphia: W. W. Woodward, 1822), 95

[363] Charles Henry Prather, *A Handbook of Classics* (Nashville, Tenn.: Pub. House of the M.E. Church, South, Smith & Lamar, 1910), 123

"Then, sir, pray excuse me, but don't you think you may as well trust Him to govern it as long as you are in it?"

To this question Whitelock had nothing to reply, but, turning about, soon fell asleep, and never awoke till he was summoned to embark.[364]

Peace

On July 21, 1683, when William Russell was led to the scaffold to be executed, he acted with surprising serenity. He wound up his watch, saying with a smile, "Now I have done with time and must henceforth think solely of eternity."[365]

Peace

George Briggs served as Governor of Massachusetts from 1844 to 1851. He was stuck by a gun that accidentally discharged and surgeons tried unsuccessfully to save him. When he realized that he was dying, he asked for a slate and wrote these words: "Be still, and know that I am God" (Psalm 46:10).[366]

Peace

When Hudson Taylor traveled to Melbourne in 1890, he stayed with pastor Hussey Macartney, who was struck with his peacefulness. He wrote of Taylor,

> He was an object lesson in quietness. He drew from the Bank of Heaven every farthing of his daily income—"My peace I give unto you." Whatever did not agitate the Saviour, or ruffle His spirit was not to agitate him. The serenity of the Lord Jesus concerning any matter and at its most critical moment, this was his ideal and practical possession: He knew nothing of rush or hurry, of quivering nerves or vexation of spirit. He knew there was a peace passing all understanding, and that he could not do without it.

[364] William Walters, *Rays of Gold from the Sun of Righteousness* (Halifax: Milner and Sowerby, 1861), 23-24

[365] Lady Rachel Russell, *Letters of Lady Rachel Russell*, (London: J. Mawman, 1801), 128

[366] William C. Richards, *Great in Goodness; A Memoir of George N. Briggs, Governor of the Commonwealth of Massachusetts, from 1844-1851* (Boston: Gould and Lincoln, 1866), 400

Now I was altogether different. Mine is a peculiarly nervous disposition, and with a busy life I found myself in a tremor all day long. I did not enjoy the Lord as I knew I ought. Nervous agitation possessed me as long as there was anything to be done. The greatest loss of my life was the loss of the light of the Lord's presence and fellowship during writing hours. The daily mail robbed me of His delightful society.

At length I said to Mr. Taylor, "I am in the study, you are in the big spare room. You are occupied with millions, I with tens. Your letters are pressingly important, mine of comparatively little moment. Yet I am worried and distressed, while you are always calm."

"My dear Macartney," he replied, "the peace you speak of is in my case more than a delightful privilege, it is a necessity."[367]

Peace

William Gladstone served as England's Prime Minister in the late 1800s. He was once asked what kept him so serene and composed in the midst of his busy life. He replied, "At the foot of my bed, where I can see it on retiring and on arising in the morning, are the words, 'Thou wilt keep him in perfect peace whose mind is stayed on Thee, because he trusteth in Thee'" [Isaiah 26:3].[368]

Prayer

English Puritan preacher Philip Henry had two children who were dangerously sick. After a time of wrestling in prayer for them, he wrote in his diary, "If the Lord will be pleased to grant me my request this time concerning my children, I will not say, as the beggars at our door used to do, 'I'll never ask anything of him again,' but, on the contrary, he shall hear oftener from me than ever, and I will love God the better, and love prayer the better, as long as I live."[369]

---

[367] Dr. and Mrs. Howard Taylor, *Hudson Taylor and the China Inland Mission* (London: China Inland Mission , 1918), 493-4

[368] William S. Sadler, *The Physiology of Faith and Fear* (Chicago: A. C. McClurg, 1912), 381

[369] Matthew Henry, *The Miscellaneous Works of the Rev. Matthew Henry, vol. I* (London: Joseph Ogle Robinson, 1833), 112

Prayer

The Scottish reformer John Knox was often in such an agony for the people of his country that he could not sleep. He passionately prayed, "O Lord, give me Scotland, or I die!" Knox was such a man of prayer that bloody Queen Mary said that she feared his prayers more than all the armies of Europe.[370]

Prayer

Andrew Fuller was at a conference when the person next to him was asked to pray. With embarrassment, he whispered to Fuller, "I do not know how to go on."

Fuller whispered back, "Tell the Lord so."

No one else heard what passed between them, but the man, taking Fuller's advice, began to confess to the Lord his not knowing how to pray as he ought, begging to be taught to pray, and proceeded with a wonderful prayer.[371]

Prayer—answered

PhilippWe can't spare you yet, Philipp." Luther then threw himself upon his knees, and wrestled with God for his recovery for upwards of an hour. He went from his knees to the bed, and took his friend by the hand.

Again he said, "Dear Luther, why don't you let me depart in peace?"

"No, no, Philipp, we cannot spare you yet," was the reply. He then ordered some soup, and when pressed to take it he declined, again saying, "Dear Luther, why will you not let me go home and be at rest?"

"We cannot spare you yet, Philipp," was the reply. He then added, "Philipp, take this soup, or I will excommunicate you."

Melancthon took the soup and soon he began to get better. He regained his health, and labored for years afterwards in the cause of the Reformation. When Luther returned home, he said to his wife with joy, "God gave me my brother Melancthon back in direct answer to prayer."[372]

---

[370] Henry Clay Fish, *Handbook of Revivals* (Boston, Mass.: James H. Earle, 1874), 283-4

[371] C. H. Spurgeon, *Feathers for Arrows* (New York: Sheldon & Company, 1870), 170

[372] William Walters, *Rays of Gold from the Sun of Righteousness* (Halifax: Milner and Sowerby, 1861), 41-42

Prayer—answered

Puritan John Flavel was once going by sea from Dartmouth to London, when the vessel in which he sailed was overtaken within five leagues of Portland by a dreadful tempest; so that, between one and two in the morning, the master and the seamen concluded that, unless God changed the wind, there was no hope of life. Flavel called all the hands that could be spared into the cabin for prayer; but the violence of the tempest was such, that they could not prevent themselves from being thrown from one side to the other as the ship was tossed, and the sea broke in upon them to threaten them with drowning right there in the cabin. Flavel took hold of the two pillars of the cabin bed, and calling upon God, begged mercy for himself and the rest in the ship. He prayed that if he and his company perished in that storm, the name of God would be blasphemed, and the enemies of religion, from whose hands he was escaping, would say that though he had escaped on shore, yet divine vengeance had overtaken him at sea. In the midst of prayer his faith and hope were raised, insomuch that he expected a gracious answer. He then committed himself and his companions to the mercy of God and concluded his prayer.

No sooner was the prayer ended than one came down from the deck, crying, "Deliverance! Deliverance! God is a God hearing prayer! In a moment the wind is become fair west!"

And so sailing before it, they were brought safely to London.[373]

Prayer—answered

The parents of the great Baptist preacher Charles Spurgeon were not Baptist. After Spurgeon was saved his mother said to him, "Ah, Charles! I often prayed the Lord to make you a Christian, but I never asked that you might become a Baptist."

Spurgeon replied, "Ah, mother! The Lord has answered your prayer with His usual bounty, and given you exceeding abundantly above what you asked or thought."[374]

---

[373] William Walters, *Rays of Gold from the Sun of Righteousness* (Halifax: Milner and Sowerby, 1861), 280-281

[374] Susannah Spurgeon, W. J. Harrald, The *Autobiography of Charles H. Spurgeon* (Cincinnati, Ohio: Curts & Jennings, 1898), 69

Prayer—continuous

A friend was once conversing with Stonewall Jackson about the difficulty of obeying the Scripture injunction, "Pray without ceasing." Jackson insisted that we could so accustom ourselves to it that it could be easily obeyed. He said,

> When we take our meals there is the grace. When I take a draught of water I always pause, as my palate receives the refreshment, to lift up my heart to God in thanks and prayer for the water of life. Whenever I drop a letter into the box at the post office, I send a petition along with it for God's blessing upon its mission, and upon the person to whom it is sent. When I break the seal of a letter just received, I stop to pray to God that he might prepare me for its contents, and make it a messenger of good. When I go to my classroom, and await the arrangement of the cadets in their places, that is my time to intercede with God for them. And so of every other familiar act of the day.[375]

Prayer—does not negate action

The great evangelist Dwight L. Moody was crossing the Atlantic when a fire broke out in the hold of the ship. The crew and some volunteers stood in line to pass buckets of water. A friend said to Moody, "Mr. Moody, let us go to the other end of the ship and engage in prayer."

Moody said, "Not so, sir; we stand right here and pass buckets and pray hard all the time."[376]

Prayer—importance of

When President Ulysses S. Grant was dying, Oliver Howard, one of his former officers known as "The Christian General," visited him. General

---

[375] J. Wm. Jones, "Appendix, Containing Personal Reminiscences," *Stonewall Jackson: A Military Biography*, John Esten Cooke (New York: D. Appleton and Company, 1876), 504

[376] John Clyde Turner *A Truth in a Smile* (Nashville, Tenn.: Broadman Press, 1941), 74

Howard reminded the president of his great service and told him that America would always hold him in grateful remembrance. Grant interrupted the general who had impressed him with both his courage and his piety, saying, "Howard, tell me more about prayer."[377]

Prayer—for others

British Major General George Gordon wrote to his sister on September 28, 1883 about some people who were exasperating him. He explained to her, "The only remedy with me...is to pray for every one who worries me; It is wonderful what such prayer does. In heaven our Lord intercedes for us, and He governs heaven and earth. Prayer for others relieves our own burdens."[378]

Prayer—for others

Union General Oliver Howard was wounded twice in his right arm during the Civil War, resulting in it being amputated. After the war, he was assigned to Fort Columbus on Governors Island in New York. Walking up and down Broadway, he was jostled in the crowds, which irritated and pained his amputation at the shoulder. Concerned that this irritation would sour his disposition, when someone would bump into him and hurt him he would pray, "God bless him!" This response became such second nature to him that he was constantly praying for those about him.[379]

Prayer—in Jesus' name

To a friend who was facing an impossible task, Amy Carmichael wrote in a letter,

> I woke between one and two o'clock and prayed oh such poor prayers for you. I was troubled about the poorness till I suddenly remembered in whose Name I prayed. That was enough. The

---

[377] n.a. *Christian Nation, vol. 29* (New York: Christian Nation Publishing Company, 1898), 10

[378] C. G. Gordon, *Letters of General C.G. Gordon to His Sister, M.A. Gordon* (London: MacMillan and Co., 1888), 351

[379] Martha Tarbell, *Tarbell's Teachers' Guide to the International Sunday-school Lessons for 1920* (New York: Fleming H. Revell, 1919), 285

Father so loves His beloved Son that the poorest little word that rises in His name touches His heart.[380]

Prayer—necessary

Gustauvus Adolphus, the King of Sweden in the 1600s, was alone in his pavilion for some time, and none of his attendants dared interrupt him. Finally, however, a favorite of his, having some important matter to tell him, came softly to the door, and looking in, beheld the king very devoutly on his knee at prayer. Fearing to disturb him, he was about to withdraw his head, when the king saw him, and bidding him come in, said, "Thou wonderest to see me in this posture, since I have so many thousands of subjects to pray for me: but I tell thee, that no man has more need to pray for himself, than he who being to render an account of his actions to none but God, is for that reason more closely assaulted by the devil than all other men beside.[381]

Prayer—need not be long

In 1885, Dwight L. Moody was holding an evangelistic meetings in London, and out of curiosity, a medical student named Wilfred Grenfell followed a crowd to hear him speak. A long-winded prayer was offered at the beginning of the meeting, and the student impatiently got up to leave. It was then that he noticed Moody rise and say, "While our brother is finishing his prayer, let us sing hymn number so and so." This startling action arrested the student, and he stayed to hear what Moody would say. The result was his conversion to Christ and a life of service as a medical missionary to the people of the Labrador peninsula of Canada.[382]

Prayer—perseverance in

George Müller began praying in 1844, for the salvation of five unbelievers. He prayed every day, and eighteen months later one came to faith in Christ.

---

[380] Amy Carmichael, *Candles in the Dark* (Fort Washington, Penn.: Christian Literature Crusade, 1982), 45

[381] n. a., *The Scottish Christian Herald, vol. I, Part II, August 6-December 31, 1836* (Edinburgh: John Johnstone, 1836) 592

[382] Paul D. Moody, *My Father,* (Boston: Little, Brown, and Company, 1938), 95

He thanked God and continued to pray for the other four. Five years elapsed, and the second one came to Christ. He thanked God and continued to pray for the other three. Six years passed before the third came to Christ. He again thanked God, and continued praying for the remaining two until he died. He had prayed for them for fifty-two years. It was not until after Müller's death that these two came to Christ.[383]

Prayer—power of

Among the stations of the China Inland Mission, one in particular had much greater results in the number and the spiritual character of converts than at the other stations. The dedication of the missionaries was just as great as at the more fruitful place, and the difference was a mystery until Hudson Taylor made a visit to England. At the close of one of his addresses a man came forward to meet him. In the conversation which followed Mr. Taylor was surprised at the accurate knowledge the man possessed concerning this Inland China Station. "But how is it," Mr. Taylor asked, "that you are so conversant with the conditions of that work?"

"Oh!" the man replied, "the missionary there and I are old college mates; for years we have regularly corresponded; he has sent me names of enquirers and converts, and these I have daily taken to God in prayer." At last, the secret was discovered![384]

Prayer—power of

Charles Spurgeon was showing a visiting friend his church, the Metropolitan Tabernacle, previous to the evening service. His friend asked him how he managed to maintain the interest of the people in the work for such a long succession of years. Spurgeon replied, "It is owing to my heating apparatus. Come and I will show it to you." He took his friend to the door of a large room in the basement of the church, and quietly opening it, said, "There it is—my heating apparatus!" It was the evening prayer meeting in which were gathered one thousand people to pray for God's blessing on the service which was to follow.[385]

---

[383] Basil Miller, *George Muller, The Man of Faith* (Grand Rapids, Mich.: Zondervan, 1946) 145-6

[384] James Hastings, *The Christian Doctrine of Prayer* (Edinburgh T. & T. Clark, 1915), 129

[385] John G. Hallimond, *The Miracle of Answered Prayer* (New York: The Christian Herald, 1916), 61-2

Prayer—priorities in

The English preacher Samuel Pearson once visited a dying Christian man. Pearson asked him what he should pray for, expecting that he would have some personal request to make. To his surprise and delight, the dying man answered, "Pray that the kingdom of Christ may be extended."

Pearson commented, "There is an exalted state of man's heart possible, when the Christian forgets himself in the thought of this Master's kingdom. It is a self-forgetful, unconscious life, the blessed life, the eternal life, in some of its fulness and joy."[386]

Prayer—priorities in

Geoffrey Studdert Kennedy was chaplain in World War I. Facing the very real possibility of death on the battlefield, he said,

> The first prayer I want my son to learn to say for me is not "God, keep Daddy safe, but, "God, make Daddy brave and if he has hard things to do, make him strong to do them." Life and death don't matter, Pat, my son, right and wrong do. Daddy dead is Daddy still, but Daddy dishonoured before God is something awful, too bad for words. I suppose you'd like to put in a bit about safety too, old chap, and mother would. Well, put it in but afterwards, always afterwards because it does not matter near so much."[387]

Prayer—unanswered

As a young girl, Amy Carmichael prayed that God would change the color of her brown eyes to blue. She says, "Without a shadow of a doubt that my eyes would be blue in the morning I had gone to sleep, and the minute I woke I pushed a chart to the chest of drawers on which there was a looking-glass and climbed up full of eager expectation and saw—mere brown eyes."[388]

---

[386] n.a., *The Evangelical Magazine, vol. 15* (London: Elliot Stock, 1885), 70

[387] G. A. Studdert Kennedy, *The Hardest Part* (London: Hodder and Stoughton, 1919) 110-111

[388] Frank Houghton, *Amy Carmichael of Dohnavur* (Fort Washington, Penn.: Christian Literature Crusade, 1953), 6

Years later, as a missionary to India, in order to gather needed information to rescue girls from temple prostitution, she stained her hands and arms with coffee and wore Indian dress to pass as a native. One of her children commented, "I know why God gave [her] brown eyes.... If her eyes had been blue someone might easily penetrate the disguise."[389]

Prayer—unanswered

In a letter he wrote in 1935 to someone discouraged over unanswered prayer, G. Campbell Morgan wrote this word of perspective and encouragement:

> When you say that your prayers seem to be quite useless you certainly are wrong. We have to remember that in prayer we talk quite freely to our Father. It may be that we ask for things that we do not receive, but in such cases we have to rest in the assurance that He who knoweth all things withholds in love. The secret of peace is never to be found by considering our own hearts, but by trusting ourselves completely to the eternal and almighty Love which never breaks down.[390]

Preaching—clarity

An old lady once walked a great way to hear the famous Adam Clarke preach. She had heard he was "such a scholar," and indeed he was. But she confessed that she was bitterly disappointed, "Because," she said, "I understood everything he said.[391]

Preaching—clarity

Puritan Richard Baxter was called to preach before the Lord Mayor, and court of Aldermen, upon some public occasion. He chose a difficult subject, in which he had an opportunity of displaying his judgment and learning.

---

389   Ibid., 7

390   Jill Morgan, ed., *This Was His Faith: The Expository Letters of G. Campbell Morgan* (Westwood, New Jersey: Fleming H. Revell, 1952), 231

391   W. J. Hoge, *Blind Bartimeus and His Great Physician* (London: T. Woolmer, 1881), 48

He was heard with admiration and applause, and received public thanks for his performance. But as be was returning home, a poor man followed him, gently pulled the sleeve of his gown, and asked him if he was the man who preached that day before the Lord Mayor. He replied that he was. "Sir," the poor man said, "I came with an earnest desire after the word of God, and in hopes of getting some good to my soul, but I was greatly disappointed; for I could not understand a great deal of what you said—you were quite above me." Baxter replied with tears, "Friend, by the grace of God, I will never play the fool to preach before my Lord Mayor in such a manner again."[392]

Preaching—compassionate

An American evangelist in Scotland, after a sermon of exceptional power, was approached by the Scottish preacher Horatius Bonar, who said, "You do love to preach, do you not?"

The evangelist replied, "Yes, I do."

Dr. Bonar then asked this searching question: "Do you love men as much as you love to preach?"[393]

Preaching—compassionate

Robert Murray M'Cheyne once asked Andrew Bonar what he had preached on Sunday. Bonar replied that his text was Psalm 9:17, "The wicked shall be turned into hell."

On hearing this, M'Cheyne asked, "Were you able to preach it *with tenderness?*"[394]

Preaching—ears to hear

John Aylmer was Bishop of London in the sixteenth century. When he noticed that his congregation was inattentive to his preaching, he began to read out of his Hebrew Bible. This immediately awakened his audience, who

---

[392] Walter Wilson, *The History and Antiquities of Dissenting Churches and Meeting Houses, in London, Westminster, and Southwark; including the Lives of their Ministers, vol. III* (London: Printed for the Author, 1810), 551

[393] Amory H. Bradford, *The Growing Revelation* (New York: Macmillan, 1897), 105

[394] *Memoir and Remains of the Rev. Robert Murray M'Cheyne*, abridged [by J. Coventry] from the larger work [ed. by A.A. Bonar]. (Edinburgh: Oliphant, 1865), 17

stared at him in amazement. Aylmer then admonished them of their folly in listening attentively to an unknown language yet neglecting the teaching of God's word so easily understood.[395]

Preaching—ears to hear

In the 1600s, the English Puritan preacher Philip Henry was struck by the confession of one of his parishioners who said, "I find it easier to go six miles to hear a sermon, than to spend fifteen minutes meditating and praying over it as I should when I come home."[396]

Preaching—ears to hear

A young man once heard Dwight L. Moody preach in Brooklyn, explaining the way of salvation. He was not affected by the truth, and returned to his boarding house only to comment with criticism and scoffing. At the table he was requested to give an outline of the sermon. As he related the points of the sermon, a young lady, who was listening, was convicted, understood the gospel, and gave her life to Christ.[397]

Preaching—engaging

A ship builder was once asked what he thought of George Whitfield's preaching. He replied, "Think! I tell you sir, every Sunday that I go to my parish church, I can build a ship from stem to stern under the sermon; but were it to save my soul, under Mr. Whitefield, I could not lay a single plank!"[398]

Preaching—faithful

Hugh Latimer was once preaching in the presence of Henry VIII when he touched upon some topics displeasing to his Majesty. He was commanded, therefore, to preach again on the following Sunday, and to introduce an

---

[395] Joseph Towers, *British Biography,* Vol III (London: R. Goadby, 1767), 229

[396] Matthew Henry, *The Miscellaneous Works of the Rev. Matthew Henry, vol. I* (London: Joseph Ogle Robinson, 1833), 109

[397] E. J. Goodspeed, *A Full History of the Wonderful Career of Moody and Sankey in Great Britain and America* (London: John O. Robinson, 1876), 396

[398] John Gillies, *Memoirs of Rev. George Whitefield* (Middletown Conn.: Hunt & Noyes, 1839), 265-6

apology for the offence he had given in this discourse.

After naming his text, the Bishop thus commenced his sermon:

> Hugh Latimer! Dost thou know to whom thou art this day to speak—to the High and Mighty Monarch, the King's most Excellent Majesty, who can take away thy life if thou offendest: therefore take heed that thou speakest not that which may displease....
>
> But then consider well, Hugh Latimer, dost thou not know from whence thou comest? Upon whose message thou art sent? Even by the Great and Mighty God, who is all present, and beholdest all thy ways—who is omnipotent and able to cast both body and soul into hell together. Therefore take heed, and deliver thy message faithfully.

Latimer then proceeded with the same sermon he had preached the preceding Sunday, and confirmed it with redoubled energy.[399]

Preaching—faithful

Lyman Beecher once engaged to preach for a country minister on exchange, and the Sunday proved to be one excessively stormy, cold, and uncomfortable. It was in mid-winter, and the snow was piled all along in the roads, so as to make the passage very difficult. Still the minister urged his horse through the drifts, put the animal into a shed, and went in. As yet there was no person in the house, and after looking about, took his seat in the pulpit. Soon the door opened, and a single individual walked up the aisle, looked about, and took a seat. The hour came for commencing service, but no more hearers.

Whether to preach to such an audience, was the question—and it was one that Lyman Beecher was not long deciding. He felt that he had a duty to perform, and he had no right to refuse to do it, because only one man could reap the benefit of it. Accordingly, he went through all the services, praying, singing, preaching, and the benediction, with only *one* hearer. And when all was over, he hastened down from the desk to speak to his congregation, but

---

[399] Edgar Sheppard, *Memorials of St. James's Palace* (London: Longmans, Green & Company, 1894), 333

he had departed.

Twenty years later, traveling in Ohio, Beecher alighted from the stage one day in a pleasant village, when a gentleman stepped up and spoke to him, familiarly calling him by name.

Beecher said, "I do not remember you"

The stranger answered, "I suppose not, but we once spent two hours together in a house alone in a storm."

"I do not recall it, sir," added the old man, "pray, when was it?"

"Do you remember preaching, twenty years ago, in such a place, to a single person?"

"Yes, yes," said Beecher, grasping his hand, "I do, indeed, and if you are the man, I have been wishing to see you ever since."

"I am the man, sir, and that sermon saved my soul, made a minister of me, and yonder is my church! The converts of that sermon, sir, are all over Ohio."[400]

Preaching—God's blessing on

Charles Spurgeon was a man who expected and experienced God's blessing in preaching. Once, in his preaching he said,

> You know the story I tell of my first student, Mr. Medhurst. He went out to preach on Tower Hill, Sunday after Sunday. He was not then my student; but one of the young men in the church. He came to me, and said, "I have been out preaching now for several months on tower Hill, and I have not seen one conversion."
>
> I said to him, rather sharply, "Do you expect God is going to bless you every time you choose to open your mouth?"
>
> He answered, "Oh! No, sir; I do not expect him to do that."
>
> "Then," I replied, "that is why you do not get a blessing." We ought to expect a blessing. God has said, "My Word shall not return unto me void" and it will not. We ought to look for a harvest.[401]

[400]   William C. Conant, *Narratives of Remarkable Conversions and Revival Incidents* (New York: Derby & Jackson, 1858) 110-111

[401]   C. H. Spurgeon, *The Metropolitan Tabernacle Pulpit, Sermons Preached and Revised by C. H. Spurgeon during the Year 1890, vol. XXXVI* (London: Passmore & Alabaster, 1891) 341

Preaching—God's Word

Robert Hall was once asked his thoughts on a sermon which excited a great sensation among the congregation. He replied, "Very fine, sir, but a man cannot feed upon flowers."[402]

Preaching—God's Word

Harry Moorehouse, the English preacher, once visited Dwight Moody at his church in Chicago. He said, "Mr. Moody, you are sailing on the wrong tack. If you will change your course, and learn to preach God's words instead of your own, He will make you a great power for good."

Moody had been accustomed to drawing his sermons from the experiences of Christians and the life of the streets, but now he began to follow this counsel and preach the word. He devoted himself to the study of the Bible as he had never done before. He explained that this became one of the secrets of his power as he began to speak with authority from God.[403]

Preaching—Gospel

A friend came to visit the Welsh Nonconformist Thomas Charles on a Sunday afternoon in 1814, after having been in church. Charles asked him, "Was there enough of gospel in the sermon to save a sinner? If not, it was of little consequence what was preached."[404]

Preaching—Jesus Christ

Thomas Manton was asked to preach upon some public occasion, and his sermon was noted as being "learned, ingenious, and eloquent." As he was returning home, an old gentleman pulled him by the coat, desiring to

[402] *The Upper Canada Christian Almanac, no. 4* (Toronto: U. C. Religious Tract and Book Society, 1836), 10 [Robert Hall may have been referring to an essay of that time which stated, "A hungry man cannot feed upon flowers; and, a soul alive to God, will disdain, with just abhorrence, a substitution of oratory for spirituality, and the display of human talent for "wisdom that is from above."
George Russell, *Letters, Essays and Poems on Religious Subjects* (London: T. Plummer, 1810), 217]

[403] Dwight Lyman Moody, *Moody: His Words, Work, and Workers* (New York: Nelson & Phillips, 1877), 257-258

[404] C. H. Spurgeon, *Feathers for Arrows* (New York: Sheldon & Company, 1870), 217

speak with him. The doctor stopped, and the stranger said, "I was one of your auditory today: I went to be fed with the gospel, as usual, but have returned empty. Dr. Manton was not Dr. Manton this morning. There was, indeed, much of the doctor, of the florid and learned man, in the discourse, but little or nothing of Jesus Christ: it was, in short, no sermon to me."

Manton answered, "If I have not preached to you, you have now preached a good sermon to me, such as, I trust, I shall never forget, but be the better for as long as I live."[405]

Preaching—need for study

In the 1800s pastor Joseph Parker was asked about the secret for the energy in his preaching. Parker answered, "There in no need of explanation. If I had talked all the week I could not have preached on Sunday. That is all. If I had attended committee meetings, immersed myself in politics and undertaken the general care of the empire, my strength would have been consumed. That is all. Mystery there is none. I have made my preaching work my delight, the very festival of my soul. That is all. Young brother, go thou and do likewise, and God bless thee!"[406]

Preaching—to edify

John Newton once listened to a sermon in which for nearly an hour the preacher occupied his message with several labored distinctions of his subject. Afterward, he asked Newton whether he thought those distinctions were complete. Newton said that he thought not, as one very important distinction had been omitted. He explained, "When many of your congregation have travelled several miles for a meal, I think you should not have forgotten the distinction between *meat* and *bones*."[407]

---

[405]   Augustus Toplady, *The Works of Augustus M. Toplady, vol. IV* (London: Printed for the Proprietors and sold by W. Row, 1794), 179

[406]   Joseph Parker, *Studies in Texts: For Family, Church, and School* (New York: Funk & Wagnalls, 1891), vol 1, viii-ix

[407]   John Newton, Richard Cecil, *The Life of John Newton* (Edinburgh: Johnstone and Hunter, 1853), 143-4

Preaching—seriousness of

When on his deathbed, Puritan preacher Thomas Shepard was visited by several young ministers. He addressed them, giving them his earnest counsel on preaching:

> Your work is great, and requires great seriousness. For my own part, I never preached a sermon which, in the composing, did not cost me prayers, with strong cries and tears. I never preached a sermon from which I had not first, got some good to my own soul. I never went up into the pulpit but as if I were going to give an account of myself to God.[408]

Preaching—truth

In 1913, G. Campbell Morgan answered someone who had questioned his preaching. He wrote,

> You ask me, "Must we be worried with such sermons on Sunday mornings?" Well, I am bound to say that the purpose of my preaching is to declare truth. If it worries people, I cannot help it; and, indeed, I should be sorry to think that my sermons never give people cause for uneasiness.[409]

Preaching—urgency of

English Puritan Richard Baxter ministered as a pastor in the 1600s and was a chaplain during the English Civil War, experiencing persecution and imprisonment during the Act of Uniformity. Yet through it all he remained fervent, expressing the urgency of preaching when he declared, "I preached as never sure to preach again, And as a dying man to dying men."[410]

---

[408] Benjamin Brook, *The Lives of the Puritans, vol. III* (London: James Black, 1813), 106

[409] Jill Morgan, ed., *This Was His Faith: The Expository Letters of G. Campbell Morgan* (Westwood, New Jersey: Fleming H. Revell, 1952), 309

[410] W. Carlos Martyn, *A History of the English Puritans* (New York: The American Tract Society, 1867), 430

Preaching—urgency of

Thomas Pentycross ministered in England in the late 1700s and early 1800s. Once, while preaching to his congregation, he was so entirely engrossed with the importance of his subject, that he exceeded his usual time, and the clock struck one. After pausing a moment, he exclaimed with great energy, "Time reproves me, but eternity commends me!" He then resumed his preaching with much earnestness, continuing to preach for a considerable time.[411]

Preaching—with conviction

Scottish philosopher and skeptic David Hume once rushed to hear George Whitefield preach. A friend challenged him if he believed what Whitefield preached. Hume replied, "No, I do not believe what he proclaims, but he does, and I want to hear a man who speaks with the authority of conviction.[412]

Prejudice

Robert Moffat was the great pioneer missionary to southern Africa in the 1800s. On his way from Cape Town, South Africa, to the interior, he stopped at the house of a wealthy Dutch farmer, the owner of many slaves. Young Moffat, then only twenty-two years old, was made welcome, and when the master of the house learned that his guest was a preacher, he proposed that a worship service should be held after supper. The request was cheerfully granted, and when the table had been cleared the Bible and psalm-books were brought out, and the farmer's family took their places. But the servants had not been asked to come, and none were present.

Moffat quietly referred to the fact, when his host gruffly retorted, "Servants, what do you mean?"

Moffat replied, "I mean the [Africans]."

In a rage, the slave owner blurted out, "Do you mean that, then! Let me go to the mountain, and call the baboons, if you want a congregation of that sort. Or stop, I have it; my sons, call the dogs that lie in front of the door—they will do."

---

[411] n.a., *The Homiletic Review* vol LXXIV July-December 1917, (New York: Funk and Wagnalls, 1914), 279

[412] n.a., *The Homiletic Review* vol LXVII January-June 1914, (New York: Funk and Wagnalls, 1914), 80

To this no reply was given, and the service was quietly begun. After singing and prayer, the preacher read the story of the Syrophenician woman, commenting especially on the words, "Truth, Lord, but even the dogs eat of the crumbs that fall from the master's table."

In a few minutes the farmer interrupted the sermon, saying, "Will [my lord] sit down and wait a little; he shall have the [Africans]."

They were summoned, and in obedience to the strange command they trooped into the master's house, whose interior many of them had never seen. At the close of the service, the astonished slaves quietly and quickly dispersed, and the farmer turned to his guest with the remark, "My friend, you took a hard hammer and you have broken a hard head."[413]

Prejudice

English pastor William Jay was talking with a friend who recounted to him, "I was exceedingly terrified, sir, this morning. I was going down to a lonely place, and I thought I saw at a distance a huge monster; it seemed in motion, but I could not discern the form of it. I did not like to turn back, yet my heart beat, and the more I looked, the more I feared; but as we approached each other. I saw it was only a man! And who do you think it was, sir?"

"I know not."

"Oh, it was my brother John!"

"Ah !" said William Jay, as his friend added that it was early in the morning, and very foggy, "Ah! How often, in a lonely place and in a foggy atmosphere, has brother John been taken for a foe! Only approach nearer each other, and see clearer, and you will find, in numberless instances, what you have dreaded as a monster was a brother—and your own brother!"[414]

Pride

As a preacher, John Bunyan was not only tempted with discouragement, but also with the opposite temptation of pride. When he was told what a sweet sermon he had delivered, he replied, "The Devil told me that before I was out of the pulpit."[415]

---

[413] A. J. F. Behrends, *Socialism and Christianity,* (New York: The Baker & Taylor Co., 1886), 97-8

[414] n.a., *Christian Pamphlets,* (Boston: John P. Jewett and Company and Cleveland, Ohio: H. P. B. Jewett and Company, 1858) 62

[415] J. M. Hare, "Memoir of John Bunyan," in John Bunyan, The Pilgrim's Progress (London

Pride

Lady Huntingdon asked the Duchess of Buckingham to come and hear George Whitefield, but the duchess was not pleased with Whitefield's preaching against sin. She replied, "It is monstrous to be told that you have a heart as sinful as the common wretches that crawl the earth. This is highly offensive and insulting, and I cannot but wonder that your ladyship should relish any sentiments so much at variance with high rank and good breeding."[416]

Pride

James Hervey, the eighteenth century preacher, was in the company of a person who was paying him some compliments on account of his writings. He, replied, laying his hand on his breast, "Oh sir, you would not strike the sparks of applause, if you knew how much corrupt tinder I have within."[417]

Pride

A lady once told Charles Spurgeon, "I pray for you every day, that you might not become proud."

Spurgeon responded, "You put me in mind of my own neglect, for I have never prayed that prayer for you, and must begin."

"Oh no," the lady protested, "there is no occasion for that, there is no danger of my being proud."

Spurgeon replied, "then I had better begin at once, for you are proud already."[418]

Pride

Renowned Scottish scientist and inventor Sir David Brewster was listening to his daughter read the memoir of a brilliant medical man, of whom it was

---

Ingram, Cooke, & Co., 1853), 15

[416]   William Edward Hartpole Lecky, *A History of England in the Eighteenth Century, vol. II* (New York: D. Appleton and Company, 1878), 671

[417]   Augustus Toplady, *The Works of Augustus M. Toplady, vol. IV* (London: Printed for the Proprietors and sold by W. Row, 1794), 175

[418]   C. H. Spurgeon, *The Metropolitan Tabernacle Pulpit, Sermons Preached and Revised by C. H. Spurgeon during the Year 1874, vol. XX* (London: Passmore & Alabaster, 1875) 263

said, "*notwithstanding* his great literary and scientific attainments, the pride of intellect was cast at the foot of the Cross of Christ."

Brewster interrupted his daughter with an outburst of vehement disapproval, saying, "That disgusts me! A merit for a man to bow his intellect to the Cross! Why, what can the highest intellect on earth do but bow to God's word and God's mind thankfully?"[419]

Priorities

Rachel Jackson was the wife of Andrew Jackson, who won the election to be the seventh president of the United States. As their friends celebrated their upcoming move to the White House, she remarked to a friend, "I assure you that I would rather be a doorkeeper in the house of my God, than to live in that palace in Washington."[420]

Priorities

Charles Spurgeon was invited to come to America to deliver fifty lectures for the then astounding amount of a thousand dollars per lecture. He responded, "No, I will do better. I will stay in London and try to save fifty souls."[421]

Protection

In the third century, Felix of Nola (near Naples) was being hotly pursued by persecutors. He took refuge in a ruinous old wall, and the opening was quickly covered by a spider's web. When his enemies saw it, they concluded that he could not have recently hid there, and left. Felix made the comment that, "With Christ, a spider's web becomes a wall, and without Christ, a wall is no better than a spider's web."[422]

---

[419] Margaret Maria Gordon, *The Home Life of Sir David Brewster: By His Daughter Mrs. Gordon* (Edinburgh: David Douglas, 1881), 177-8

[420] Laura Carter Holloway, *The Ladies of the White House* (Philadelphia: Bradley & Company, 1881), 296

[421] Frank L. Martin, Walter Williams, *The Practice of Journalism, a Treatise on Newspaper Making* (Columbia: E.W. Stephens, 1911), 69

[422] *William White, Notes and Queries, third series, vol. 2* (London: Bell & Daldy, 1862), 355-6

Protection

On March 15, 1752, John Gill left his study in order to go to preach. Soon after, a stack of chimneys, being blown down by a violent hurricane, forced their way through the roof of the house, and into the study, breaking his writing-table to pieces, and falling on the very spot where Gill was sitting a few minutes previously. Some time before one of Gill's friends had mentioned to him a saying of Dr. Halley, the celebrated astronomer, that "close study preserves a man's life, by keeping him out of harm's way."

Gill, with gratitude to God, remarked, "What becomes of Dr. Halley's words now, since, it seems, a man may come to danger and harm in the closet as well as in the highway, if he be not protected by the special care of Divine Providence?"[423]

Regeneration

In the second century, Celsus, an adversary of Christianity, complained, "Jesus Christ came into the world to make the most horrible and dreadful societies; for he calls sinners, and not the righteous, so that the body he came to assemble is a body of profligates, separated from good people, among whom they before were mixed. He has rejected all the good, and collected all the bad."

The church father Origen replied, "True, our Jesus came to call sinners—but to repentance. He assembles the wicked—but to convert them into new men, or rather to change them into angels. We come to him covetous, he makes us generous; lascivious, he makes us chaste; violent, he makes us meek; impious, he makes us religious."[424]

Repentance

In the fourth century the emperor Theodosius ordered the killing of seven thousand citizens of Thessalonica. Bishop Ambrose wrote the emperor a letter of severe rebuke, warning him not to approach the holy communion

---

[423]   John Young, *The Record of Providence; or, The Government of God Displayed in a Series of Interesting Facts from Sacred and Profane History* (London, Houlston and Son: 1832) 88

[424]   J. B. Sumner, *The Evidence of Christianity, Derived for its Nature and Reception* (London: J. Hatchard and Son, 1824), 402

having hands stained with innocent blood. When Theodosius came to the church of Milan Ambrose refused him entry. The emperor pleaded that David, the man after God's own heart, had been guilty both of murder and adultery. Ambrose boldly replied, "You have imitated David in his crime; imitate him in his repentance."[425]

Repentance

"The sacrifices of God are a broken spirit; a broken and contrite heart, O God, thou wilt not despise" (Psalm 51:17). The church father Augustine found so much sweetness in this promise that he had it written on the wall opposite his bed where he lay sick, and died.[426]

Repentance

As a faithful preacher in the 1600s, Thomas Fuller exhorted people to repentance. He said, "You cannot repent too soon, because you do not know how soon it may be too late."[427]

Repentance

In 1680, Puritan Philip Henry preached over the doctrine of faith and repentance from several texts of Scripture. He said "Some people do not like to hear much of repentance. But I think it so necessary, that if I should die in the pulpit, I should desire to die preaching repentance, and if I should die out of the pulpit, I should desire to die practicing it."[428] Henry had been told concerning the Puritan John Dod, that some called him in scorn "faith and repentance," because he insisted so much upon those in all his preaching.

---

[425] John Aikin, William Enfield, *General Biography; or, Lives, Critical and Historical, of the Most Eminent Persons of all Ages, Countries, Conditions and Professions, vol. I* (London: G. G. and J. Robinson, 1799), 230

[426] James Comper Gray, *The Biblical Museum: A Collection of Notes Explanatory, Homiletic, and Illustrative, on the Holy Scriptures, Old Testament, Vol. VI* (London: Elliot Stock, 1879), 126

[427] C. H. Spurgeon, *The Treasury of David, Vol. IV* (London: Passmore and Alabaster, 1874), 328

[428] J. C. Ryle, *Expository Thoughts on the Gospels, St. Luke, Vol. II* (Ipswich: William Hunt, 1859), 112

"But," Henry said, "if this be to be vile, I will be yet more vile, for faith and repentance are all in all in Christianity."[429]

Responsibility

A young minister once complained to the eighteenth century Scottish preacher John Brown of Haddington regarding the smallness of his congregation. Brown replied, "It is as large a one as you will want to give account for in the day of judgment."[430]

Reward

When the order for his banishment from Geneva was brought to John Calvin, he replied, "Certainly, had I been the servant of men I had obtained a poor reward, but it is well that I have served Him who never fails to perform to his servants whatever he has promised."[431]

Sacrifice

Justinian Von Welz was a baron in the Netherlands in the 1600s. He unsuccessfully pleaded with the state church to bring the gospel to the world, and was stigmatized as "a dreamer." His response was a determination to go himself to Dutch Guinea (now Suriname, South America). He renounced his title of baron and his estates, and gave himself, going at his own expense to Dutch Guinea, where he soon filled a lonely missionary grave. He said,

> What to me is the title "well-born," when I am one born again in Christ? What to me is the title "lord," when I desire to be a servant of Christ? What to me to be called "your grace," when I have need of God's grace, help and succor? All these vanities I will away with, and everything besides I will lay at the feet of Jesus, my dearest Lord, that I may have no hindrance in serving him aright.[432]

---

[429] Matthew Henry, *The Life of the Rev. Philip Henry* (London: William Ball, 1839), 80

[430] C. H. Spurgeon, *Feathers for Arrows* (New York: Sheldon & Company, 1870), 199

[431] John Calvin, *Tracts Relating to the Reformation with His Life by Theodore Beza, Translated from the Original Latin by Henry Beveridge* (Edinburgh: Calvin Translation Society, 1844), xxxiii

[432] A. J. Gordon, *The Holy Spirit in Missions* (New York: Fleming H. Revell Company, 1893),

Sacrifice

Dondaba was Brahmin of India who came to Christ and was baptized in the early 1800s. As a result, he lost his houses, his fields, his wells, his wife, and his children. When he was asked how he bore his sorrows, he replied, "Aye, I am often asked that, but I am never asked how I bear my joys, for I have joys within with which a stranger [knows] not. The Lord Jesus sought me and found me, a poor strayed sheep in the jungles, and He brought me to His fold and He will never leave me."[433]

Sacrifice

Lough Fook was a believer who came to Christ in Canton, China in 1861. He had a fervent heart of compassion for the salvation of the Chinese who were taken to South America to work in the mines. The problem was he could find no way to reach them. He finally found a way—he sold himself into slavery in order to preach the gospel to them.[434] He lived as a slave, preaching Christ while he toiled. He died in a foreign land, but not until he had won nearly two hundred to Christ.[435]

Sacrifice

Lilias Trotter gave up a promising career in art to minister to prostitutes in London, and then to bring the gospel to Algiers in 1888. Despite a weak heart, she labored for forty years in the filth, disease, ignorance, bigotry, and violence of the Algerian coast towns. She was recognized as a woman of literary gifts, rare artistic ability, undaunted courage, unlimited common sense, and a faith like an apostle's. Miss Trotter was the favorite pupil of the famous artist John Ruskin. When she departed to Africa, Ruskin remarked to a friend, "I have lost the one pupil I had of real talent. She has decided to throw away her life teaching Arabs."[436]

43-4, 83

[433] n.a., *Church Missionary Paper* no. CXLIII (London: L & G Seeley, 1851), 2

[434] Edmund Franklin Merriam, *A History of American Baptist Missions*, (Philadelphia: American Baptist Publication Society, 1900), 63-64

[435] A. J. Gordon, *The Holy Spirit in Missions* (New York: Fleming H. Revell Company, 1893), 131

[436] Cornelius H. Patton, *The Lure of Africa* (New York: Missionary Education Movement of

Sacrifice

In the 1800s when Frederick Temple was the Anglican Bishop of London he sent a young man to a position involving much hardship. The young man's friends tried to dissuade him from accepting it, and he went to the bishop and told him that he believed he would not live two years if he accepted the appointment. Dr. Temple listened and replied, "But you and I do not mind a little thing like that—do we?"[437]

Salvation

Charles Wesley took the gospel to the outcasts of society, preaching July, 1738, at Newgate, the infamous London prison. It was a cruel penitentiary where men, especially slaves, were condemned for the most minor offenses. Hangings were conducted for townspeople to view like sporting events. Charles took a special interest in a poor African slave condemned to hang for stealing from his master. The hopeless man listened in astonishment as Charles told him about Christ who came from heaven to die an agonizing death for him. He listened with eager astonishment as the tears streamed down his cheeks. He cried, "What! Was it for me? Did God suffer all this for so poor a creature as me?" He soon found salvation in Christ, as did several other prisoners. The next week, on the day of execution, Charles prayed and sang hymns with the men as they were loaded onto a cart, their hands tied behind their backs. Charles wrote in his journal that they "were all cheerful; full of comfort, peace, and triumph; assuredly persuaded Christ had died for them, and waited to receive them into paradise." He also recorded, "that hour under the gallows was the most blessed hour in my life."[438]

Salvation—by regeneration, not religion

Bishop John Taylor Smith, former Chaplain General of the British Army, was once preaching in a large cathedral using John 3:7 as his text, "Ye must be born again." In order to drive it home, he said, "My dear people, do not

---

the United States and Canada, 1917), 53

[437]   J. R. Miller, *The Glory of the Commonplace*, ed., by John T. Faris (New York: Thomas Y. Crowell Company, 1913), 130

[438]   Charles Wesley, *Journal, Etc: To which are Appended Selections from His Correspondence and Poetry* (London: James Nichols, 1849), 120-123

substitute anything for the new birth. You may be a member of a church, even the great church of which I am a member, the historic Church of England, but church membership is not new birth, and 'except a man be born again he cannot see the kingdom of God.'"

The rector was sitting at his left. Pointing to him, he said, "You might be a clergyman like my friend the rector here and not be born again, and 'except a man be born again he cannot see the kingdom of God.'"

Then he pointed directly at the archdeacon in his stall and said,, "You might even be an archdeacon like my friend in his stall and not be born again and 'except a man be born again he cannot see the kingdom of God.' You might even be a bishop, like myself, and not be born again and 'except a man be born again he cannot see the kingdom of God.'"

A day or so later he received a letter from the archdeacon, in which he wrote:

> My dear Bishop: You have found me out. I have been a clergyman for over thirty years, but I had never known anything of the joy that Christians speak of. I never could understand it. Mine has been hard, legal service. I did not know what was the matter with me, but when you pointed directly to me and said, "You might even be an archdeacon and not be born again," I realized in a moment what the trouble was. I had never known anything of the new birth."

He went on to say that he was wretched and miserable, had been unable to sleep all night, and begged for a conference, if the bishop could spare the time to talk with him.

The next day they got together over the Word of God and after some hours, were both on their knees, the archdeacon taking his place before God as a poor, lost sinner and telling the Lord Jesus he would trust Him as his Saviour. From that time on everything was different.[439]

Salvation—Effectual Calling

Thomas Doolittle, a godly minister of the seventeenth century, used to catechise the members, and especially the young people of his congregation,

---

[439] H. A. Ironside, *Illustrations of Bible Truth* (Chicago: Moody Press, 1945), 47-8

every Lord's day. One Sunday evening, after having received an answer in the words of the Assembly's Catechism, to the question, "What is effectual calling?" and having explained it, he proposed that the question should be answered by changing the words "us" and "our," into "me" and "my." Upon this proposal a solemn silence followed; many felt its vast importance; but none had courage to answer.

Finally a young man rose up, and with every mark of a broken and contrite heart, by divine grace, was enabled to say, "Effectual calling is the work of God's Spirit, whereby, convincing *me* of *my* sin and misery, enlightening *my* mind in the knowledge of Christ, and renewing *my* will, He doth persuade and enable *me* to embrace Jesus Christ, freely offered to *me* in the gospel."

The scene was truly affecting. The proposal of the question had commanded unusual solemnity. The rising up of the young man had created high expectations, and the answer being accompanied with proof of unfeigned piety and humility, the congregation was bathed in tears. This young man had been convicted by being catechised; and to his honor, Doolittle says, "from being an ignorant and wicked youth, he had become a true believer, to God's glory."[440]

Salvation—joy over

Harry Ironside had the joy of leading a wild, reckless man to faith in Christ. As tears ran down his face, the man exclaimed, "Oh, if my dear mother were only living that I might send her a telegram tonight to let here know that I had yielded to Christ. She prayed for me for many years; my ungodliness broke her heart. She died praying that I might be saved. How glad I would be if I could only get word to her that at last her prayers are answered."

Ironside said to him, "My dear young man, you need not grieve over that. I am certain she knew the moment you trusted Christ. Up there in heaven every redeemed one is rejoicing over another sinner that repenteth."[441]

---

[440]   William Carruthers, *The Shorter Catechism of the Westminster Assembly of Divines* (London: Publication Office of the Presbyterian Church of England, 1897), 37

[441]   H. A. Ironside, *Death and Afterwards* (Neptune, New Jersey: Loizeaux Brothers, 1900), 13-4

Salvation—not by works

When Puritan Thomas Hooker was dying, mourners gathered around his bedside. One that stood weeping said to him, "Brother, you are going to receive the reward of all your labors."

Hooker looked at him and replied, "Brother, I am going to receive mercy."[442]

Salvation—not by works

Bishop Taylor Smith mentioned the subject of salvation to the barber who was giving him a shave. The barber snapped, "I do my best and that's enough for me. The bishop was quiet until the shave was over.

When the next man was seated the bishop asked, "May I shave this customer?"

"No, you mustn't," replied the barber.

"But I would do my best," answered the bishop.

"So you might," the barber replied, "but your best would not be good enough for this gentleman."

The bishop responded, "No, and neither is your best good enough for God."[443]

Salvation—not by works

Shortly before his death, John Knox seemed to fall into a slumber, interrupted with heavy moans. When asked why he sighed so deeply, he replied,

> I have during my life sustained many assaults of Satan, but at present he has assailed me most fearfully, and put forth all his strength to make an end of me at once. The cunning serpent has labored to persuade me that I have merited heaven and eternal blessedness by the faithful discharge of my ministry. But blessed be God, who has enabled me to quench this fiery dart, by suggesting to me such passages as these: "What hast

---

[442] William Buell Sprague, *Annals of the American Pulpit* (New York: Robert Carter & Brothers, 1857) 34-5

[443] Rollin T. Chafer, ed., *Bibliotheca Sacra, vol. 95* (Dallas: Dallas Theological Seminary, 1938), 366

thou that thou hast not received" and, "By the grace of God I am what I am."[444]

Salvation—now is the day of

On October 8, 1871, Dwight L. Moody preached to the largest congregation that he had ever addressed in Chicago, having taken for his text, "What then shall I do with Jesus which is called Christ" [Matthew 27:22]. After preaching with all his power of entreaty, presenting Christ as a Savior and Redeemer, he said, "I wish you would take this text home with you and turn it over in your minds during the week, and next Sabbath we will come to Calvary and the cross, and we will decide what to do with Jesus of Nazareth."

That night the Great Chicago fire swept through the city, killing hundreds. Reflecting on that night, Moody said, "What a mistake! I have never dared to give an audience a week to think of their salvation since."[445]

Salvation—of God's grace

Thomas Bilney sought for peace of soul for a long time through religious works. Hearing of Erasmus's translation of the New Testament, he purchased a copy and bolted himself in his room to begin reading it. The very first sentence he read was 1 Timothy 1:15, "This is a faithful saying, and worthy of all acceptance, that Christ Jesus came into the world to save sinners, of whom I am chief." Bilney cried,

> What, St. Paul the chief of sinners, and yet St. Paul is sure of being saved! O assertion of St. Paul, how sweet art thou to my soul! I also am, like Paul, and more than Paul, the greatest of sinners; but Christ saves sinners. At last I have heard of Jesus. Jesus Christ, yes, Jesus Christ saves. I see it all—my vigils, my fasts, my pilgrimages, my purchase of masses and indulgences were destroying instead of saving me.[446]

---

[444] Thomas M'Crie, *Sketches of Scottish Church History: Embracing the Period from the Reformation to the Revolution* (Edinburgh: John Johnstone, 1841), 93

[445] William R. Moody, *The Life of Dwight L. Moody* (New York: Fleming H. Revell, 1900), 144-5

[446] Eri Hulbert, *The English Reformation and Puritanism* (Chicago: The University of Chicago Press, 1908), 74-75

Falling on his knees, he joyfully prayed, "O Thou who art the Truth, give me strength that I may teach it and convert the ungodly, by means of one who has been himself ungodly."[447]

Salvation—of God's grace

The Calvinist preacher Charles Simeon had an encounter with John Wesley that affirms the truth that as sinners we contribute nothing to salvation—it is entirely God's work and grace.

After having been introduced to Wesley, Simeon said to him, "Sir, I understand that you are called an Arminian, and I have sometimes been called a Calvinist, and, therefore, I suppose we are to draw daggers. But before we begin the combat, with your permission I should like to ask you a few questions, not for impertinent curiosity but for instruction."

Permission was readily and kindly granted by Wesley, and Simeon asked, "Pray sir, do you feel yourself a depraved creature, so dependent you would never have thought of turning to God if God had not put it into your heart?"

Wesley answered, "Yes, I do indeed."

"And do you utterly despair of recommending yourself to God by anything you can do, and look for salvation solely through the blood and righteousness of Christ?

"Yes, solely through Christ."

"But sir, suppose you were first saved by Christ, are you not somehow or other to save yourself afterward by your own works?"

"No," replied Wesley.

"Allow then, you were first turned by the grace of God, are you not in some way to keep yourself by your own power?"

"No," Wesley answered again.

"What then? Are you to be upheld every hour and every moment by God, as an infant in its mother's arms?"

"Yes, altogether."

"And is all your hope in the grace and mercy of God to preserve you into His eternal kingdom?"

"Yes, I have no hope but in Him."

---

[447] Jean Henri Merle d'Augibné, trans. by H. White, *History of the Reformation of the Sixteenth Century* (New York: Robert Carter & Brothers, 1879), 167

Simeon responded,

> Then sir, with your leave, I will put up my dagger again, for this
> is all my Calvinism; this is my election, my justification by faith,
> my final perseverance. It is in substance all that I hold and as
> I hold it; and, therefore, if you please, instead of searching out
> terms and phrases to be a ground of contention between us, we
> will cordially unite in those things wherein we agree.[448]

Salvation—requires humility

When Prince Edward Augustus, the father of Queen Victoria, expressed
in the prospect of death concern about the state of his soul, his physician
endeavored to soothe his mind by referring to his high respectability, and his
honorable conduct in the distinguished situation in which God has placed
him. Prince Edward stopped him short, saying, "No; remember, if I am to be
saved, it is not as a prince but as a sinner."[449]

Salvation—requires understanding sinfulness

George Whitefield had a brother who had gone far from the ways of
godliness. He had heard his brother preach the day before, and his conscience
had been cut to the quick. He groaned and cried, "I am a lost man," and could
neither eat nor drink.

Lady Huntingdon, opposite him at tea asked, "What did you say Mr.
Whitefield?"

He answered, "I said I am a lost man."

She responded, "I'm glad of it."

Whitefield replied, "Your ladyship, how can you say so?"

"I repeat it, sir," said she; "I am heartily glad of it."

He looked at her, more and more astonished. She continued, "I am glad
of it because it is written, 'The Son of man came to seek and to save that
which was lost.'"

---

[448]   Richard Pike, *Remarkable Religious Anecdotes,* (London: Hamilton, Adams & Co., 1882),
38-39

[449]   n.a., *Anecdotes Illustrative of New Testament Texts* (Hartford, Conn.: S. S. Scranton, 1900),
98

With tears rolling down his cheeks, he said, "What precious Scripture; and how is it that is comes with such force to me? O! madam, madam, I bless God for that; then he will save me, I trust my soul in his hands; he has forgiven me."[450]

Sanctification

Two or three years before John Newton's death his sight had become so dim that he was no longer able to read. At breakfast, the portion of Scripture for the day was read to him. It was 1 Corinthians 15:10: "By the grace of God I am what I am." It was Newton's custom on these occasions, to make a short familiar exposition on the passage read. After the reading of this text, he paused for some moments, and then exclaimed, "I am not what I ought to be. Ah! how imperfect and deficient. I am not what I wish to be. I abhor what is evil, and I would cleave to what is good. I am not what I hope to be; soon, soon, I shall put off mortality, and with mortality all sin and imperfection. Yet, though I am not what I ought to be, nor what I wish to be, nor what I hope to be, I can truly say, I am not what I once was—a slave to sin and Satan; and I can heartily join with the apostle, and acknowledge, "By the grace of God, I am what I am."[451]

Sanctification

James Buckley was once asked to conduct a testimony meeting for a church. A woman rose and bore witness to the preciousness of her religion as a light bringer and comfort giver.

Dr. Buckley commented, "That's good, sister! But now about the practical side. Does your religion make you strive to prepare your husband a good dinner? Does it make you look after him in every way?"

Just then Dr. Buckley felt a yank on his coat tails by the preacher of the church, who whispered, "Press them questions, doctor, press them questions, doctor. That's my wife!"[452]

---

[450] William C. Conant, *Narratives of Remarkable Conversions and Revival Incidents* (New York: Derby & Jackson, 1858), 196

[451] Ashbel Green, *The Christian Advocate, vol. II* (Philadelphia: A. Finley, 1824), 75

[452] *Life*, vol. 73, no. 1901, ed. by Charles Dana Gibson, (New York, Life Publishing Co., April 3, 1919), 670

Sanctification

Archbishop James Ussher was a man of distinguished learning, piety, and diligence. A friend of his frequently urged him to write his thoughts on sanctification, which finally he agreed to do. After a considerable time had elapsed, the performance of the promise was claimed. Ussher replied,

> I have not written, and yet I cannot charge myself with a breach of promise, for I began to write; but when I came to treat of the new creature which God formeth by his own spirit in every regenerate soul, I found so little of it wrought in myself that I could speak only as parrots, or by rote, but without the knowledge of what I might have expressed, and therefore, I durst not presume to proceed any farther upon it.

Upon this, his friend stood amazed to hear such a humble confession from so holy a person. Ussher added,

> I must tell you, we do not well understand what sanctification and the new creature are. It is no less than for a man to be brought to an entire resignation of his own will to the will of God; and to live in the offering up of his soul continually in the flames of love, as a whole burnt offering to Christ; and oh, how many profess Christianity are unacquainted, experimentally, with this work upon their souls.[453]

Serving God

In the eleventh century King Henry, Duke of Bavaria, grew weary of the pomp of court life and the cares of being a monarch. As he visited the Abbey of Verdun, he asked the prior there if he would be accepted into the monastery as a monk. The prior, Richard, told him that the first vow would be one of obedience. The monarch promised his willingness to follow his will in every detail. The prior said, "Then back to your throne and do your duty in the station God assigned you."[454]

---

[453] *The American Flint,* vol. 11, ed. Joseph M. Gilooly, ed., (Toledo, Ohio: 1919) 20

[454] James Hastings, ed., *The Expository Times,* Vol. 16 (Edinburgh T. & T. Clark, 1905), 303

Serving God

When Puritan Richard Baxter was on his death bed, a friend sought to comfort him with the thought of the good many had received by his preaching and writings.

Baxter replied, "I was but a pen in God's hands, and what praise is due to a pen?"[455]

Serving Others

Puritan John Howe briefly served as chaplain to Oliver Cromwell. During this time he was often approached for assistance by others, and he never refused any worthy request.

One day Cromwell said to him, "Mr. Howe, you have asked favors for everybody except yourself; pray when does your turn come?"

Howe replied, "My turn, my lord protector, is always come when I can serve another."[456]

Sin

When Chrysostom was threatened with death by the Empress Eudoxia, he sent word to her saying, "Go tell her that I fear nothing but sin."[457]

Sin

In 1662, 2,000 Puritan pastors in England were ejected from their ministry because they refused to compromise with the mandates imposed by the Act of Uniformity legislated by Parliament. And as one of those pastors, Edmund Calamy, faced the loss of his ministry, his livelihood, and the grief that this meant for himself and his church, he warned his congregation of something that was far worse. In his last sermon that he preached he said, "There is more evil in the least sin than in the greatest calamity."[458]

---

[455] Richard Baxter, William Orme, *The Practical Works of Richard Baxter, vol. I* (London: J. Duncan, 1830), 400

[456] R. C. Waterston, *Thoughts on Moral and Spiritual Culture* (Boston: W. Crosby, 1844), 103-4

[457] T. De Witt Talmage, *The Pathway of Life* (Philadelphia: Historical Publishing Company, 1894), 383

[458] James Reid, *Memoirs of the Lives and Writings of those Eminent Divines who Convened in the Famous Assembly at Westminster in the Seventeenth Century, vol. 1* (Paisley, England:

Sin

In the 1800s, evangelist John Bartholomew Gough was talking with a young man who said, "I do not think I am a sinner."

Gough asked him if he would be willing his mother or sister should know all he had done, or said, or thought—all his motives and all his desires.

After considering this, he said, "No, indeed, I should not like to have them know; no, not for the world."

Gough replied, "Then can you dare to say, in the presence of a holy God, who knows every thought of your heart, 'I do not commit sin'?"[459]

Sin

In the early 1900s the Australian pastor Henry Howard once preached a strong message on sin. Afterwards, an officer of his church said to him, "Mr. Howard, we don't want you to talk as plainly as you do against sin. Call it a mistake if you will, but do not speak so plainly about sin."

Howard took down a small bottle and showed it to the man. It was a bottle of strychnine, and was marked, "Poison." He said, "I see what you want me to do. You want me to change the label. Suppose I take of this label of 'Poison' and put on some mild label, such as 'Essence of Peppermint;' don't you see what happens? The milder you make your label, the more dangerous you make your poison.[460]

Sin

Alexander Whyte once astonished his audience by saying that he had found out the name of the wickedest man in Edinburgh, and had come to tell them. As all eyes were on him, he bent forward and whispered, "His name is Alexander Whyte!"[461]

Stephen and Andrew Young, 1811), 177

[459] John B. Gough, *Sunlight and Shadow or, Gleanings from my Life Work* (London: R. D. Dickinson, 1881), 117

[460] John Wilbur Chapman, *Revival Sermons* (New York: Fleming H. Revell, 1911), 21-22

[461] G. F. Barbour, The Life of Alexander Whyte, D. D. (New York: George H. Doran Company, 1925) 316

Sin—deceptiveness of

Andrew Bonar was speaking with a lady who told him that for six months she had not consciously committed any sin. Dr. Bonar replied, "And are you not very proud of it?" "Yes," she answered, "I am!"[462]

Sin—hiding

During the early months of World War II, Pastor John Bonnell received an urgent long-distance call from a combat officer. He came almost a thousand miles to New York to see him. The officer had just been granted embarkation leave, but was so upset that he could not go home to his wife and children. As he spoke of his assignment to command an advance party to a Pacific island, the officer declared, "My nerves are shot to pieces. I can't depend on myself any longer. I am afraid that I may crack up in an emergency—I dare not fail my men."

Bonnell asked him, "What is the trouble?"

The officer replied, "I've lost my faith. I can no longer believe in the Bible or in prayer, and I never go to chapel services. All this has upset me dreadfully."

Bonnell answered, "I understand you are under great pressure in the matter of time. Let's get down to business quickly. You have told me about your doubts. Now tell me of the thing that is far more important than your doubts—the thing that has prompted them. Tell me about your sins."

There was a long pause as the officer remained silent. Finally Bonnell said, "Let me see a picture of your wife and children." The officer reached into his pocket and drew out a picture. After another period of silence, Bonnell asked, "Have you been true to her?"

Instantly the officer dropped his head and replied, "I guess that's where all the trouble lies."[463]

Sin—slaves of

In the 1800s in East London, Henry White, a minister, was wakened in the dead of the night and urgently implored by a woman at the door to come and

---

[462] Marjory A. Bonar, ed., Reminiscences of Andrew A. Bonar (London: Hodder and Stoughton, 1895), 137

[463] John Sutherland Bonnell, *Psychology for Pastor and People* (New York: Harper & Brothers Publishers, 1948) 38-9

see her husband, who, she said, was dying. Mr. White hastily dressed, and fastening his watch in his waistcoat pocket, went out into the dark streets. The woman led him to the door of a squalid house in a court. Following the woman's lead he entered, went upstairs, and found, lying on a wretched bed in a corner of the room, a man of about forty years of age, with just minutes of life left in him. Glancing round the room, the young minister was surprised to observe some articles a little out of place with such surroundings. There stood on the table a silver dish of considerable value, clothes of good style were heaped about the room, and there were one or two small pictures—the man was a lifelong thief. But Mr. White's concern was for the man's soul. He bent over the bed, talked to the man, and offered to pray with him. As he spoke he observed a sudden gleam in the man's eyes, and noted that they were fixed on his watch chain. The young minister prayed as his wife stood near, sobbing her heart out. When he finished he found the man was dead, and rising from his knees discovered that the fingers of the corpse were clasped in his watch-chain. Even as he was dying, the sight of a preoccupied man's gold watch chain was too much for him, and as the minister was praying to God to forgive him his sins, the dying thief tried to steal from him.[464]

Sinners—children of the devil

Lemuel Haynes was an African-American preacher in the 1800s. After the publication of his sermon on the devil, two reckless young men conspired to vex him, saying, "Father Haynes, have you heard the good news?"

"No," said Mr. Haynes, "what is it?"

"It is great news, indeed," said the other, "and, if true, *your* business is done."

"What is it?" Haynes asked again.

"Why," said the first, "the devil is dead."

In a moment the old preacher replied, lifting up both his hands and placing them on the heads of the young men, and in a tone of solemn concern, "Oh, poor fatherless children! What will become of you?"[465]

---

[464]   Henry W. Lucy, *A Diary of the Salisbury Parliament: 1886-1892* (London: Cassell and Company, 1892) 217

[465]   Timothy Mather Cooley, *Sketches of the Life and Character of the Rev. Lemuel Haynes* (New York: John S. Taylor, 1839), 123

Sinners—Christ calls to

A woman once came to Dwight L. Moody and said, "Mr. Moody, I would like to become a Christian, but I'm so hard-hearted."

He replied,

> My good woman, did the Master say, 'You soft-hearted people, come?' Nothing of the kind. He said, "Come unto me"— all black hearts, vile hearts, corrupt hearts, deceitful hearts—"all." If your heart is hard, who will soften it? You can't. The harder the heart the more need there is for the Saviour; so come along and get rest. If you can't come as a saint, come as a sinner; if you can't run, walk; if you can't walk, creep to him; but come.[466]

Skepticism

A man once said to Dwight L. Moody, "If you will answer this list of questions, I will become a Christian."

Mr. Moody replied, "If you will become a Christian, and start tonight, then come to me tomorrow morning, I will answer every question on your list."

That night the man trusted Christ as his Savior. The next morning he came to Mr. Moody's house, his face shining, and said, "Mr. Moody, I will not have to put you to the trouble of answering the questions. They have all been answered in the night, and the way is clear."[467]

Speaking the truth in love

At a minister's meeting, an erroneous opinion was spoken. Andrew Fuller, zealous for the truth, censured the brother so heavily that Dr. Ryland cried out, "Brother Fuller, brother Fuller! You can never admonish a mistaken friend but you must take up a sledge hammer and knock his brains out!"[468]

---

[466] G. B. F. Hallock, *The Evangelistic Cyclopedia* (New York: George H. Doran Company, 1922), 43

[467] J. Wilbur Chapman *Revival Sermons* (New York: Fleming H. Revell Company, 1911), 114

[468] *The Sword and the Trowel ed. by C. H. Spurgeon,* (London: Passmore & Alabaster, February 1865), 42

Speech

Someone once commented to Charles Spurgeon that a certain preacher had no more gifts for the ministry than an oyster. Spurgeon remarked, "In my own judgment this was a slander on the oyster, for that worthy bivalve shows great discretion in his openings, and he also knows when to close."[469]

Speech

Harry Ironside was attending a conference at the home of a very devoted believer. One of the ladies said, "Well, now, we will go out and help our hostess with dinner," leaving the men together.

One of the men then said, "since the ladies have gone out, there is a story I got hold of today I would like to tell you."

Before anyone else had a chance to speak, one of Ironside's friends said, "Just a minute brother; there are no ladies here, but the Holy Spirit is here and is more sensitive than the most fastidious lady. Is your story fit for Him?"

The man was humble enough to say, "Thank you, I accept the reproof. I will never tell such a story again."[470]

Study

When James A. Garfield, who afterward became president of the United States, was president of Hiram College in Ohio, a man brought his son for entrance as student, for whom he desired a shorter course than the regular one. "The boy will never take all that in," the father said. "He wants to get through by a shorter route. Can you arrange it?"

"Oh, yes," replied the president. "I can arrange for it. Your son can take the shorter course. It all depends on what you want to make of him. When God wants to make an oak, he takes a hundred years; but when he wants to make a squash he requires only two months."[471]

---

[469] Charles Haddon Spurgeon, *Second Series of Lectures to My Students* (London: Passmore and Alabaster, 1877), 28

[470] H. A. Ironside, *In the Heavenlies* (Neptune, New Jersey: Loizeaux Brothers, 1937), 243

[471] n.a., *The Homiletic Review* vol LXVII January-June 1914, (New York: Funk and Wagnalls, 1914), 80

Testimony

In one of his last visits to America, evangelist George Whitefield spent a day or two at Princeton with the college president, Dr. Finley. At dinner, Finley remarked, "Mr. Whitefield, I hope it will be very long before you are called home, but when that event shall arrive, I should be glad to hear the noble testimony you will bear for God."

"You would be disappointed, doctor," Whitefield predicted, "I shall die silent. It has pleased God to enable me to bear so many testimonies for him during my life, that he will require none from me when I die."[472]

Transformation

Anskar was a French missionary to Scandinavia in the ninth century. When he was asked by the unbelievers there if he could perform miracles, he replied, "If God were indeed to grant that power to me, I would only ask that I might exhibit the miracle of a holy life."[473]

Transformation

In the 1800s, Charles Bradlaugh, a prominent atheist, made known a challenge in all England to Hugh Price Hughes, a Welsh minister, to a public debate on the value of the Bible. Hughes, believing that a debate would accomplish nothing, responded saying,

> I propose to you that we bring some concrete evidences of the validity of the Bible's purpose in the form of men and women saved from lives of sin and shame. I will bring one hundred such men and women saved by the Bible, and I challenge you to do the same saved by atheism that denies the Bible. If you cannot bring one hundred to match my hundred, I will be satisfied if you will bring fifty men and women who will stand and testify that they have been lifted up from lives of sin and shame by the influences that deny

---

[472] A. C. Thompson, *Last Hours, Or, Words and Acts of the Dying* (Boston: Perkins & Whipple, 1851), 17

[473] A. J. Gordon, *The Holy Spirit in Missions* (New York: Fleming H. Revell Company, 1893), 213

the Bible's teachings. If you cannot bring fifty, I challenge you to bring twenty people who will testify with shining faces, as my one hundred will, that they have a great new joy in a life of self-respect as a result of your teachings. If you cannot bring twenty, I will be satisfied if you bring ten. Nay, if you cannot bring ten, I challenge you to bring just one man or woman who will make such testimony regarding the uplifiting influence of your teachings.

The challenge, known to all England, was never accepted.[474]

Transformation—only through God's word

As he passed through the great Kalahari desert in Africa, missionary David Livingstone was warmly welcomed by a tribal chief named Sekomi. On one occasion that they were together, Sekomi, said to Livingstone, "I wish you would change my heart. Give me medicine to change it, for it is proud, proud and angry, angry always." Livingstone lifted up his New Testament and was about to tell him of the only way in which the heart can be changed, but he interrupted him by saying, "Nay, I wish to have it changed by medicine, to drink and have it changed at once, for it is always very proud and very uneasy, and continually angry with someone." He then rose and went away."[475]

Treasure

As Colonial patriot Patrick Henry wrote his will, he wrote this in the closing paragraph:

> I have now disposed of all my property to my family. There is one thing more I wish I could give them and that is the Christian religion. If they had this and I had not given them one shilling they would be rich, and if they had not that and I had given them all the world they would be poor.[476]

---

[474] James G. K. McClure, *The Supreme Book of Mankind* (New York: Charles Scribner's Sons, 1930), 209-210

[475] William Garden Blaikie, *The Personal Life of David Livingstone* (London: John Murray, 1880), 47-8

[476] L. Carroll Judson, *The Sages and Heroes of the American Revolution* (Philadelphia: Moss &

Treasure

After the great Chicago fire, someone said to Dwight L. Moody, "I understand you lost everything."

Moody replied, "I have got much more left than I lost, I am a good deal richer than you could conceive, and here is my title deed: 'He that overcometh shall inherit all things' (Revelation 21:7)."[477]

Trials

During his ministry in Burma, missionary Adoniram Judson was locked up in a foul prison for a year and seven months. He was chained so that he could move only with great difficulty, breathing hot, fetid air, and surrounded by the filth of native criminals of the lowest class. The jailers gave him no food, and he would have starved if his wife had not brought provisions for him. When her money was exhausted, she was forced to beg for food from house to house to keep her husband alive. Once thieves broke into their house and stole everything that could be taken. Twice Mrs. Judson was dangerously ill, once by confinement and once by spotted fever.

In the midst of all this, one of Judson's fellow prisoners sneered, "What about the prospects of the conversion of the heathen?"

The missionary calmly replied, "The prospects are just as bright as the promises of God."[478]

Trials

When William Carey established his pioneer missionary work in India, he set up a printing house for the printing of Bible portions. But on the evening of March 11, 1812, the printing house was destroyed by fire. Two thousand reams of paper and many volumes of Scripture fed the flames. Fonts of type in thirteen languages and manuscripts in seven languages were consumed, along with Carey's manuscript dictionary of Sanskrit, the work of many years

Brother, 1854), 160-161

[477] Dwight Lyman Moody, *Pleasure and Profit in Bible Study* (New York: Fleming H. Revell, 1895), 96

[478] Samuel Marinus Zwemer, Arthur Judson Brown, *The Nearer and Farther East: Outline Studies of Moslem Lands and of Siam, Burma, and Korea* (New York: The Macmillan Company, 1908), 240-241

and nearly ready for the press. The next morning Carey walked over to the smoking ruins with a friend. With tears in his eyes he said, "In one short evening, the labors of many years are consumed. How unsearchable are the ways of God! The Lord has laid me low that I may look more simply to him."[479]

But the Lord had good in mind with this disaster. Little did Carey dream that this fire would prove to be the means of making them and their work famous all over Europe and America, as well as India. Men of every Christian school, and men interested only in the literary and secular side of their enterprise, had their active sympathy called out. The mere money loss, at the exchange of the day, was not under ten thousand pounds. In fifty days this was raised in England and Scotland alone, till Andrew Fuller, the leader of his mission in England, declared, "We must stop the contributions."[480]

Trials

When the puritan pastor Joseph Alleine was imprisoned because of his beliefs in the 1600s, he was a great source of encouragement his fellow prisoners. He once asked them,

> Shall I tell you a story that I have read? There was a certain king that had a pleasant grove, and that he might make it every way delightful to him, he caused some birds to be caught, and to be kept up in cages, till they had learned sundry sweet tunes; and when they were perfect in their lessons he let them abroad out of their cages into his grove, that while he was walking in this grove he might hear them singing those pleasant tunes, and teaching them to other birds that were of a wilder note. Brethren, this King is God, this grove is His church, these birds are yourselves, this cage is the prison; God hath sent you hither, that you should learn the sweet and pleasant notes of His praise.[481]

---

[479] George Winfred Hervey, *The Story of Baptist Missions in Foreign Lands, From the Time of Carey to the Present Date* (St. Louis, Miss.: Chancy R. Barns, 1884), 31

[480] George Smith, *The Life of William Carey* (London, J. M. Dent & Co., 1913), 184-5

[481] Charles Stanford, *Joseph Alleine: His Companions & Times* (London: Jackson, Walford, and Hodder, 1861), 333

Trusting God

When Martin Luther was writing to his friend, the chancellor, at the Diet of Augsburgh, many reformers at the time had their minds filled with great anxieties— Phillipp Melancthon was very fearful, and many of the Protestant princes were fearful, too; but Luther's heart was stout as a castle wall. He trusted in the Lord his God; nothing made him afraid; and he wrote in his letter to the chancellor,

> I fear not, and why should I fear? I have seen two miracles lately. I looked up, and saw the clouds above me in the noontide; and they looked like the sea that was hanging over me, and I could see no cord on which they were suspended, and yet they never fell. And then when the noontide had gone and the midnight came, I looked again, and there was the dome of heaven, and it was spangled with stars and I could see no pillars that held up the skies, and yet they never fell. Now He that holds the stars up and moves the clouds in their course, He can do all things, and I trust Him in the sight of these miracles."[482]

Trusting God

Richard Cecil taught a lesson of faith and trust in God to his daughter when she was very young. He explains,

> She was playing one day with a few beads, which seemed to delight her wonderfully. Her whole soul was absorbed in her beads. I said, "My dear, you have some pretty beads there."
>
> She answered, "Yes, Papa!"
>
> "And you seem to be vastly pleased with them."
>
> "Yes, Papa!"
>
> "Well now, throw them behind the fire." The tears started into her eyes. She looked earnestly at me, as though she ought to have a reason for such a cruel sacrifice.
>
> "Well, my dear, do as you please; but you know I never told

---

[482] James Comper Gray, *The Biblical Museum: A Collection of Notes Explanatory, Homiletic, and Illustrative, on the Holy Scriptures, Old Testament, Vol. VI* (London: Elliot Stock, 1879), 176

you to do any thing, which I did not think would be good for you."
She looked at me a few moments longer, and then summoning
up all her fortitude—her breast heaving with the effort—she
dashed them into the fire.

"Well," I said "there let them lie: you shall hear more about
them another time; but say no more about them now."

Some days after, I bought her a box full of larger beads and
toys of the same kind. When I returned home: I opened the
treasure and set it before her: she burst into joyful tears.

"Those, my child," said I, "are yours, because you believed me,
when I told you it would be better for you to throw those two or
three paltry beads behind the fire. Now that has brought you this
treasure. But now, my dear remember, as long as you live, what
faith is. I did this to teach you the meaning of faith. You threw
your beads away when I bid you, because you had faith in me that
I never advised you but for your good. Put the same confidence
in God. Believe every thing that he says in his word. Whether you
understand it or not, have faith in him that he means your good."[483]

Trusting God

In 1846 George Müller had a very difficult time in purchasing a field to
build a house for orphans. But through it all his heart was at peace, trusting
the Lord. He wrote that he was "fully assured that if the Lord were to take
this piece of land from me it would be only for the purpose of giving me a
still better one; our heavenly Father never takes any earthly thing from his
children except he means to give them something better instead."[484]

Trusting God

George Mueller trusted God as a pastor and as a director of an orphanage
that cared for thousands of destitute children. His partner in ministry was
his wife, Mary. Their marriage was so happy that Mueller testified that he

---

[483] Richard Cecil, *The Works of the Rev. Richard Cecil, M. A. With a Memoir of His Life, vol. III*
      arranged and revised by Josiah Pratt (New York: John P. Haven, 1825), 334-5

[484] George Müller, *The Life of Trust: Being A Narrative of the Lord's Dealings with George Müller,*
      ed. by H. Lincoln Wayland (Boston: Gould & Lincoln, 1868) , 335

never saw her at any time without a new feeling of delight.[485] When she died in 1870 after thirty-nine years of marriage, he continued to trust in God and His goodness. The Scripture he chose for the funeral sermon that he preached was Psalm 119:68, "Thou art good and doest good." The three divisions of his sermons were: "The Lord was good and did good: first, in giving her to me; second in so long leaving her to me; and third, in taking her from me."[486]

Trusting God

Knowing that he would soon face death, John Brown of Haddington summoned his two oldest boys in his room, and encouraged them to trust in the Lord and do good. He said to them, "No doubt, I have met with trials as well as others, yet so kind hath God been to me, that I think, if God were to give me as many years as I have already lived in the world, I would not desire one single circumstance in my lot changed—except that I wish that I had less sin."[487]

Unity

Once an assembly of ministers met with John Eliot, the apostle to the Indians, with a bundle of papers containing the particulars of a contention between some individuals. Eliot, threw the papers in the fire. saying, "Brethren, wonder not at what I have done; I did it on my knees this morning before I came among you."[488]

Unity

George Whitefield once stepped into a stagecoach about to leave Edinburgh. A lady who belonged to a different denomination happened to step into the same coach. Observing Whitefield, she started up with alarm, and asked, "Are you not Mr. Whitefield?"

---

[485] Arthur T. Pierson, *George Müller of Bristol* (London: James Nisbet & Co., 1899), 235

[486] Ibid., 238

[487] John Brown, Thomas Brown, *A Compendious History of the British Churches in England, Scotland, Ireland and America, vol. I* (Edinburgh: Machlachlan & Stewart, 1823), xvii-xviii

[488] Martin Moore, *Memoirs of the Life and Character of Rev. John Eliot* (Boston: Flagg & Gould, 1822), 157

"Yes, Madam," he replied.

"Oh," she exclaimed, "then let me get out."

"Surely, Madam." he calmly replied. "But before you go let me ask you one question. Suppose you die and go to heaven, and then suppose I die and go there also; when I come in, will you go out?"

Struck by his words, the lady then cordially shook his hand and they proceeded together on their journey.[489]

Unity

A woman once asked Harry Ironside, "What denomination are you?"

He responded, "Well, I belong to the same denomination that David did."

The lady replied, "What was that? I didn't know that David belonged to any."

Quoting from Psalm 119:63 Ironside answered, "David said, "I am a companion of all them that fear Thee and keep Thy precepts."[490]

Witness

Thomas Bilney, a Roman Catholic, came to faith in Christ and joyfully prayed, "O Thou who art the Truth, give me strength that I may teach it and convert the ungodly, by means of one who has been himself ungodly."[491] He soon set his sights on Hugh Latimer, a priest who was religiously zealous but, as he would later describe himself, "as obstinate a papist as any in England." Bilney reflected, prayed, and at last planned a very creative means to proclaim the truth of the gospel. He went to the college where Latimer resided and said to him, "For the love of God, be pleased to hear my confession."

Latimer eagerly yielded to this request, and Bilney, kneeling before him, related to him with touching simplicity the anguish he had once felt in his soul, the efforts he had made to remove it, their unprofitableness so long as he determined to follow the precepts of the church, and, lastly, the peace he had felt when he believed that Jesus Christ is *the Lamb of God that taketh*

---

[489] *The Bible Class Magazine, vol. I ed. by C. H. Bateman* (London: Sunday School Union, 1848), 75

[490] H. A. Ironside, *In the Heavenlies* (Neptune, New Jersey: Loizeaux Brothers, 1937), 175

[491] Jean Henri Merle d'Aubigne, trans. by H. White, *History of the Reformation of the Sixteenth Century* (New York: Robert Carter & Brothers, 1879), 167

away the sins of the world. He described to Latimer the spirit of adoption he had received, and the happiness he experienced in being able now to call God his father.

Latimer, who expected to receive a confession, listened without mistrust. His heart was opened, and the voice of Bilney penetrated it without obstacle. From time to time the confessor would have chased away the new thoughts which came crowding into his bosom; but the penitent continued, assisted by the Holy Spirit. At length grace prevailed: the penitent rose up, but Latimer remained seated, absorbed in thought. The strong defender of Rome contended in vain against the words of the feeble Bilney. Like Paul on the way to Damascus, he was conquered, and his conversion, like the apostle's, was instantaneous. He stammered out a few words; Bilney drew near him with love and God scattered the darkness which obscured his mind. He saw Jesus Christ as the only Savior given to man: he contemplated and adored him.

Latimer afterwards said, "I learnt more by this confession than by much reading and in many years before. I now tasted the word of God, and forsook the doctors of the school and all their fooleries."[492] And so it was not the penitent but the confessor who received absolution, and Latimer went on to become a strong champion and martyr of the faith.

Witness—unspoken

In the early 1500s, there were two monks named Martin. The first, Martin Basle, was convinced of the truth of the gospel but hesitated to proclaim it. He wrote this confession on a piece of parchment: "O most merciful Christ, I know that I can be saved only by the merit of thy blood. Holy Jesus, I acknowledge thy sufferings for me. I love thee! I love thee!" Then he removed a stone from the wall of his chamber and deposited his confession there. It was discovered a hundred years later. Meanwhile no one knew that Martin Basle had found Christ.

About the same time there was another monk, Martin Luther, who also saw clearly from the Scriptures the doctrine of justification by faith, and did not fear to confess the truth. He said, "My Lord has confessed me before men; I will not shrink to confess him before kings." The world was

---

[492] Ibid., 220-222

unchanged by Martin Basle. By God's grace the world was transformed by Martin Luther.[493]

Witness—of everyone

Lyman Beecher was once asked how he was able to do so much in his church. His answer was, "Oh, I preach Sundays, and four hundred of my church members preach every day."[494]

Work

English reformer Hugh Latimer ministered during the 1500s. He rejected the notion that only vocational ministry was pleasing to God. He declared,

> This is a wonderful thing, that the Savior of the world, and the King above all kings, was not ashamed to labor; yea, and to use so simple an occupation. Here he did sanctify all manner of occupations, exhorting and teaching as with this [example] every man to follow and keep the state whereunto God hath called him.[495]

Work

Puritan pastor John Carter once visited a tanner who was busily employed in the humble work of tanning a hide. Giving him a pleasant tap on the shoulder, the man startled, looked behind him, and, with a blushing countenance, said, "Sir, I am ashamed that you should find me thus."

Carter responded, "Let Christ, when he cometh, find *me* so doing."

"What," replied the man, "doing thus?"

Carter answered, "Yes, faithfully performing the duties of my calling."[496]

---

[493] David James Burrell, *A Quiver of Arrows* (New York: Funk & Wagnalls, 1902), 46

[494] J. C. Ferdinand Pittman, *Bible Truths Illustrated* (Cincinnati, Ohio: The Standard Publishing Company, 1917), 59

[495] George Elwes Corrie ed., *Sermons and Remains of Hugh Latimer* (Cambridge: The University Press, 1845), 158-159

[496] Benjamin Brook, *The Lives of the Puritans, vol. II* (London: James Black, 1813), 411

Worldliness

Since the early days of the church, one of the issues has been how to understand the relationship of Christian belief with the world's philosophy. Some have seen common ground between the two, looking to the philosophy of the world for wisdom to bolster the wisdom of Scripture. The church father Tertullian, born in the second century, fought against this, maintained that the wisdom of man corrupts the truth of God. He asked, "For by whom has truth ever been discovered without God?"[497] Tertullian called the Grecian philosophers the patriarchs of all heresies, and scornfully asked, "What has the academy to do with the church? What has Christ to do with Plato?"[498]

Worldliness

Rowland Hill had a member of his church who was in the habit of going to the theater. Mr. Hill went to him and said, "This will never do — a member of my church in the habit of attending the theater!" The member replied that it surely must be a mistake as he was not in the habit of going there, although it was true he did go now and then *for a treat.*

"Oh!" said Rowland Hill,

> then you are a worse hypocrite than ever, sir. Suppose any one spread the report that I ate carrion, and I answered, 'Well, there is no wrong in that; I don't eat carrion every day in the week, but I have a dish now and then *for a treat.'* Why, you would say, 'What a nasty, foul, and filthy appetite Rowland Hill has to have to go to carrion for a treat!' Religion is the Christian's truest treat, Christed is his enjoyment.[499]

---

[497] Tertullian, *A Treatise on the Soul,* chapter 27 in *Ante-Nicene Christian Library,* ed. A. Roberts and J. Donaldson, vol. XV (Edinburgh, 1870), 6

[498] Philip Schaff, *History of the Christian Church, From the Birth of Christ to the Reign of Constantine, A.D. 1-311* (New York: Charles Scribner, 1859), 515

[499] Vernon J. Charlesworth, *Rowland Hill: His Life, Anecdotes, and Pulpit Sayings* (London: Hodder and Stoughton, 1876), 147-8

Worldliness

A man who had become a Christian came up to Dwight L. Moody and asked, "Mr. Moody, now that I am converted, have I to give up the world?"

Moody answered, "No, you haven't to give up the world. If you give a good ringing testimony for the Son of God, the world will give you up pretty quick; they won't want you."[500]

Worship

Henry Ward Beecher was a very famous and popular preacher of the 1800s. One Sunday, his brother Thomas was preaching for him in his absence. There were many, as usual, who had come to hear Henry preach, and as soon as Thomas rose to the pulpit, they started to leave. At this Thomas announced, "All those who came here this morning to worship Henry Ward Beecher may now withdraw from the church—all who came to worship God may remain."[501]

Worship—giving our best

Isaac Watts was born in 1674, the son of a schoolmaster who was imprisoned for his faith. During this time, the Psalms, which were the only songs used in his church, were poorly paraphrased for singing. Typical of the crude lyrics is this:

> Ye monsters of the bubbling deep,
> your Maker's praises spout;
> Up from the sands, ye codlings, peep,
> and wag your tails about.[502]

Watts once wrote, "While we sing the praises of our God in his church, we are employed in that part of worship which of all others is the nearest

---

[500] D. L. Moody, *The D. L. Moody Year Book, sel. by Emma Moody Fitt* (East Northfield, Mass: the Bookstore, 1900), 147

[501] Lyman Beecher Stowe, *Saints, Sinners and Beechers* (Indianapolis: The Bobbs-Merrill Company, 1934), 380

[502] Joseph Belcher, *Historical Sketches of Hymns, Their Writers, and Their Influence* (Philadelphia: Lindsay & Blakiston, 1859), 352-353

a-kin to heaven; and it is pity that this, of all others, should be performed the worst upon earth."[503]

One Sunday, when he was eighteen, he complained to one of his fellow-worshippers of the character of the hymns at their church, where his father was deacon. Watts was given the reply, "Give us better, young man." He accepted the challenge, and that evening the church was invited to close its evening service with his first hymn,[504] which was received enthusiastically by his church. The passion of Isaac Watts for worshiping Christ with excellence resulted in hymns which are still sung and loved to this day, include "When I Survey the Wondrous Cross," "Jesus Shall Reign," "O God Our Help in Ages Past," and "Joy to the World."

Worship—pleasing the king

When King George III of England was repairing his palace, one of the workmen, a devout Christian, caught his attention, and he often held conversations with him at some length upon serious subjects. One Monday morning, the king went as usual to watch the progress of the work, and not seeing this man in his customary place, enquired the reason of his absence. The king was answered evasively, and, for some time, the other workmen avoided telling him the truth. After further questions, they acknowledged that not having been able to complete a particular job on the Saturday night, they had returned to finish it on the following morning. This man alone had refused to comply, because of the Lord's day. In consequence of what they called his obstinacy, he had been dismissed entirely from his employment. The king exclaimed, "Call him back immediately! The man who refused doing his ordinary work on the Lord's day is the man for me. Let him be sent for." The man was accordingly replaced, and the king ever after showed him particular favor.[505]

---

[503] Isaac Watts, *The Works of the Rev. Isaac Watts D.D. in Nine Volumes, vol.9* (London: William Baynes, et. al., 1813), 127

[504] Charles F. Bradley, Amos W. Patten, Charles M. Stuart, *Life and Selected Writings of Francis Dana Hemenway* (Cincinnati, Ohio and Chicago: Cranston & Stowe, 1890), 244-255

[505] Ingram Cobbin, *Georgiana: or, Anecdotes of George the Third* (London: John Hill, 1820), 51

Zeal

The seal of John Calvin was a hand holding a burning heart, which symbolized the purpose of his life: "I give Thee all; I keep back nothing for myself!"[506]

Zeal

It is said of Puritan Samuel Crooke that he did not serve God with that which cost him nothing, but labored much in his ministry. His constant motto was, "I am willing to spend and be spent." In a time of sickness, the physician told him that he might live longer if he would preach less. Crooke replied, "Alas! If I may not labor I cannot live. What good will life do me, if I be hindered from the end of living?"[507]

Zeal

When the Scottish reformer Andrew Melville was accused of being too fiery he replied, "If you see my fire go *downward*, set your foot on it and put it out; but if it go *upward*, let it go to its own place."[508]

Zeal

Rowland Hill was a zealous preacher and evangelist in the 1700 and 1800s. He was once preaching in a town in England when he said,

> Because I am in earnest, men call me an enthusiast; but I am not; mine are the words of truth and soberness. When I first came into this part of the country, I was walking on yonder hill; I saw a gravel-pit fall in, and bury three human beings alive. I lifted up my voice for help so loud that I was heard in the town below, at the distance of a mile; help came, and rescued two of

---

[506] Paul Henry, "The Life and Times of John Calvin," trans. by Henry Stebbins, *The Theological and Literary Journal*, ed. David N. Lord, *vol. V* (New York: Franklin Knight, July 1852- April, 1853), 538

[507] Benjamin Brook, *The Lives of the Puritans, vol. III* (London: James Black, 1813), 108

[508] Thomas M'Crie, *The Story of the Scottish Church: From the Reformation to the Disruption* (London: Blackie & Son, 1875), 85

the poor sufferers. No one called me an enthusiast then; and when I see eternal destruction ready to fall upon poor sinners, and about to entomb them irrecoverably in an eternal mass of woe, and call aloud on them to escape, shall I be called an enthusiast now! No, sinner, I am not an enthusiast in so doing; I call on thee aloud to fly for refuge, to the hope set before thee in the gospel of Christ Jesus.[509]

Zeal

After preaching more than 18,000 sermons—an average of ten a week—evangelist George Whitefield preached one final time in 1770. The people assembled in such throngs that it was necessary to preach in the open air. Before commencing the service, a concerned friend said to Whitefield, "Sir, you are more fit to go to bed than to preach."

He replied, "True, sir," and turning aside, he clasped his hands together and exclaimed, looking upwards, "Lord Jesus, I am weary in thy work, but not of thy work. If I have not yet finished my course, let me go and speak for thee once more in the fields, seal the truth, and come home and die." His prayer was answered— Whitefield preached his last sermon and the next morning he died.[510]

Zeal

After John Newton had turned eighty, some were concerned about his health. One of his friends, Reverend Richard Cecil, advised him to consider his work as done and that he cease from preaching.

"I cannot stop," Newton said. Then, raising his voice exclaimed, "What! Shall the old African blasphemer stop while he can speak?"[511]

---

[509] Edwin Stanley, *The Life of the Rev. Rowland Hill, A.M.* (London: Baldwin & Cradock, 1834), 198

[510] Edwin Holt, *Historical Sketch of the North Church* (Portsmouth, New Hampshire: Published by Author, 1838), 17-18

[511] Richard Cecil, *Memoirs of the Rev. John Newton* (New York: Thomas A. Ronalds, 1809), 164

Zeal

In 1883, Wilfred Grenfell came to Christ as a result of hearing a sermon by Dwight L. Moody. Much later in life, he saw Moody in a Boston hotel. Coming up to him, he said, "Mr. Moody, fourteen years ago I put my faith in Jesus Christ after hearing you preach."

Moody replied, "Oh, and what have you been doing since?"[512]

---

[512] Wilfred T. Grenfell, *A Man's Faith* (Boston: The Pilgrim Press, 1908), 35

Biographical Index

Adalbert (956-997, First known Missionary to the Prussians, Bishop of Prague)

Adolphus, Gustauvus (1594-1632, King of Sweden)

Alexander, Archibald (1772-1851, American preacher and first professor of Princeton Seminary, father of James Alexander)

Alexander, Charles (1867-1920, American gospel singer, associate of J. Wilbur Chapman)

Alexander, James (1804-1859, American preacher and seminary professor, son of Archibald Alexander)

Alleine, Joseph (1634-1668, English Puritan preacher and martyr)

Allen, Ethan (1738-1789), American Revolutionary War Leader

Ambrose (c. 340-397), Archbishop of Milan

Amphilochius (c. 340-c. 394-403), Bishop of of Iconium

Anskar (801-865, French missionary to Scandinavia and Archbishop of Hamburg)

Asbury, Francis (1745-1816, one of the first American two bishops of the Methodist Episcopal Church)

Athanasius (296-372, presbyter and bishop of Alexandria, defender of orthodoxy)

Augustine, Aurelius (354-430, Bishop of Hippo, theologian, one of the greatest of the church fathers)

Augustus, Prince Edward (1767-1820, Duke of Kent and Strathearn, Earl of Dublin, son of King George III and father of Queen Victoria)

Aylmer, John, (1521-1594), Bishop of London

Bacon, John (1740-1799), British sculptor

Basil (c. 330-379, presbyter and bishop of Caesarea, archbishop of Cappadocia)

Baxter, Richard (1615-1691, English Puritan preacher and author)

Beecher, Henry Ward (1813-1887, American preacher, son of Lyman Beecher and brother of Harriet Beecher Stowe)

Beecher, Lyman (1775-1883, American preacher, father of Harriet Beecher Stowe and Henry Ward Beecher)

Bilney, Thomas c. 1495-1531, English Puritan preacher and martyr)

Bonar, Andrew (1810-1892, Scottish preacher and author, youngest brother of Horatius Bonar)

Bonar, Horatius (1808-1889, Scottish preacher, author, and hymnist, older brother of Andrew Bonar)

Bonnell, John Sutherland (1893-1992, American preacher and author)

Booth, Marie (1864–1937, Staff Captain, The Salvation Army, daughter of William Booth)

Bradford, John (1510-1555, English Puritan preacher and martyr)

Brainerd, David (1718-1747, Missionary to the Native Americans)

Bray, Billy (1794-1868, English preacher)

Brewster, David (1781-1868, Scottish scientist and inventor)

Briggs, George (1796- 1861, United States Congressman, 1831 to 1843, Governor of Massachusetts, 1844 to 1851)

Brooks, Phillips (1835-1893, American preacher and author)

Brown, John (1722-1787, Scottish preacher and author)

Buchanan, Claudius (1766-1815, Scottish theologian, chaplain and vice-principal of the College of Fort William, Calcutta, India)

Buckley, James (1836-1920, Methodist minister, author)

Bunyan, John (English Puritan preacher and writer, author of *The Pilgrim's Progress*)

Burke, Grafton (1886-1938, Alaskan missionary doctor)

Burnet, Gilbert (1643-1715, Scottish theologian, Bishop of Salisbury, author of *History of the Reformation of the Church of England*)

Burr, Jonathan (1604-1641, English non-conformist and New England Puritan preacher)

Calamy, Edmund (1600-1666, English Puritan minister)

Calvin, John (1509-1564, French Reformer and author)

Campbell, Alexander (1788-1866, American preacher, early leader of the Restoration Movement)

Campbell, Willielma, Viscountess Glenorchy (1741-1786, patroness of evangelical missionary work in Scotland and beyond)

Carey, William (1761-1834, English missionary to India, called "the father of modern missions")

Cargill, Donald (c. 1610-1681, Scottish preacher and martyr)

Carmichael, Amy (1867-1951, Irish missionary to Japan and India)

Carter, John (c. 1540-1634, English Puritan preacher)

Cecil, Richard (1748-1810, English preacher)

Chalmers, James (1841-1901, Scottish Missionary to New Guinea)

Chalmers, Thomas (1780-1847, Scottish preacher and leader of the Free Church)

Chapman, J. Wilbur (1859-1917, American preacher, evangelist, and author)

Chapman, Robert (1803-1902, English pastor)

Charles, Thomas (1755-1814, Welsh Nonconformist preacher, author of the corrected edition of the *Welsh Bible*)

Chrysostom, John of Antioch (343-407, preacher and author, was given the name "Chrysostom" which means "golden-mouthed")

Clarke, Adam (1762-1832, English preacher, theologian, and commentator)

Coleridge, Samuel Taylor (1772-1834, English poet)

Condor John, (1714-1781, English pastor)

Cotton, John (1585–1652, Colonial Puritan preacher, father-in-law of Increase Mather)

Cranmer, Thomas (1489-1556, English Puritan preacher and martyr, first Archbishop of Canterbury)

Cromwell, Oliver (1599-1658, British soldier and statesman, Lord Protector of the commonwealth of England, Scotland, and Ireland)

Crooke, Samuel (1574-1649, English Puritan preacher)

de Fénelon, François (1651-1715, French archbishop of Cambray)

de Muler, Geleyn (?-1562, Netherlands martyr)

Deering, John (1513-1576, English Puritan preacher)

Dod, John (c. 1549-1645, English Puritan preacher)

Doolittle, Thomas (1630-1707, English Puritan preacher)

Duncan, John (1796-1870, Preacher and missionary of the Free Church of Scotland, Professor of Hebrew and Oriental Languages at New College, Edinburgh)

Duff, Alexander (1806-1878, First Missionary from Scotland to India)

Edwards, Jonathan (1745-1801, American preacher and theologian)

Egede, Hans (1686-1758, Norwegian preacher, first missionary to Greenland)

Eliot, John (1604-1690, Colonial Puritan pastor and missionary to the American Indians)

Faraday, Michael (1791-1867, English chemist and physicist)

Felix of Nola (?-c. 353, Presbyter of Nola, Italy)

Fisher, John (1469-1535, Bishop of Rochester, martyr)

Flavel, John (1630-1691, English Puritan preacher and author)

Fletcher, John (1729-1781, Swiss preacher in England, associate of John Wesley)

Fook, Lough (?-1884, Chinese missionary to South America)

Foote, Andrew Hull (1806-1863, American Admiral)

Foxe, John (1516-1587, English Puritan preacher, author of "History of the Acts and Monuments of the Martyrs," commonly known as "Foxe's Book of Martyrs.")

Fuller, Andrew (1754-1815, English preacher and author, one of the founders of the Baptist Missionary Society which sent William Carey to India)

Fuller, Thomas (1608-1661, English preacher)

Gardiner, Allen (1794-1851, missionary to South America)

Garfield, James A. (1831-1881, 20th President of the United States)

George III, King (George William Frederick, 1738-1820, King of Great Britain)

George IV, King (George Augustus Frederick, 1762-1830, King of Great Britain)

Gill, John (1697-1771, English preacher and commentator)

Gillespie, George (1613-1648, English Puritan preacher)

Gilpin, Bernard (1517-1583, English Puritan preacher)

Gladstone, William (1809-1898, Prime Minister of England 1868–1874, 1880–1885, 1886 and 1892–1894)

Good, John Mason (1764-1827, English medical doctor and author)

Goodwin, Harvey (1818-1891, Bishop of Carlisle)

Goodwin, Thomas (1600-1690, English Puritan preacher, president of Magdalen College, London)

Gordon, George (1833-1885, British Major General and administrator)

Gouge, William (1575-1653, English Puritan preacher and author)

Gough, John Bartholomew (1817-1886), American evangelistic temperance speaker and author)

Gough, Henry Dorsey (1745-1808, American plantation owner)

Gray, Horace (1828-1902, United States Supreme Court Justice)

Gregor, William (1754-1833, Scottish Presbyterian preacher)

Grenfell, Wilfred (1865-1940, English Medical Missionary to Newfoundland and Labrador

Grimshaw, William (1708-1763, English preacher)

Hall, John (1829-1898, American Presbyterian preacher)

Hall, Newman (1816-1902, English preacher and author)

Hall, Robert (1764-1831, English preacher)

Halyburton, Thomas (Scottish preacher and professor, 1674-1712)

Hamlin, Cyrus (1811-1900, Missionary to Turkey, founder and president of Robert College, Constantinople)

Hastings, Selina, Countess of Huntingdon (1707-1791, Philanthropist, Patroness of Whitefield and Wesley)

Haussmann, Nicholas (?-1522, Pastor of Zwickau, Germany)

Havergal, Frances Ridley (1836-1879, English poet and hymn writer)

Haynes, Lemuel (1753-1833, African-American preacher)

Henry, Matthew (1662-1714, English preacher and commentator)

Henry, Patrick (1736-1799, Colonial patriot and American politician)

Henry, Philip (1631-1696, English Puritan preacher, father of Matthew Henry)

Herbert, George (1593-1633, English preacher and hymnist)

Hervey, James (1714-1758, English preacher and author)

Heywood, Nathaniel (1633-1677, English Puritan preacher)

Hill, Rowland (1744-1833, English preacher, one of the founders of the Religious Tract Society)

Hooker, Thomas (1586-1647, Colonial Puritan preacher, one of the founders of the Colony of Connecticut)

Hooper, John (1495-1555, English Puritan preacher, bishop of Gloucester, martyr)

Houston, Samuel (1793-1963, American soldier, US Senator, President of the Republic of Texas, Governor of Texas)

Howard, Henry (1859-1933, Australian preacher and author)

Howard, Oliver Otis (1830 -1909, Union Civil War General, Medal of Honor recipient)

Howe, John (1630-1705, English Puritan preacher)

Hughes, Hugh Price (1847-1902, English preacher)

Huss, John (1369-1415, Bohemian reformer and martyr)

Ignatius (c. 35-c.107, student of the apostle John, Bishop of Antioch, and martyr)

Ironside, Henry (Harry) A. (1876-1951, American preacher and author)

Innes, William (1770-1855, Scottish preacher and author)

Jackson, Thomas Jonathan "Stonewall" (1824–1863, Confederate general during the American Civil War)

Jackson, Rachel (1767-1828, wife of General and President-elect Andrew Jackson)

Janeway, John (1633-1657, English Puritan preacher)

Jay, William (1769-1853, English preacher)

Jenkyn, William (1612-1685, English Puritan preacher and martyr)

Johnson, Samuel (1709-1784, English writer, poet, author of *A Dictionary of the English Language*)

Jones, Mary (1784-1864, Welsh girl, whose love for God's word led to the formation of the British and Foreign Bible Society)

Judson, Adoniram (1788-1850, American missionary to Burma)

Knox, John (c. 1513-1572, Scottish Reformer)

Lawrence (225-258, Deacon of the church of Rome and martyr)

Latimer, Hugh (c. 1485-1555, English Bishop, Reformer, and martyr)

Livingstone, David (1813-1873, Scottish missionary to Africa)

Lorimer, George (1838-1904, American preacher and author)

Love, Christopher (1618-1651, Welsh Puritan preacher and martyr)

Luther, Katharina (1499-1552, Wife of Martin Luther)

Luther, Martin (1483-1546, German Reformer and author)

Mann, Horace (1796-1859, American education reformer and abolitionist)

Manton, Thomas (1620-1677, English Puritan preacher)

Mariani, Marco (?-1890, Italian evangelist)

Marsh, William, (1775-1864, English preacher)

Marshall, William (1628-1680, English Puritan preacher)

Martyn, Henry (1781-1812, English missionary to India)

Mather, Cotton (1663-1728, Colonial Puritan preacher)

M'Cheyne, Robert Murray (1813-1843, Scottish preacher)

Melancthon, Philipp (1497-1560, German Reformer and theologian)

Miller, Peter (1710-1796, Colonial preacher)

Moffat, Robert (1795-1883, Scottish missionary to Africa)

Mompesson, William (1639-1709, English preacher)

Monier-Williams, Monier (1819-1899, English professor and author)

More, Hannah (1745-1833, English author and philanthropist)

Morrison, Robert (1782-1834, first Protestant missionary to China)

Moody, Dwight L. (1837-1899, American evangelist)

Mueller, George (1805-1898, English evangelist and philanthropist)

Naimbanna II (1720-1793, Prince of Sierra Leone)

Newton, John (1725-1807, English preacher and hymnist)

Newton, George (1602-1681, English Puritan preacher)

Norton, Hermon (1799-1859, American preacher, author, and corresponding secretary of the American and Foreign Christian Union)

Norton, Ralph (1869-1934), Evangelist and founder of Belgian Gospel Mission

Origen (c. 185-c. 254, Early Christian preacher and author)

Owen, John (1616-1683, English Puritan preacher and author)

Page, Harlan (1791-1834, Agent of American Tract Society, Sabbath School Superintendent)

Parker, Joseph (1830-1902, English preacher)

Parnell, John Vessey (1805-1883, Second Baron Congleton of England, 1805-1882)

Paton, John (1824–1907), Missionary to the New Hebrides

Payson, Edward (1783-1827, American preacher, father of hymnist Elizabeth Payson Prentiss)

Pearson, Samuel (1647- 1727, English preacher)

Penry, John (1559-93, Welsh preacher and Wales's most famous Protestant martyr)

Pentecost, George Frederick (1842-1920, American Civil War chaplain, pastor, evangelist, and author)

Perkins, William (1558-1602, English Puritan preacher, professor, and author)

Raikes, Robert (1736-1811, Owner and publisher of the Gloucester Journal, founder of Sunday School movement)

Reynolds, Richard (1735-1816, English iron manufacturer and philanthropist)

Rinkart, Martin (1586-1649, German pastor and hymnist)

Robinson, Robert (1726-1790) English preacher, author of "Come Thou Fount of Every Blessing")

Robinson, William (?-1746, American Presbyterian evangelist)

Rogers, John (c.1500-1555, English reformer and first English Protestant martyr under Queen Mary)

Rogers, John (c. 1572-1636, English Puritan preacher)

Rogers, Richard (1550-1618, English Puritan preacher)

Romaine, William (1714-1795, English preacher and author)

Russell, William (1639-1683, English politician)

Saunders, David (1717-1796, English shepherd)

Savonarola, Girolamo (1452-1498, Italian reformer and martyr)

Schauffler, William (1798-1883, Russian missionary to Turkey)

Selwyn, John (English missionary to Melanesia)

Shepard, Fred (1855-1915, American Medical missionary to Turkey)

Shepard, Thomas (1605-1649, Colonial Puritan preacher and author)

Simeon, Charles (1759-1836, English preacher)

Smith, John Taylor (1860-1937, Anglican Bishop and Chaplain-General to the Forces)

Smith, Rodney "Gypsy" (English evangelist, 1860-1947)

Spafford, Horatio (1828-1888, American attorney, church elder, and hymnist)

Spurgeon, Charles (1834-1892, English preacher and author)

Stearns, Daniel M. (1844-1926, American preacher)

Studdert Kennedy, Geoffrey Anketell, (1883-1929, Anglican priest and poet, World War I chaplain) Sumner, Charles Richard (1790 – 1874, Bishop of Llandaff and Bishop of Winchester)

Talmage, Thomas De Witt (1832-1902, American preacher, Civil War chaplain, author)

Temple, Frederick (1821-1902, Archbishop of Canterbury)

Tennent, William, junior (1705–1777, Colonial preacher, son of William Tennent)

Tertullian (c. 160-c. 220, Latin church father and apologist)

Thornton, John (1720-1790, English merchant and philanthropist)

Thorpe, John (1730-1776, English preacher)

Trotter, Lilias (1853-1928, English missionary to Algeria)

Toplady, Augustus (1740-1778, English preacher and hymnist)

Tucker, Frederick (Booth) (1853-1929, Salvation Army Commissioner)

Tyndale, William (1484-1536, Father of the English Reformation)

Ussher, James (1581-1656, Archbishop of Armagh and Primate of All Ireland)

Vassar, John (1813-1878, American evangelist)

Venn, Henry (1725-1797, English preacher)

Von Dannecker, Johann (1758-1841, German sculptor)

Von Welz , Justinian (1621-1688, Dutch baron and missionary)

Watts, Isaac (1674-1748, English preacher and founder of modern English hymnody)

Webster, Daniel (1782-1852, American lawyer and statesman)

Wellesley, Arthur (1769-1852, The Duke of Wellington, British Field Marshall and statesman)

Welsh, Elizabeth (1570-1625), Daughter of John Knox, wife of John Welsh

Welsh, John (1624-1681, Scottish preacher, great-grandson of John Knox)

Wesley, Charles, (1708-1788, English preacher, hymnist of the English revival, younger brother of John Wesley)

Wesley, John (1703-1791, English preacher, father of Methodism, older brother of Charles Wesley)

Wesley, Martha (1706-1791, Sister of John and Charles Wesley)

Wesley, Samuel (1662-1735, English preacher and poet, father of John and Charles Wesley)

Wesley, Susanna (1669-1772, Mother of John and Charles Wesley)

Westover, Oscar (1883-1938, Major General, fourth chief of the United States Army Air Corps.

White, Henry (1834-1890, Chaplain of the House of Commons)